Praise for Sketches

"Miner combines his father's writings and interviews with WWII veterans to craft a loving tribute to the young men who fought in WWII…He does his father and other WWII veterans proud."

Publishers Weekly

"An inherently fascinating and impressively informative read from cover to cover. Thoroughly 'reader friendly'… **Sketches of a Black Cat** is unreservedly recommended for personal, community, and academic libraries…"

Midwest Book Review

"…This book is sure to prove to be an invaluable glimpse into a pilot's daily life. Brilliant in its composition and heart-wrenching in its forthrightness, Miner's compilation is sure to stand the test of time."

U.S. Review of Books

"…this is a story that has heart, action, and is in constant flux."

Eric Hoffer Book Awards

"**Sketches of a Black Cat** is a unique and fascinating memoir of a World War II combat aviator ~ with original and previously unpublished sketches and photographs. This artfully crafted book is a must-read for anyone in search of a new and completely different view of war in the Pacific and on the home front during America's greatest conflict."

LARKIN SPIVEY
military historian and author

"From boxes of notes and drawings comes a book illuminating a WWII pilot's experiences as part of the Black Cat Squadron…accounts of support missions, rescues of airmen and interactions with indigenous island peoples told in vivid but unembellished detail…a handsome volume that reads breezily and is punctuated with photos and drawings from Howard's war years."

MIKE FRANCIS
the Oregonian

"**Sketches of a Black Cat** is a worthy addition to the fascinating true story of the Navy's black painted, night-flying Catalinas and the courageous men who flew them into the darkness."

RICHARD KNOTT
author **Black Cat Raiders of WWII**

"…A refreshing and insightful look at what it took to be a Navy pilot in the Pacific during WWII…a delightful and easy read… It should be noted that Howard Miner was an excellent artist…Along with these artful depictions are plentiful photographs of Mr. Miner and his Navy friends as they advance through the Pacific Islands during WWII. Many of these stories are left untold. Fortunately Ron Miner has brought forth at least one gem for us to follow and cherish.

RICHARD C. GESCHKE
Vine Voice and Military Writers Society of America

"As a former flight engineer aboard a PBY in WWII… I can truly say I felt as though I was on Howard's Catalina…so many similarities to my own experiences. I can almost hear the drone of the engines in synchronization. Many episodes were warm and compelling. I highly recommend this book to vets, historians, and students. You won't put down **Sketches of a Black Cat** till you've read it cover-to-cover!"

WIN STITES, VP-91, VP2-1
served in both Atlantic and Pacific regions during WWII,
Former President PBY Memorial Foundation and Museum

"Wonderful and beautifully real stories such as this are dying every day as we lose our WWII veterans. Kudos to Ron Miner for preserving and sharing with the rest of us the gold of his father's journals, photos, and drawings to bring us such a compelling look at life during the war. This is not only a valuable and insightful historical document but a dramatic and warm personal story."

DON KEITH
author of **Undersea Warrior**

"...Howard Miner's memoirs are a wonderful view into the world of a patrol squadron at war...Miner sees the war through the eyes of an artist, revealing details of day-to-day life that are often overlooked in war time narratives. A wholly enjoyable story!"

STEWART BAILEY
Curator, Evergreen Aviation and Space Museum

"Howard was a careful observer and chronicler, both in prose and pictures, of a war experience that is at once singular and reflective of thousands of other young men belonging to what Tom Brokaw has famously called the 'Greatest Generation.' Every reader will be grateful to Ron Miner for adapting his father's journals and seeing this material into print."

JIM HILLS
Professor of Humanities, Corban University

" ...Only after his death did Howard's family discover a treasure trove of his handwritten journals, logs, artwork, and photographs from his time serving in the Pacific Theater. Thanks to Howard's son, Ron, the legacy of another 'greatest' man now is available for all to read, appreciate, and treasure. Enjoy!"

DAVID SANFORD
author, editor, and educator

2017 Gold Medal - *National Indie Excellence Awards*
2017 Gold Medal - *Reader's Favorite Book Award*
2017 Double Medal winner - *Next Generation Indie Awards*
Indie Brag Medallion
2017 Gold Medal - *IAN Book Awards*

Sketches of a Black Cat: Story of a night flying WWII pilot and artist
By Ron Miner

 Copyright © 2016 Ron and Howard Miner.
All rights reserved.
Riverdale Press

Cover and interior design by Anneli Anderson, www.designanneli.com
ISBN-13: 978-1535055284
ISBN-10: 1535055286
Printed in the United States of America

"**Sketches of a Black Cat: Story of a night flying WWII pilot and artist**" is the product of a long and continuing review of my father's journals, writings, log entries, and personal interviews. It is, to the best of my knowledge, a representative account of his life and times during WWII. Please see *Acknowledgements and Notes* section at the end of the book for more information.

This book may not be reproduced or otherwise transmitted without the expressed written consent of the author except in the case of brief quotations in critical articles and reviews.

You can write to the author at BlackCatWWII@gmail.com

Additional copies of this book are available for sale online at
www.Amazon.com
www.BarnesandNoble.com
www.BooksaMillion.com
and other popular online retailers
as well as SketchesOfABlackCat.com

*Thank you, Dad,
for this unexpected gift*

SKETCHES OF A BLACK CAT

Story of a night flying
WWII pilot and artist

By Ron Miner

Author's Note

I think it is fair to say that in the years since this *Introduction* was first written, I have learned a great deal more about the Black Cat story. Since then, I've had the pleasure of meeting and interviewing quite a few "Cats," some of them members of my father's squadron. One was kind enough to forgive me for mistakenly implying in the *Epilogue* that he was no longer with us when I said, "Dad was the last of the 'Seven' to pass away." At ninety-five, Del Fager and his wife, Bebe, invited us to their home in San Francisco to straighten me out and reminisce over sandwiches and cake. I instantly understood why he and Dad were such close friends.

It seemed nonfiction was becoming a living, growing entity, and while I felt tremendous pride as copies of the book circulated among family and friends, something still gnawed at me. I wondered how much I still didn't know?

When we first visited my father's house in Massachusetts, there wasn't enough time to thoroughly work through all the boxes, drawers, and storage areas, and it required a follow-up trip a year later, together with my brother, Mike, to really feel we had completed the task. This episode was again full of surprises.

We unearthed four years worth of letters — over a hundred of them — that my dad had written home from locations throughout the United States and the South Pacific area. The letters were all in mint condition and lend wonderful specifics to portions of the story that were previously more anecdotal. Yes, even then my father was a prolific writer.

A fantastic but tiny flight notebook turned up deep in the recesses of a large envelope of papers. He carried it with him on every flight during the war. In it were complete sets of notes describing everything from semaphore signals and Morse code to how to start a Corsair. There were detailed drawings of celestial skies for navigation and a "Recognition" section with hand drawn images of all enemy and friendly ships, as they would appear from a flying PBY. Other art pieces and souvenirs have surfaced as well.

All the while, my education continued to flourish, encompassing insightful books and articles, interaction with museums, and over twenty hours of filmed interview footage with squadron members.

Chapter Two, *The Discovery,* now elaborates on the scant details of the *Introduction* and gives what I've come to feel is a necessary explanation of the circumstances leading to the writing of the original book. The insights I've acquired during the interviews with these veterans coupled with the surprising amount of new material that we had yet to discover made me realize that *Sketches of a Black Cat* could offer readers much more detail and supplemental storytelling than it had in version one. Given what I know now, the book felt incomplete. Here was a chance to tell readers more about some of Dad's friends and colleagues, visit unknown locations, and share many additional experiences. This contributed fresh content to every chapter, changed many substantially, and provided a couple of new ones.

I am still hitting the road in search of other squadron members, but of course, this becomes more difficult with each passing day. Dad's story probably still has a few unexpected twists and turns to it, but I feel the Black Cats have, in large part, spoken and these pages accurately reveal their story, as told to me through their collective voices. I hope you enjoy the flight.

I would like to thank Del Fager, Elliot Schreider, Bob Pinckney, and Harold Koenig —all members of VP-54 — Win Stites of VP-91, and John Love's son, Andy Love, for their valuable contributions. And special thanks to VPB-54's Alex Catlow, who was the first to introduce himself and has pointed me in the right direction so many times. He and his wife, Margaret, were instrumental in locating other squadron members, and they continue to be dear friends and supporters. Alex passed away in January of 2018.

Introduction

It's Veterans Day. We've been working on a little project at a local, country cemetery, and throughout the day we see them come and go — the families, the spouses, sometimes the veterans themselves who pay their respects. A cemetery is an appropriate place for us to be on this day, a place of observance and reflection.

A few weeks back, I found myself in another cemetery in Otis, Mass., along with members of our family, celebrating my father's life. Dad had passed away unexpectedly in 2011 at age ninety-two, so this was, similarly, a time of reflection for us and we found ourselves immersed into his life through the stories of friends and coworkers who knew him from the Norman Rockwell Museum where he volunteered, or the Berkshire Scenic Railway, where he had achieved a lifelong dream of being an engineer. There was much to learn, and my lesson was just beginning.

Dad never talked much about the war. I guess that was typical of many WWII vets, but I had memories from my childhood of occasional glimpses of souvenirs, or sometimes a carefully worded anecdote with an upbeat ending. I also had more vivid memories of the file cabinet downstairs where — as I followed him around like a puppy — he, at once, showed me a large, manila folder containing a variety of odd sized sheets of very worn paper. To my surprise, the pages were actually drawings, sketches of planes, ships, jungles, and soldiers. I can remember smiling widely and wanting to touch them and being very proud. Over the years, I would continue to sneak downstairs with friends and show them the cabinet with the sketches, and we would carefully pore over them, imagining what stories they were begging to tell. Then one day, when I tiptoed into his office to take a look, the cabinet was locked. It would be many years before I saw them again.

Dad came out to Oregon for a visit in 1992. I hadn't seen him for quite some time, and we explored the Willamette Valley, checked out some waterfalls, and reminisced. We met up with my brother and his wife in Multnomah the morning he was to fly out of Portland. As we sat around talking, the subject of the war came up, more or less out of nowhere, and slowly he revealed some elaborate tales of his exploits in the South Pacific. It wasn't as if he had been quietly suffering and harboring secrets, it just seemed like it was time. He spoke easily and frankly, as if he knew the stories well, and we were fixated on every word. I desperately wanted to capture these narratives.

Over the years, we would get together as travel would allow, sometimes at reunions at the family house in Northern Georgia. I now came armed with a recorder, and in the evening over my wine and Dad's Scotch, I would try to steer the conversation a bit to see if he would bite. He usually did, and I slowly compiled revealing reflections of his experiences through college and the war. But he also was a product of the Depression era, growing up in austere conditions with a habit of collecting and keeping almost everything. His professed difficulties in retaining information at the college level caused him to become a prolific note taker and, ultimately, writer. During his long career in aviation, he developed a pattern of keeping journals and accurate records for every trip and encounter. He was an enthusiastic family history buff and had quite a remarkable memory. Recently, as we went through some of his things, we found out just how extensive this collection of writing, artwork, documents, and personal photos was.

He was a Navy pilot, a member of VP-54, one of the Black Cat squadron of PBY amphibious aircraft that flew their missions at night, without lights, in lumbering planes painted entirely black. The "Dumbos," as they were lovingly called, flew sorties that would take them on reconnaissance, rescue, and limited bombing runs (only four bombs apiece), frequently scouting enemy positions and communicating what they would find to nearby fighters and bombers, and sometimes illuminating these targets with flares. Later, during his second tour, the unit was reformed and used primarily for rescue and recon patrols.

His story gives us a behind-the-scenes look at one soldier's evolution from enlistment and training to the military camps and missions during the combat years. For me, this overview of life in the Pacific while on-and-off duty was sometimes blunt, awkwardly romantic, and not always politically correct, but it remains a study of the love of flying and the friendships gained during turbulent, unpredictable times — relationships that would continue on at reunions until each of them were finally gone. The tales, sometimes heroic and often laughable, made this an adventure to uncover and explore.

This is a story of heroes, not in the sense of an Audie Murphy or a Congressional Medal of Honor winner, but rather of countless, otherwise average people plunged into an impossible situation. "Pearl" evokes the memory of where each one was when they first heard the news, as "9-11" does today. Like members of our armed forces thrust into multiple tours in Iraq and Afghanistan, the soldier's struggle with the danger, weather, loneliness, and yearning for family is a shared burden all military heroes somehow endure, many throughout their lives.

Dad captured so much of WWII's Pacific Theater in his own hand, both as an artist and a writer. As I thumb through the tattered manila pages, often struggling to make out his words in now faint pencil, I feel honored. And looking at pencil sketches and watercolors that were conceived in tents and Quonset huts on a Pacific island somewhere, I feel blessed. My task was to piece it all together — the notes, letters, and log entries with abundant, detailed first-hand accounts — into a chronicle that is both enjoyable and worthy. Through these "sketches" of his life, I hope to introduce you, as I have been introduced, to my dad in his twenties.

Chapter One

Using the fuselage frame, I tried to steady myself and struggled to stay slightly out of the blustery airstream racing by the open blister hatch as I took my last sighting. Our airspeed was just over one-hundred knots, but the ride was remarkably smooth. There was only a sliver of a moon visible behind me through the port side blister, the other bubble shaped glass hatch that housed our .50 caliber machine guns and served as a doorway for supplies or passengers. The two of them together appeared something like insect eyes protruding from the plane's waist, part of what gave the old PBYs their unmistakable profile.

Tonight the Navigator's table was my office, located in an adjacent compartment behind and somewhat below the pilot's seat, and on it were all the tools necessary to plot our location using charts, hazy radar images, and sometimes star sightings at this exact time of night. I had spent considerable effort in flight school learning the intricacies of celestial navigation, and these ten-hour flights gave me ample time to sharpen my skills. A thousand miles to the south was the Great Barrier Reef's coast of Australia and due west it was about a five-hour flight to New Guinea. We had slinked our way up the "Slot," the long water passageway that stretched northwest from Guadalcanal to Bougainville Island, the largest island of a group dotted with 10,000-foot mountains and active volcanoes. For something over four hundred miles, this corridor passed between Japanese held islands, large and small, forming a gauntlet of sorts but also providing prime hunting ground for enemy activity and shipping. According to my octant, the southern-most islands of Choiseul lay just ahead.

> At first I thought I had spotted a ship or two, but they had apparently gone dead in the water...

"Pilot to Navigator..." John Erhard's voice in my headphones broke my concentration, and for a moment I thought he was addressing someone else, as I frequently sat beside him in the first officer's seat. He was a skilled aviator and a lieutenant, but we enjoyed a certain amount of informality on these long flights. I gave him our position.

"Ensign, head back into the tail cone and have a look."

I made my way back through the plane's darkened interior and past several crew members, stepping through the familiar bulkhead hatches separating each compartment. I could make out the silhouette of our waist gunner in the starboard blister, intently scanning the near invisible ocean surface with his eyes. Once in the tail, I opened the hatch and casually sprawled out so I could peer down at the blackness less than 3,000 feet below.

After a few minutes, I again got the word from John, "See anything down there, Howie?"

At first I thought I had seen a ship or two, but had noticed nothing unusual since. If anything was down there, it had apparently gone dead in the water, as I could no longer make out any sign of the wakes.

"I'm not sure. They may have spotted..." Suddenly, from directly below, came flashes of anti-aircraft fire. Tracers were racing up at us, something plunked into the sidewall, and instinctively, I reared up and slammed shut the belly hatch. John instantly reacted, winging us hard to the left. "You O.K. Howard?" As we slowly pulled away from the explosions that were all around us, I thought, "You just slammed a door. What good was that?"

I had been at this for several months now, along with an eclectic mix of experienced pilots like John and flight school graduates like myself, yet there were times the intensity of things was still beyond anything I had ever experienced before. Secretly, I wondered, "Would I ever get used to it?"

CHAPTER ONE • 3

PBY silhouette over island palms

The Discovery

"His ashes are in the bathtub?" Melissa's tone said it all. I felt it too and was equally astonished at our inability to navigate the muddle of responsibilities that family members typically face in the days and months following a parent's passing.

In my mother's case, she had made sure of every detail and left nothing to chance, fearful of anything that might saddle her children with an additional burden when they least needed it. My father was a very different story. Almost two weeks had now gone by, and we still didn't really know what arrangements had been made, what legal steps had been taken, what details had been released to newspapers, or even where the Hell he was.

My home in Oregon was 3,000 miles from Miami Springs, and the assumption, based on the latest hearsay, was that our father's remains were gracing the porcelain of the Miami house's clawfoot bathtub and we might need to make another trip down there.

"Well, I think they're probably in an urn ..." I offered, trying to give my sister some comfort.

It was only a month ago in February of 2011 that Melissa and Mike, two of my three siblings, and I had flown to Miami to visit with Dad ahead of a serious surgery. At his age, almost 92, major abdominal surgery was really a last resort and we didn't have a good feeling about this one. We jumped a flight and appeared, unannounced, the night before he was scheduled to go in. He and Alayne were together in his room at the hospital nervously passing the time, as going to sleep now would only mean the morning would arrive all the more quickly. I'll always remember the look on their faces as the three of us gently pushed opened the door and poked our heads into the room, an amusing combination of confusion, surprise, and then delight. The positive energy we generated in those few hours and again the next morning might have been enough to get him through the surgery and into recovery. Dad, by all appearances, was in pretty good shape for a ninety-something and tough enough to surprise even the surgeons. But the cancer they found was never part of the equation, and we soon learned there was nothing more they could do.

As he was undergoing the procedure, the three of us had decided against languishing in the hospital's waiting room and tried to prepare Alayne for the possibilities that lay ahead. We spent part of the afternoon cleaning out and sprucing up their minivan, including a time-bomb thermos of coffee and cream that had sat in the Florida sun for ten days. We tried to keep her busy, taking her to lunch and just talking. Mike and I conspired to meet with a counselor hoping to make some inroads toward a suitable place for her to now call home. Although she did not drive and we knew living at the house would no longer work for her, she would have no part of a discussion about leaving it. She was my father's second wife, and we didn't have any real right to make decisions for her.

Dad woke up on March 10, his 92nd birthday and the day we were to catch our flight home. He was very weak and we shared a tearful farewell without really discussing what this all meant. On our return trip, I left knowing the situation was teeming with loose ends and, once in the air, there was a growing sense of helplessness due to distance and an inability to stay involved.

He passed away two weeks later.

A year earlier my wife, Heidi, and I had flown to Massachusetts where Dad had built a cabin in the woods as a New England getaway for the two of them. He had roots in this area and it had always been his dream to have a place in ski country. At that time, they had told us about a little cemetery, and he had even drawn a detailed map indicating their preferred resting place on a lovely hillside in a tiny Berkshire town near Stockbridge.

Now that the summer was nearly upon us, I could sense an unfamiliar tension in my telephone conversations with Alayne, probably the understandable product of feeling lost, afraid, and uncertain about her life. I tried to keep this in mind, but our frustration about the lack of direction and the feeling that nobody was in charge of a host of important end-of-life obligations was becoming more troubling.

Our first concern was Alayne's well being, and at this point she seemed to be moving around to the Senior Center or to friends' homes, but the conversation would always involve a desire to eventually return to her house. None of us could imagine how she would make it work there. She was in a very fragile state and increasingly hard of hearing. It was becoming difficult to have a productive discussion with her about the houses and the other various legalities. While I was sure she wanted this resolved as much as any of us, it was unclear whether we were making any headway. There was anxiety about his will. I wished I could see it. The two of them did not live a lavish lifestyle and I doubted there was much to his estate, and as his spouse, we were happy to allow Alayne the benefit of whatever they shared as a couple. For us as children, it was access to personal family things and family history that was most important. We were reasonably confident that she would always intend for us to have such things, but we just weren't feeling any of this access. Confusion reigned.

Alayne's sister had come into the picture and was extremely active in trying to help out. For some reason, the two of them didn't get along, but Janet could drive and was a good communicator and slowly, a few details that had been bugging me were addressed. She soon managed to get Alayne at least temporarily situated in an assisted living facility. I hoped that we were finally on the right path.

I guess it is closure you want above all — an obituary, a service, the passing on of family heirlooms. My memory of a small collection of artwork, much of it from my dad's WWII years as a pilot in the Navy, was still as clear as the day I first saw it. I probably was about six and we were in the basement in what was considered his office.

In another seven years we would refer to it as the "fallout shelter" as we were all among the duck-and-cover children of the early sixties. He had a file cabinet with important papers and keepsakes of all kinds, boring stuff in large part, but on this occasion he lifted a worn manila folder from the cabinet drawer. Curious, I watched intently as he slid out a small stack of worn pages and turned one over. To my surprise, there was the image of three planes flying through the clouds, each with a striking but bizarre toothy expression near the propellers. "These are *Flying Tigers*," he explained. Then page-by-page we looked through the assorted watercolors and pencil sketches of jungles, planes, soldiers, and tent encampments. Other folders had locomotives or cowboys. It was fantastic! I dearly hoped his artwork would turn up somewhere despite all this confusion since his death, and that it would still be reasonably intact.

The difficulty in gaining any traction with the situation had continued throughout the summer, and while there was some progress with a will and a few boxes that Janet had managed to ship, things appeared to be stalled again. I hadn't been able to speak with Alayne and was no longer even sure of her whereabouts. Our letters and cards to her were now coming back to us. After several weeks of kicking around the possibilities, it was decided that we would go to the Berkshires and have a service. I hoped that most of the immediate family, including Alayne, would be able to make the trip, and we would somehow find the long-lost ashes in time, but another Berkshire winter was looming and it was time to make a move. I had been in touch with others in my family including Dad's sister, Marian, expressing our exasperation with it all. She sent email after email filled with support and wisdom, not the least of which was this: "I know ashes are important, especially to Melissa. However, my feelings about ashes and bodies are that they are somewhat irrelevant compared to the memories people share of the person. That's why I am so happy that you all will get together and do just that! Wish I could be with you!"

On a sunny, seventy-degree October day, a small group of us gathered at that scenic hillside cemetery overlooking the mountains painted in autumn color a short distance away and shared our favorite stories, anecdotes, and memories. With one final emotional group embrace, we concluded our ceremony.

This region included postcard New England communities like Stockbridge, Lenox, Lee, Otis, and Williamstown and was an area with a considerable history for the Miner family. Ancestors had taught, preached, and farmed in communities throughout the Berkshires. Mt. Greylock, the state's tallest mountain, had an ancestor's family farm on its flanks in early times and was a favorite recreational hiking and skiing destination for generations to come. This was Dad and Alayne's stomping grounds and they were active citizens and volunteers. We visited a few places that were important in their lives, like the Norman Rockwell Museum where the staff welcomed us with a tour. They told us a tale of my dad painting Christmas cookies that Alayne had baked with the faces from a variety of Rockwell characters, mimicking artwork hanging there in the Gallery. These cookies were used as ornaments on the museum's tree. At Lenox, the Berkshire Scenic Railroad treated us to a round-

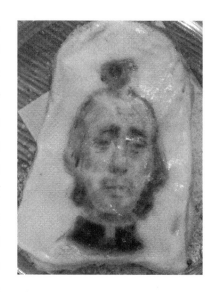

trip train ride to Stockbridge. In retirement, Dad had been one of their engineers.

My other sister, Susan, and her son, Mike, also had made the trip and Alayne's sister, Janet, had joined us. Alayne herself was unable to fly and we were still unsure how she felt about any of this. Cell phone service around the area was spotty at best, and although Janet had a key, we didn't yet know if we could visit the house. At our hotel, there seemed to be one sitting room, specifically one couch in that sitting room, where you could make a call. That evening, we tried again. Alayne sounded clear, spoke warmly, and sounded like herself again, and she said she was happy we made the trip and wished she could have been with us. She was concerned about the house and wondered if we could check on it. Apparently, Janet had told her that flying squirrels might have found their way in and if that was the case, could we deal with it. Of course we could!

It was as I remembered it. Dad had put so much of himself into the house and grounds, creating a small rustic cabin with many handmade touches both inside and out. Extensive trails and native landscaping meandered throughout the rocky glens of hemlock and maple. It showed signs of wear and neglect, but otherwise was in good shape. She was right about the flying squirrels.

It may have been a result of living through the Great Depression and growing up without, but whenever I visited, I always found myself overwhelmed by the crowded clutter that dominated their lives. Very little was thrown away, and it was difficult to know where to begin. Treasure, trash, or both? Relentless.

Other times it was more poignant. About the time I heard Susan say, "Hey you guys, do you remember this?" we noticed Heidi trotting up the stairs clutching the WWII artwork album. This was a great relief to all of us, but the futility of sorting everything was becoming obvious, so we focused on looking for any of Dad's keepsakes and inspecting the general well being of the place.

"Hey Ron, check this out." Mike had found a large box, one of several, and carried it over to the bed. "Some interesting things in here."

Inside, there was a variety of large envelopes and folders, scores of smaller ones containing photos, and a number of red spiral notebooks, perhaps half a dozen. The cover of each had a title in black magic marker and inside was a table of contents with chapter names. Two of them had references to his WWII experiences.

This was new ground. I remembered as a child seeing a wooden locker with Japanese souvenirs in it and, of course, the artwork, but Dad hadn't really spoken much about the war until the last few years and that always took a little gentle prodding.

Mike pulled some final boxes loose and we resolved to give them more scrutiny later and continued on to the next pile. By late afternoon, we were all beat and tired of breathing stale, moldy air, preferring to see what wine might be available back in town. We'd box up everything we could find of importance in the morning and mail or pack it home.

Families sometimes grow stronger out of adversity, and talking together about our collective past gave us comfort. Walking in our father's preferred footsteps, seeing glimpses of his life, and exchanging stories with his friends was nurturing and gave us the closure we were seeking. Alayne's considerate and accommodating eleventh-hour consent was the final piece of a complicated puzzle and we felt the satisfaction of a shared adventure beyond expectations.

I had always felt Dad's artwork deserved a forum of some kind and the idea of a book showing it off with appropriate text or captions had been among my mental musings for some time. Given the underwhelming way things had gone before our trip, it felt like a deserving tribute to him. I spread the boxes around my small office and took inventory, beginning with the photos. There were many hundreds of them. Often, the quality was poor, blurry, the victim of dampness of the tropics, or sometimes just nonsensical groups of guys mugging for the camera. Others were quite good, some powerful and exceptional.

In the folders were stacks of assorted sized pages, most in worn pencil making them difficult to read. A few were photocopied to help with clarity I suppose, and several contained one word titles like "Tarawa" or "Nadia" — titles that were not yet recognizable to me. The red spiral notebooks were jammed with writing, roughly organized by chapter and index. They were predominantly short stories and spontaneous pieces. On the cover of one notebook he had written "Log of My Life." In it were entries, pilot-style, beginning with "Born" and clicking through the months and years with highlights and occasions, each given its rightful place along with a few words of explanation. It was a life calendar. The back of each page was left blank, providing a clear space for additional new entries as they might occur to him.

When I reached the "Forties" the pages included what must be flight log entries, each with corresponding dates, hours, and destinations, but they were somewhat incomplete. In 1944 I saw "Tarawa" again. I examined some of the assorted, small hand written pencil pages more closely, turning over the last page. At the bottom it was signed Lt.(jg) Howard Miner, 1944. There were other groups of pages fastened together with rusty staples, mostly untitled, with short and long descriptions of other locations, islands, and missions. Dates were sometimes there: 1943, Jan. 1945, and others. On the backs of some of the photos were names: Bonnett, Fagerburg, Peckham, Maravich, Peleliu, Guadalcanal. The sheer amount of writing and information was startling. Dad's entire wartime story was likely distributed throughout all these pages and boxes, some of it stored here for over sixty years like assorted jigsaw pieces just waiting for light of day and a willing hand. I only needed to figure out how to put these pieces together.

One of the red spiral notebooks came to the rescue. There were twenty or so chapters on assorted subjects that my dad must have written over a number of years and perhaps after he had retired. One chapter jumped out at me: "Off to the Pacific."

I knew now I had what I'd been looking for — the story that could bring his artwork to life for family, friends, and, I hoped, many others. I opened to Chapter IIA, page one and began to read...

School Days

Our biggest social event of the year at Wabash was the weekend of December 6th, 1941. Margaret came down for this special affair and looked stunning with her long blond hair and evening gown. I was in love. That evening, I gave her my "Sword and Shield" pin before arriving at the hall on campus where my Phi Delta Theta "brothers" sang romantic ballads to us as we danced the night away. We all hit the local snack shop before I finally bid her good night at the door of the rooming house where I had arranged her accommodations. The following day, we again eagerly met for a late Sunday brunch, enjoying conversation and pancakes as the radio played in the background the big band tunes of Jimmy Dorsey and Benny Goodman. It was exciting to think about our future together and playfully speculating about the life we might now share as a couple. Then, almost mysteriously, all about the room a humming sound, the buzz of voices increasing in volume, some kind of commotion, an announcement, slowly more information, and now the smiles had left our faces. The President's voice would confirm our worst fears. Some time later, as Margaret and I talked it over, she gave me my pin back.

It is interesting to contemplate where things might have ended up had World War II not intervened, but with a very low draft number, I knew I would soon be in uniform. I had already turned twenty-one when twenty million of us, from my age through age thirty-six, were given a number and a drawing was held in the fall of 1940. More than 7,000 capsules, each with a different number inside of it, were placed in a giant fishbowl, stirred with a spoon made from part of a beam taken from Independence Hall in Philadelphia, and then hand drawn to determine the order our respective draft boards would use to send out induction notices.

My first experience flying had really impressed me, so earlier during the summer of '41, I had worked on letters and an application for the Army Air Corps at Randolph Field in Texas. When I returned to campus in the fall, the Navy Air Force had come up with a recruiting poster that pointed a provocative finger at me daily saying, "Are you good enough?" I was sure I wasn't. But the concept of flying was so appealing I decided to give it a shot. As the Navy recruiter took my name and personal information, he dismissed my Army flight application with a smile, "Screw 'em," and I was soon on my way to the Navy.

The first hurdle was the physical. When it came to the part where the medic asked, "I don't suppose you can read the bottom line," I was able to easily rattle the letters off correctly, quickly adding, "And down in the lower right hand corner it says, 'Property of the U.S. Navy'." Apparently, they loved good eyesight. I was informed I could expect my orders after the first of the year, so I finished the term knowing "We were at War!" and that I was really a navy cadet. Counting down to my first day at Naval Air Station Glenview (NAS Glenview), I still couldn't believe it, but now I was determined to fly.

The Navy recruiters had arranged a most peculiar swearing-in ceremony, obviously wanting to reap all the publicity they could from this event. A dozen or so of us were treated to a dirt-track auto race and stunt show at the big grandstand at the Indiana State Fairgrounds. Six years earlier, I competed for the second year running in the student category for some pencil drawings of locomotives and horses and was lucky enough to earn blue ribbons both years, giving me free admission every day. I had sneaked into the fringes of this very grandstand to glimpse the chorus girls in their skimpy costumes, a totally new experience for me. Today, the emotions were very different.

As a child I was very interested in both railroading and aviation. I spent hours and hours playing with toy trains and building model airplanes at our home in Indianapolis, right on the line between Fort Benjamin Harrison and the Motor Speedway. On Memorial Day each year we waited with anticipation for the dirigibles and biplanes to fly almost directly above our house, and I even ventured over to

Ohio to watch the USS Macon being built, more than 750 feet long from nose to tail. The blimps were impressive and very captivating to a young enthusiast like myself, and I could almost imagine taking a turn at the controls of one of these giant aircraft.

However, I came from a rather sheltered background with conservative parents, not even owning a bicycle and certainly never attending the Indy 500. Entering the field of aviation was already something of a breach of my protective armor. So here were the race cars, roaring around the track, dust flying everywhere, and the noxious odor of burning oil enveloping us. Cars crashed together, violently, like nothing I'd ever seen. This spectacle was quickly gaining steam and now included an ancient Waco biplane winging low across the infield. He came in lower and lower, and abruptly and deliberately smashed into a newly erected frame building with a horrible impact. A couple of dynamite charges were simultaneously triggered for effect, with smoke and sirens. Rescuers raced onto the scene. They pulled the body of the pilot from the wreckage and, then amazingly, he bounded forward and bowed to the crowd. My nerves were shattered and I was starting to feel nauseous.

Suddenly our group was ushered onto the racetrack, single file, and lined up as the crowd hushed. The color guard marched in to play the "Star Spangled Banner". I was talking to my stomach. Now our right hands were raised and we were taking the oath. I was hanging on. Flash bulbs were popping everywhere. The thing was like a bizarre dream.

As it turned out, one of those flash bulbs belonged to a girl I was not to meet for five years. As luck would have it, we would both stop for hamburgers and somehow begin talking. We went together for many months afterward, and one day she gave me a snapshot she had taken of a line of enlistees as they took the oath. Fortunately, it was a black and white photo, concealing the fact that my face was actually green.

So what were we to make of this? Was I excited, anxious, or just plain scared? The passions young Americans felt about the atrocity at Pearl Harbor gave most of us plenty of motivation, but the anxiety of family and friends was real and difficult to ignore. I was in it now, for better or for worse, so I became determined to do what I could to enjoy the moment and appreciate each day as it came.

Things began with a choice of duty: lighter or heavier than air? While dirigibles had fascinated me back in school, they were brought nearly to termination upon the crash of the Hindenburg at Lakehurst. Only the Navy continued to make use of some for training and eventually a few rigid and non-rigid blimps for patrols. But it didn't seem the way to go, and by and large these patrols were taken over by the PBY Catalina flying boats I would soon know so intimately.

> A stagger-wing Beechcraft biplane was landing towards us and it quickly became obvious he had miscalculated.

By now the number of Indianapolis Naval cadets awaiting flight training had grown to perhaps forty. Our parents organized an "Indianapolis' Own" Squadron, and they designed and issued each of us a gold pin. The night before we shipped out, they held a first rate "bash" for us at the local Naval Armory on White River. The following day, I was picked up by Jack Evans and his parents, and we drove to NAS Glenview north of Chicago. This seemed appropriate, as the image of his brother, Bob, standing and saluting during the National Anthem at a Wabash-Butler football game had largely persuaded me to go Navy in the first place. It was January 29, 1942.

Our stint at "Elimination Base" was pretty impressive but no easy task. Boot cadet training started promptly. We were the lowest of the low on the military scale, and a marine sergeant with a squeaky but stern voice gave us the word on making up bunks, tight with forty-five-degree corners and all, or waxing barrack floors slick enough to skate on. He formed us into platoons and barked in shrill, hieroglyphic voice commands, "Hun, who, heep, hoe," and then for good measure, "to the rye, Har!" Ted Shadinger, my upper bunkmate, found this hysterically funny, and he and I would sneak looks at each other to see if either of us would lose it, which made it all the funnier. "Howie, Harch!" he'd loudly whisper, upping the stakes, and we'd both bite our lips and look away for fear of getting guard duty or worse.

Our first reveille was as advertised, early, dark, and loud like a stick beating in a bucket. I still don't know why the Navy calls a washroom the head, but it was a hell of a different experience for a "protected" kid like myself: forty or so young men sitting on johns, standing at urinals, brushing teeth at wash basins, all with different techniques, shapes, sizes, and routines. It was evident there was to be very little privacy. And, of course, there was among us one individual of such considerable size and girth that he was the subject of endless speculation.

Inspections were held almost daily, and every item of gear had to be in order. Rifles were issued and the Marines showed us the fine art of field stripping them. A few of the rebellious personalities were already marching the ramp with rifles on their shoulders, so it seemed best to play along.

As ground school got underway, I found the classes in Morse code kind of appealing — "Dit-dah-dit-dit" endlessly, earphones on, right hand on the key. I was engrossed in my tapping, seated by the window of the little frame radio shack during an afternoon class beside the grass airfield, and looked up from the keys for a moment. A stagger-wing Beechcraft biplane was landing towards us and it quickly became obvious he had miscalculated, bouncing and bobbing along with very little slowing to show for it. He got the thing stopped about one half a plane length from our windows. As the wobbly pilot made his way out of the biplane, the look on his face was enough to get a few of us wondering what we had gotten ourselves into.

In 1938, when I was still at Williams College in Williamstown, Mass., I experienced my first real taste of the approaching conflict. Up until then, I had little interest in foreign affairs, having quite enough on my plate just trying to stay in school. My studies were compromised by a combination of poor grades and gross financial problems and, of course, my expanding awareness of women. This particular evening there was a student bonfire and rally where Adolph Hitler was hung in effigy, a very strange display of passion by a group not all that crazy about a war. After transferring to the more moderate Wabash in Indiana for the '39-'40 term, I became interested in Zoology, finally landing a scholarship for a summer of study at Woods Hole (Mass) in 1941. It was a coed group, involving hard work (and play), but by this time, all the men in the group were solidly focused on the growing hostilities and world situation. It was back at Williamstown, however, where I took that first airplane ride, an adventure that persuaded me to pursue the life of a pilot. And now here I was.

It was the dead of winter on the edge of Lake Michigan, perfect weather for flight training, according to the Navy. Straightaway, upon our arrival at the base, we were lined up at muster and issued winter coats. Some were given leather sheepskin-lined flight jackets, but at this early stage of the war, supplies were limited and there were too few to go around. The rest of us were handed blue Navy submarine pea coats with an apologetic "Lots of luck." Standing and shivering at morning muster while trying to convince our bodies that we were warm was one thing, but for flying in the open cockpit of our trainer, a Spartan NP-1 biplane, there was no choice. The subzero temperatures required the complete sheepskin flying suits with helmets, goggles, scarfs, and fur mittens. The planes had to be warmed up for thirty minutes or longer before they were safe to fly, and from the ready room we would take turns performing this chore, ten minutes on and ten minutes off. We hated it.

The flying itself was a combination of terror and incredible excitement! The instructor sat in the forward cockpit, the student in the aft. On my first flight with an instructor in the open cockpit, the temperature was way below zero and my goggles fogged up and froze from nervous sweat. I couldn't understand the one-way conversations through the Gosport, a system of rubber tubes fastened near our ears. Everything was strange, the smell of the aircraft, the engine "blatt," the stomach sensations and nausea, the sights (when airborne, we were instantly, totally lost). The instructor tried to point out the importance of the sound of the airflow on the guy wires to determine speed and of keeping our eyes out of the cockpit.

And the landing. Harrowing seems the word. At the end of one period, our hotshot instructor decided to land on the only short paved landing strip on the base, which happened to be somewhat out of the wind. He probably hadn't had much more flying time than I did because as he rolled to a stop, the crosswind got

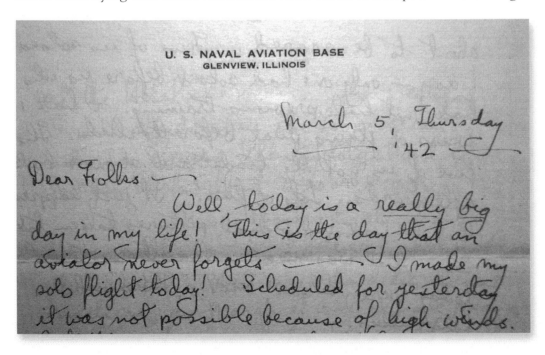

the better of him and he spun around in a wild, dust-spewing skid. To his credit, his composure now back in hand, he announced into the Gosport, "This is known as a ground loop. We don't do this here!"

After a few periods, I was "kicked off the perch" to solo in the NP-1. High winds had interfered for a couple of days, but today it was still — perfectly clear, spring-like weather. After a half hour warm up with my instructor, I went up with a different one for a check. He had me make a couple of landings, gave me a few cut throttles (forced landings) and generally found plenty to gripe about. I was getting worried about a "down check" as we taxied into the ramp, then I realized he was singing.

He paused, and then got out. "Take her around the field once." I was on my own.

It was both a thrill and no different at the same time, with too much to think about to be scared. Five of us soloed that day and all got the traditional shower bath afterwards.

The ensuing sessions were used to build up experience on our own. Usually we practiced during the noon hour as the instructors were at chow and the field was uncrowded. On one of my early flights, I guess the wind had shifted and no one had reset the tetrahedron. My take off seemed awfully slow and dragged out, and before I knew it, the hangar building was dead ahead and I was barely airborne. On the roof was a pole with a red obstruction light on it. Since it was obvious that my wing would clip it, I simply raised the wing till I cleared it and then put it back on level. It seemed quite the logical thing to do. It was after I landed that I got the shaky knees, and quickly taxied back to the line and called it a day. Somehow, though, I felt like a pilot.

Imagine for a moment the feeling you may have had as a child dangling upside down from playground bars or trying to stand on your head. Blood rushes down and eyes bulge, a combination of unpleasant disorientation, dizziness, and maybe even a little humor. This was what was in store for us the day we were upgraded into the Navy's traditional acrobatic biplane trainer, the N3N, or the "Yellow Peril," a name that suited it for more than one reason. Since Ted had already accomplished his airline flight training, he had soloed easily in a couple of hours. He was idly waiting for us to catch up at every milestone, and his coaching became invaluable as our difficulty intensified. My squeamish stomach was becoming an issue again, but he had a plan. "Howie, let's get you doing a series, instead of one move. We start out at 6,000 feet, right? Dive into the loop, then follow it right away with a snap roll, a couple of 'em, then go for the big ending. A two-turn spin and now you're down to 2,000 feet. It's so fast you'll forget to puke!" Sure enough — shaken but intact.

By far the most insidious and revolting maneuver of all was the inverted spin. This was essential, they told us, because in some higher performance aircraft, during a loop, it was possible to end up in a stall while on our backs. Recovering from this predicament took an inverted spin; all control functions were reversed, you pulled back on the "joy stick" instead of pushing forward, as in a normal spin. During a particular training session, as I made a half loop and kicked into an inverted spin, debris was falling from the bilges of the aircraft past my goggles, I was hanging from my seat belt, and my head was reeling as I looked down at the approaching ground "above" my head.

There was a monastery. I could even see the monks walking about with their Bibles in the gardens, and I thought, "What a pity, crashing into such a peaceful setting." Then I rallied myself and hit the opposite rudder, pulled back on the stick, and was able to recover into normal level flight. I wondered what they thought.

During my free time, I would occasionally stroll down to the flight line and admire the transient combat planes. Sometimes it was fun to sit and sketch the F4F carrier fighters and larger, newer attack aircraft with their sophisticated flush rivets. On occasion, for liberty weekends I would take the train to Chicago with Ted and another buddy, Robin Sims, and stay at a German hotel in the Loop. Ted's dad was a chemistry professor at Butler University, and he and Sims were both Chemistry majors who attended school there until joining the Navy — two very sharp fellows indeed. Ted was charismatic and handsome with a luminous smile and magnetic personality, charming to women and a solid friend to men. Robin left school during his junior year and was a Sigma Chi. He was a bit shorter than the other two of us, and I found I got kind of a kick out of him. We all had been part of Indianapolis' Own and had family who kept close tabs on what we were up to and how our training progressed, but when it came to these liberty weekends, all we wanted to do was forget about training for a while. Granted, our lowly cadet "tans" were even below the "boots" of the Lake Michigan Naval Training Base, but still, the United States was at war and military men were on stage. At this point, I was still not drinking, so we would hit the strip joints and light up a cigarette over a Coke and look around, hoping for some action.

On a Sunday night, I met a feisty little brunette and things seemed to be going well enough, until I discovered midnight had come and gone and I had missed my train back to the base. When I finally arrived at the gate, the Marines opted to ignore my tardy return. Making my way into the barracks and back to my bunk, I thought I was home free until Ted sleepily advised me, "Hey, man, they made bed check and you are AWOL." To prevent the kindly Marines from being fingered, I walked all the way back to the gate and told them to log me in late. I paid dearly for my indiscretion with ten hours of marching with a shoulder rifle on the hangar ramp.

Ground school continued with semaphore flag and blinker light communications and more Navy regs. Flight training advanced into cross country runs up to Milwaukee and wherever, and before long it was possible to find Glenview in the blinding snow squalls of February: just fly down the shore of Lake Michigan to the "Temple," turn west, and there it was.

So after six weeks, Elimination Training was complete, and the cadet-fliers all boarded a train and headed south. I had 10.4 hours dual, 6.7 hours solo, and we were now pilots, or so we thought. The trip was a chance to relax a little, maybe with a bit of new swagger, and I watched Ted operate with every female on the train, white teeth shining behind that totally confident grin. Sims was doing OK, too. But, still encumbered with my conservative and insecure social background, I was getting nowhere.

Dallas "Pool" Base — an entire month devoted to waiting for space at Corpus Christi. Our weeks were filled with ground school — aerodynamics, aerology, enemy aircraft and ship identification, engines, weapons, and celestial navigation. No flying and the celestial navigation was tough and boring. At least there was downtown Dallas with its reputation for lovely ladies, and Ted continued his winning ways with them; I so envied him. It was also the occasion of my first (and then second) beer, a breakthrough of sorts, I suppose.

To most military guys, alcohol and cigarettes were as important as a rifle. If you didn't enjoy either when you got in, you likely did before you got back out. Before enlisting, I visited a close friend in Olney, Ill., a city of albino squirrels. His father was an undertaker there and, over the course of the weekend, they showed me around, eventually heading downstairs and through the basement. There, spread out on white linens, was a body, the first up close view I'd ever had of a dead person. We made our way upstairs and sat down to talk a while. "What would you like to drink?" Innocently enough, I replied, "What would you suggest?"

"How about a Margarita?" I nodded, not even knowing what one was. It was good and went down a little too quickly, and I wasn't prepared for the feeling it gave me. This first experience with drinking had been both unsettling and unpleasant, and I hadn't tried it again until Dallas. I suppose the time away and the dangers faced affect the things you do to relax. At any rate, Navy guys liked their alcohol.

The month ended and it was on to Corpus Christi Naval Training Center in Texas. Here our work really intensified and ground school became heavily involved with celestial navigation. We peered at the stars through sextants and octants and even spent late night hours in sophisticated simulators high in the darkened interiors

of domed buildings. The mathematics involved almost defeated us, especially Sims, but Ted, with his head start in aviation, was able to fill in the gaps where we needed it, and somehow we made it through.

The group continued flying the "Yellow Perils," practicing a couple hours at a time, and returning to base, the whole swarm of us in our little N3Ns arrived together. Guidelines dictated we stagger ourselves right and left to land on the mat in a continuous stream. As I rounded out to try for the typical Navy tail wheel landing, I was alarmed to discover that the plane wanted to become airborne again. I couldn't seem to whip it. After bouncing a couple of times with throttle completely closed, I was still skimming the hot pavement. The planes in front of me were somehow coming to a stop, but I was merrily sailing toward them. Growing desperate, I steered a course to zigzag around each one and ultimately got the beast slowed to a standstill. After taxiing to the line and shutting down, I was advised that the commander of operations wanted me in his hangar office, "Pronto!" Terrified, I appeared on the carpet giving my name, rank, and serial number, as prescribed.

"Just what in the Hell were you doing?" he blared. "Don't you know how to make a wheel landing?"

"I thought all landings were wheel landings," I stammered.

Apparently, during the two hours I was away from the field, the wind had picked up substantially, and the customary tail wheel type landing we were trying to master for carrier operations would not work. Easing back on the stick would only propel the lightweight aircraft back into the sky, and I needed to land on the front wheels, nose low, and allow the plane to slow to a crawl. This procedure had been omitted from our curriculum, until now. At length, the commander bought my explanation and assigned me to further training in "wheel landings."

"Spot landings" were equally humbling. Picture, if you can, flying downwind above a circle marked on a grass field. At this point, you cut your engines and glide, power-off, without benefit of flaps (which you didn't have on an N3N) or slipping (which involved crossed controls to come down rather sideways, increasing drag at will, which was not easy), yet still managing somehow to plunge the thing into the circle without crashing. I couldn't seem to judge the maneuver well enough to hit the necessary two of three, and I thought I had washed out for sure. I was granted extra time and assigned to another instructor, Lt. Blackmore, an ex-airline pilot. He was infinitely patient and nursed me through the necessary skills to pass the test.

While the flight suits did the job in the N3Ns, for anything else we needed our local "uniform shop." The process of getting fitted for uniforms was an elaborate one: dress blues, dress whites, working greens, working suntans, it all took time and was expensive. Along the way, I became acquainted with a girl named Henricia, who worked there. I was able to persuade her to go on a date, quite an accomplishment considering the flow of cadets through the shop. We spent time together over the next few weeks, dining at some intriguing restaurants or lolling around the stepped concrete breakwater along the city's lovely waterfront. Corpus Christi was an interesting change for me and having her to spend time with and show me around town made it special. Ted had, by now, become involved with a lovely girl named Nancy. On one occasion Sims had a blind date, and the six of us all had dinner and hit a few nightclubs. It was a memorable evening. Ted and Nancy invited us all to Sunday brunch the next morning at a petite little hotel next to the high-rise Driscoll Hotel and we toasted with champagne, my inaugural acquaintance with that bubbly beverage.

According to rumor, Mrs. Driscoll, a multimillionaire, had once been insulted by the management of this smaller establishment and vowed to "Pee on their roof!" She acquired the property next door and built a multistory building with her penthouse on the top floor — and indeed one day stepped outside and proved she wasn't bluffing. At least that was the legend. Ted and I enjoyed teasing the girls about exactly how they might go about accomplishing that. It was funny how the time away from training, with the stresses and apprehension about the future that it seemed to bring on, was becoming as important as the training itself.

There were numerous satellite bases scattered around the southern foot of Texas, and one or another would be selected for a certain phase of training, for example, so called "basic" training. Here we moved into heavier, low wing SNV trainers, a type of Vultee aircraft, and became familiar with the use of flaps and changeable pitch propellers — props with blades able to twist slightly along their length to allow the pilot to adjust the thrust produced by the engine. On my first solo practice flight in one of these new dream machines, I felt I was truly in Heaven. I was really enjoying myself out in one of the big grass fields shooting "touch and go" landings, but after a time, became concerned because the takeoffs were so dragged out, barely clearing the far fence. Eventually, I headed into the base and sought my instructor's advice. "Did you shift the prop into low pitch before each takeoff?" With all the new gadgetry, and my concentration elsewhere, I had forgotten the prop and was in low RPM. My growing pains were teaching me the wisdom of a checklist. I also began keeping more notes and compiling some ledgers.

In many ways, Cabaniss Field was an enjoyable place. Originally, about 500 of us moved into the newly constructed barracks there, and other than a lack of hot water for a few days, I found the smaller size of the place appealing in the way that a small college might feel when compared to a large university.

There were two squadrons of a hundred planes each, meaning plenty of flying for everybody in those blue Texas skies, playing tag with cotton-like clouds for four or five hours a day. It was easy to forget you were strapped into a ton and a half of steel fabrication that was, according to the laws of physics, going just fast enough to stay up there.

Ted and I were talking as we headed back to the Field after a relaxing afternoon and a much needed liberty. We were still in shock at the loss of a shipmate, George, who had apparently let his airspeed drop too much and lost control of his plane. I had a flight in the morning and needed to pick up some cards for my folks' anniversary afterward, so we agreed to head over to Ship's Service first and then see what we could do about flowers.

Back at the barracks, about a half hour before taps, there was a blackout. "Not again!" came a voice out of the dark. "How am I supposed to study for this damn exam tomorrow!"

"I'm sure they spotted that sub again. You know, the one down in the West Indies, 2,000 miles away," Russ, my other roomie, chimed in.

It was over in another fifteen minutes — we never really knew if these things were practice or the real deal. Then about five minutes after taps, the whistle blew again.

"Aaggghh!" I figured it was another blackout and hopped out of bed to turn out what few lights were still on. Suddenly, the fire truck that usually chases around with its sirens blaring when the blackout is called stopped — directly in front of Ship's Service. A few of us poked our heads out to see what was up.

"Holy cow, there's smoke up in the cupola!"

I rushed out along with several other cadets, all still in our shorts, and we pulled the hoses loose and snapped them onto the hydrant just as the enlisted men began swarming in from their barracks. It was a crazy scene, smoke filling the cafeteria and the general merchandise rooms with everything getting soaked down, including us. After an hour or so, things seemed under control, and I headed back to bed — I had a check to take in the morning. So much for my folks' anniversary cards.

It was usually during the other form of "basic," those abominable training drills on the ground that you realized how deathly hot Texas could be. "Cokes" were the preferred way of replenishing fluids, most of us downing three or four a day, about a nickel each, and they were at their refreshing best when those bits of ice would make their way up the neck of the bottle to the surface. Our cadet working uniforms were suntans, which had a tendency to quickly blotch around the arms. The sergeant called us in to hand out some additional equipment; "I have, here, official Navy issue rain gear for each of you." Sims looked at me, and then we both looked at the sky. I suppose it might have been slightly threatening, although the Navy selected Corpus, in part due to the low incidence of cloudy days. "You will bring it along for today's hike." And so we did. This wartime garment was some sort of fabric painted with battleship gray flexible enamel. It was unquestionably close to waterproof, but every bit as effective as an evaporation barrier. A drop must have hit the sergeant in the nose somewhere along the way, and he barked out an order to don the rain gear. We continued to march along, singing and swinging as the gear rustled to our movements and the sun continued to beat down. When it finally ended and we removed the stinking stuff, our suntans were chocolate browns and couldn't have been wetter if he had marched us into the bay.

The next real step was into the first service type aircraft, the OS2U Vought Kingfisher (a nifty little thirty-foot seaplane that looked more like a fighter carrying a way too big twenty-nine-foot bomb. It was often used in a float version based on cruisers). What an exciting prospect! "Go out and climb aboard, I'll join you in a bit," the instructor said to Ted and me. I scrambled into the forward cockpit, Ted in the aft. We were looking over all the controls, levers, and unfamiliar gun and bomb arming switches, and underneath the seat, I discovered a mysterious, cone-shaped device connected to a hollow tube. My first thought was that it was some sort of Gosport communicator, like in the biplanes. Then I noticed the encrusted yellow

Greetings!

Lineup of biplane trainers

"Spot Landings" Circle

Some flier classmates that would become part of the VP-54 squadron (arrows courtesy of Howard's mom)

John Love, future governor of Colorado, and Ray Peckham were VP-54 Black Cats

stuff within it and it dawned on me that this was for those "longer" flights. Just then, I heard Ted, "Hey Howard, look!" I spun around to see him with the cone to his mouth. "A speaking tube!" Ted was inclined a bit to jump first and think later. It was a trait that was, one day, to do him in.

The Nordon bombsight was a fascinating optical device with crosshairs and a couple of control knobs. You preset the crosshairs and fixed on a target, and then steering was done by an "auto pilot" guided by the sight. However, our initial experience with it came not in an aircraft, but on moving stands in an empty hangar. These were set on rubber wheels, probably battery propelled, and stood some eight or more feet high, where the student sat on a platform to peer into his bombsight instrument. On the "deck" there was a map painted with various "targets" illustrated in a crude image. When activated, the stand would creep ahead and be guided by the knob adjustments on the bombsight. At the estimated release point, a switch was pushed to drop a miniature missile. It was fun. Ironically, this poorly done map of bombing targets was of the Corpus Christi area. It seemed to me that it might as well look pretty authentic, so I requested and got permission to redo it, perhaps leaving my own mark on the base for posterity.

It was the summer of '42. After a brief stay at Cuddihy Field, I had moved again to another part of the base. A few days later, a hurricane passed through the area, coming ashore at one of our favorite swimming beaches at Aransas Pass, about forty miles by car, fifteen by air. The seven-mile causeway to Mustang Island was knocked out and it flooded miles and miles of oil country. From above, it still looked wet down there.

We had been given a choice of carrier aircraft or flying boats. I chose the boats, as did Ted, both of us feeling that, if all went well, the larger twin-engine aircraft might be more in line with any ambitions we had about future airline careers. We began taking instruction in the PBY Catalina seaplanes right in Corpus Christi Bay, and it was a tremendous thrill. There were now two throttles instead of one, and six to eight people in the crew, generally including a couple of trainees to swap off with an instructor. We focused on three types of landings: power on, normal, and stall. Each was most appropriate to a certain water and wind condition. The power

> NAVAL AIR STATION
> "UNIVERSITY OF THE AIR"
>
> September 18, Friday '42
>
> Dear Folks —
>
> You'd never in the world guess where this is being written, but it might be interesting to you to mention it — about 7200 feet over the Gulf of Mexico breezing along at about 110 knots in a "flying boat." I am sitting at the navigator's desk killing time while awaiting my turn at the controls. You see it is really very smooth sailing! And if the pilot knows his business pretty well I can't even tell when we are climbing, gliding, or standing on one wing tip in a deep bank. In fact there is only one interruption occasionally, and that is when we make a full-stall landing — that shakes us up considerably and makes about as much racket as though we were landing in a pile of gravel!

landing was used on smooth or glassy water with little or no wind. A certain power was set up with a "sink rate" of 175 feet per minute down, and the plane was flown until you heard the pat-pat-pat of the wavelets under the step of the hull. You would pull off the power and that was it. The normal landing was from a "power off" glide, where you came down and rounded out and put it on the water. You needed good depth perception and had to have enough wind to make the water choppy, perhaps six to fifteen knots. In rougher seas, a full stall landing was used. This was more like the tail-wheel landings we had learned from day one at Glenview. You would hold the plane off the surface with no power until it finally stalled just above it and came crashing down with a horrendous splash, sounding more like you had landed in a gravel pile than in water. Each style was fun and we practiced them all. Then we worked with plane-mounted bombsights, dropping lead weights with shotgun shells to mark the "hit." We also began applying our celestial navigation on three-hour flights. Ted, Sims, and I were all sometimes on the same crew. Ted and I had been bunkmates since Glenview. He was a sidekick and good friend to me during our training together, but while I liked him a lot, I was more and more struggling with what seemed to be his growing tendency toward overconfidence and impulsiveness. I watched as he pulled several careless boners on flights with crews, and I started to fear flying with him.

Link trainers were like imitation airplanes and we had four large rooms each containing about twelve of them. Each cadet would sit alone in the things with a cover over his head, staring ahead at the mass of instruments that represented a particular aircraft's cockpit dashboard. The device would allow us to do everything but go onto our backs — we could spin, stall, change airspeed, even bounce and buck along in very rough air — all while an instructor sat at a nearby desk talking back and forth with us. A remarkable gadget called a "crab" traced our exact path on a sheet of paper. Radio work required orienting yourself on a radio range and riding a beam into a selected airfield. Once we had fifteen hours or so on the links, we transferred to the real planes and did it all over again. It was a thrill to feel my way along the Rockport radio range while under a hood and totally blind, then nervously begin my timed let-down and announce, "I should be over the field..."

My instructor said, "Come on out of the hood," and dipped a wing revealing the gorgeous sight of the airfield right below us. You could have knocked me over with a feather.

The low-pressure chamber was a chance for ten of us to find out what the air was like at high altitude. A doctor started with a simple little mental exam, and then took us up to 18,000 feet where atmospheric pressure is only half and no one could remain conscious over fifteen minutes or so. He gave us another exam after only five minutes, then took us all the way up to 28,000 feet for a third exam.

We all scored similarly on the first and third, but for some reason on the second at 18,000, my score was somewhat lower, maybe an indication that I was slightly more susceptible to the affects of altitude. Regardless, it was a fun way to spend an afternoon.

Curiously, as our training progressed, it became obvious that the training squadron was up to something, and slowly, a spanking new obstacle course materialized beside our barracks complex. Earth was mounded up, sections of sewer pipe were arranged, a wall was erected, and an enormous cargo net made of hemp rope was strung over a high cable like a tent. We watched with both interest and trepidation. As it was completed, they announced it would be christened the following day and our group would have the honor of the first run under the watchful eye of the admiral and his daughter in the reviewing stand. It was a wild day. We had no time to practice the obstacles individually or train and condition ourselves. They rather preferred to line us up and turn us loose. The several gazelles among us took off and set a furious pace while the rest of us scrambled along behind them. Some fell along the way. I nearly met my maker on the cargo net, but somehow we staggered on in, completely exhausted, and hating the admiral's daughter.

Our several months of operational training in the PBYs neared completion. Soon it would be graduation day, and we would be given our Golden Wings. The camp was buzzing with anticipation and I had my four different colored Navy uniforms waiting and ready. Ted had opted to go Marine after graduation. He had discovered that the Marines offered a six-month training course in transport type R4Ds* flying instruments around the country, and he felt it would be invaluable for airline careers. I also think the snazzy dress blue uniform with the red stripe may have tipped him. But I was pretty damn proud of my Blue and Gold!

The two of us went out for a final weekend on the town. Flying was finished and we had made it. "Let's do it up right," he suggested, and we booked rooms at the more expensive Driscoll (remember Mrs. Driscoll) and headed to the lounge for champagne cocktails. He was in high form, smiling and chatting it up with everything in a skirt and, of course, persuaded one young lady over to the table where he turned on the full power of his charm. I watched in scientific wonder as

---

* R4D was the Navy's version of a DC-3 like those used for passengers on commercial airlines throughout the U.S. The army designation was C-47.

she melted under his gaze, and it wasn't long before they took off together "to see her car."

So I was on my own again and decided to head upstairs and grab a nap in preparation for a late night.

I was soundly sleeping when there was a knock at the door. I was surprised to find Nancy standing there. "I was looking for Ted," she started. "Would you know where he is? He's not in his room." This was awkward. I assured her that I did not know his whereabouts, although he was in town.

"Would you like to come in? We can call his room from here," I suggested. She quickly sat down and explained that she had traveled from Dallas and expected him to meet her at the bus station. "I know he understood I was arriving today. He's just so unreliable," she lamented. "Did I do something? Is it me?"

She had come all this way to help him celebrate his crowning achievement, and where was he? Over the past few months, I had gotten to know Nancy really well, and I felt tremendous compassion for her at this moment. I was miffed about my role as go-between, Father confessor, or whatever. Ted had really blown it here and it bothered me.

I looked at her and there were tears in her eyes — and that did it. I had to do something, so I drew her to my shoulder to comfort her. "You haven't done anything wrong," I said. " I think you are wonderful."

"Well, I wish Ted did, too," she whispered.

"I think he really does," I reassured her. She walked a few steps away with a gesture of frustration, then turned abruptly and stared at me helplessly. "In fact, I know he does ... you're very beautiful." What was I saying?

I may have been admiring her and she caught me and raised a brow, and I suddenly realized my off-hand remark may have surprised us both. I tried to clarify things. "I mean, look at you ... your hair, your figure, everything ..." Now I was fumbling around trying to hide my embarrassment and only making things worse.

It was one of those moments that comes along, maybe once in a lifetime. You have bared your soul to someone and could very well never live it down, a "shake your head" memory that will always stick with you. Or she could bare hers as well. And that, to my astonishment, is what she did, slowly at first, until in a few moments, she stood before me, a stunning silhouette in the twilight of my room. I felt I needed to move toward her. We gently embraced. I was still amazed by the pace of the encounter but felt helpless to resist it. As the interlude continued, the tiny voices that always found me at times like this prattled in my ear, "What are you doing?"

I negotiated. "Ted can be a jerk."

"He's your buddy. How will you ever face him? Or her?" It was no use.

"I can't," I whispered. "Not today. Perhaps, someday if you and Ted … I'm sorry, you are special to me. Let me help you with your things."

She looked me in the eye and smiled, kind of proudly. There was no embarrassment, and we held each other warmly one last time before she went through the door. I never saw her again.

The Navy Corps Band was playing loudly on the parade grounds, and Ted and I stood side by side at attention. It was Graduation Day. The admiral pinned the Golden Wings on our chests, our throats trembling with emotion. We faced each other smiling widely, saluted smartly, and then pulled Sims over and all bear hugged with a howl. A few days before, we had attended a mandatory lecture in the big auditorium. A fleet carrier pilot had returned from Pacific combat duty and he had much to say about the Navy action. We devoured his war stories eagerly. In his closing remarks, he brought us back to earth with a stunning analysis: "Only a third of you guys will return, you know. The Japs will get the other two-thirds."

I met Ted's parents briefly less than a year after he had joined the Marines. Ironically, he had been switched from transport planes into SBD dive bombers. It was on his first solo flight around North Island in San Diego that he grabbed the wrong handle, the dive brakes popped on instead of the landing flaps, and he went straight in.

I requested and received permission to bring the body back to Indianapolis for burial at Crown Hill Cemetery. It was a full military funeral. As I saluted the casket during taps, there in my dress blues, I recalled the Navy officer at the Wabash/Butler football game. It was at once a proud, sad, and very scary moment for me. I spent a few days with Ted's family before returning to the Pacific for another three years. It was only a short time later that I received word that Sims, too, had bought the farm out there somewhere. Two of the three of us were now gone.

BT-13 Valiant, an advanced trainer used by the Navy

Ensign Howard Miner with biplane trainer

VMAIL shows redacted text for security. Nothing revealing location or activities was permitted

MR. AND MRS. H.D. MINER
5141 PARK AVENUE
INDIANAPOLIS, INDIANA

ENS. H.D. MINER (Sender's name)
FLEET WING TWO (Sender's address)
% FLEET POST OFFICE
SAN FRANCISCO, CAL.
DECEMBER 6, 1942 (Date)

Dear Folks —

I am writing you from our stateroom on a certain U.S. Army Troop Transport. The stateroom is somewhat larger than our living room, has two showers, eight bunks and lockers, four dressers. ▓▓▓▓▓▓▓▓▓▓▓▓▓▓▓▓▓▓▓▓▓▓▓▓ 's quarters, while ▓▓▓▓▓▓▓▓▓▓▓▓▓▓▓▓ It is very crowded but perfectly comfortable. Meals served in a regular dining room are excellent.

The trip so far has been quite pleasant and uneventful. Although the first night out was very rough and many were sick, none of the fliers had any trouble, and the others soon recovered. The weather is warmer, and we are in khakies.

The view from the deck is of course rather monotonous — no land, inky waves, ▓▓▓▓▓▓ nearby, overcast above. At night the foam is luminescent. We spend most of the day on deck — nothing else to do. Everyone is happy and worried about nothing.

We expect to make port tomorrow night, and I will mail this when we dock. Let me know how it comes thru.

Love — Howie

V—MAIL

C. Times   CORPUS CHRISTI, TEXAS, FRIDAY, SEPTEMBER 11, 1942

CRPUS CHRISTI TIMES 10/30/42
GRADUATION DAY

HOWARD D. MINER, Jr.
Indianapolis, Ind.
USNR

"COMMANDO" MINER

ALL IN A MESH—One of the Navy's toughest obstacle courses is the military track recently opened at the Corpus Christi Naval Air Station. The horseshoe-shaped course is more than 350 feet long, and offers mental as well as physical hazards, requiring the runner to think fast as he encounters new obstacles. One of the most impressive is the rope climb, shown above, consisting of a cargo net 30 feet high, which the runners are required to climb. They go up one side, down the other. Other obstacles are hurdles, water jumps, tunnels and sand pits. The course is designed as a method of toughening the men who are being trained as the Navy's future flying officers. (Official U. S. Navy

The First Tour

I stepped off the launch into the darkness of the dock at Alameda Naval Air Station with some thirty other brand new officers. We were all reporting to our first duty assignment since recently receiving our wings and were a little uneasy as we took in the details of this strange, new environment. Towering above us was the superstructure of an aircraft carrier, enormous and waiting with ramp lowered. It was confounding; I had not trained for carrier duty. I was a seaplane pilot somehow misplaced and heading aboard the wrong ship. Mechanically, I moved along with the group. They were all complete strangers. There was no one I had trained with or felt I could ask or confide in.

The group of us walked along for fifty paces or so and came to an intersection. To the left, the ramp ascended sharply into the ship, and to the right, it went ashore among a shadowy group of palm trees and buildings. Those palm trees kind of whispered to me, a lucky break as it turned out, and I wandered among them in the darkness and felt my way along. By midnight I had found my assigned quarters and was able to relax a little and review this particularly long day.

It had, in fact, been an incredible eight months, and by October 1942, I was taking my final training run in a PBY. I had opted for the South Pacific instead of the Aleutians, I guess primarily because given the choice of simmering at the equator or getting frost bitten near the North Pole, I preferred to take my chances at a simmer.

About a month later, I logged a couple more hours at Rodd Field in one of the N2S biplanes I had originally soloed in, and the next day, flew another two hours in the Vultee, presumably for familiarization. It wouldn't be a stretch to admit it was satisfying and rewarding to see just how far things had come. I had accumulated about 200 hours of flying time by now and had earned a few weeks of leave, so I caught the train back to Indiana to see my family before shipping out.

My mother was understandably torn between her happiness at seeing me home in one piece, and anxiety about my leaving again. "Why did you need to go in the Air Force?" She was not enthusiastic about flying or planes, but Dad seemed able to put her more at ease. In time, like many moms, she became ardently supportive and began compiling every news clip, photo, and letter she could into an elaborate scrapbook. Unfortunately, having two sons away (my brother, Mac, was entering the Army) took its toll on my parents. Dad barely lived to see the conflict end, and Mom died shortly after we both returned.

But that first leave was memorable. I was persuaded to give a talk at Park School, the school I attended through high school and where my dad had taught for many years. It was different returning there in my Naval pilot's uniform. I felt almost a celebrity status, even among the various "social" cliques that I might never have been a part of as a student. It was cool. I had stood at that podium many times over the years, but this time it came easy. At last, I felt I had something to say.

Just before leaving Corpus Christi for home, I had stumbled across another good friend, Bill, and invited him to spend the week in Indianapolis. He and I seemed to have unlimited things in common. We had a great time together, double dating and taking in the town. When the leave ended, he went to Atlantic duty and I was assigned to the Pacific. Bill never returned.

Then it was on to Alameda NAS in San Francisco, where our stay was brief. The first evening, I met several of the other junior officers as we signed in and we gathered the next morning for breakfast. We wandered into the officers' mess, took our trays through the line, and settled down at one end of an available table. As we dug in and talked a little, two officers from the far end of the table headed our way, grumbled a few words, and nodded at the sign by the table: "Senior Officers' Table." Oops! The next day before we were able to do anything else wrong we were all aboard a troop ship headed for "somewhere." Our orders came neatly enclosed in a manila envelope informing us we were part of VP-54, "V" for heavier than air and "P" for patrol.

The troop ship, a U.S. Army Troop Transport, was one of the many ways that huge numbers of soldiers, troops, and even Navy PBY crews were moved around to new training locations and eventually into action. It seemed that virtually every ship large and fast enough was being pressed into service. Some squadron members had hopped a United Fruit banana boat a few weeks before we shipped out and jig-jagged along to avoid detection from submarines. By now, even the Queen Mary, renamed the "Grey Ghost," had been painted black and grey and fitted with anti-aircraft guns to serve as a huge transport capable of carrying 10,000, even 15,000 troops at a time. Both she and her sister, the Queen Elizabeth, traveled at high enough speeds on the water that they were relatively safe and able to outrun U-boats and subs.

Our transport lacked the glamor of those vessels, but was surprisingly comfortable given the crowded nature of the place. There was even a dining room and the chow was reasonably good, although the sea was rough enough during our first night that many on board were sick. I couldn't help noticing that none of our fliers were affected.

Day by day the big ship chugged along, and despite some nerves and occasional seasickness, the friendships that were going to last throughout the war and into the years of peace afterward began forming. We talked by the hour, comparing notes and speculating about the future while anchoring our hats with chin straps against the wind. These graduates may have only had a couple of hundred hours apiece as pilots but we were united in a bond shared by men who fly.

It was Hawaii. We dropped anchor at Pearl Harbor and were conveyed by ship's boat to the recently sullied soils of that historic island, Oahu. There were occasional glimpses of the hulking battleships, their sunken wreckage a vivid reminder of what had occurred there less than a year before. It was an unforgettable feeling.

Once ashore, we were treated to a bountiful breakfast, then whisked away in buses through winding, tropical forests to the top of Pali Lookout. The road rounded the curve and in past the sentries, approaching the promontory. My God, what a view! From the top of the sheer cliff, you could see out across the pineapple and papaya fields to the turquoise Pacific. There in the distance was our destination, the Air Station at Kaneohe Bay. And we assembled on that afternoon, a new group of friends.

There was Jack and Pete, Del and Gewin, Art and Ray, and of course Willie and Bob, John, Mel, and Jim[*] and so many others. I developed a particularly close relationship with the first six of these guys. We became the "Big Seven." VP-54 had arrived.

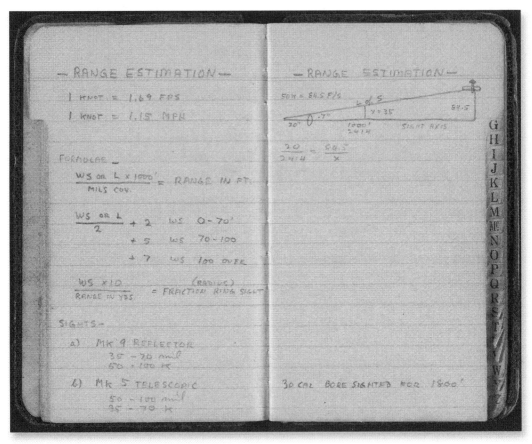

Gunnery notes in notebook carried on all flights during WWII

Early on, we fell into a routine of flying and additional instruction. One of our first sessions was gunnery training, so it was off for a couple of weeks to learn how to handle .45 caliber automatics, shotguns, and .30 and .50 caliber machine guns. I was not a natural, had no background in firearms, and in truth, was terrible at the skeet shooting challenges. Yet for some strange reason, I did well with automatic weapons, well enough to finish with the top grade in this class, a peculiar piece of

---

[*]Jack Beuttler, Pete Maravich, Del Fager, Gewin McCracken, Art Bonnet, Ray Peckham, Willie Sneed, Bob Pinckney, John Love, Mel Goers, and Jim Hanson.

irony. The second highest was Mel, and the two of us were promptly selected by our new executive officer, John Erhard, for his two pilot/navigators. He would never admit it, but we felt he was influenced by the gunnery stuff.

We were now a crew and the flying began in earnest. At this point in the war, the majority of the pilots and crewmen were drawn from flight training facilities like we were, so most us had limited flying or combat experience. Our squadron had thirty or so PBY-5A, amphibious type Catalinas. We soon learned these would not be ordinary PBYs. Not only were they painted black, they were totally "blacked out" for night operation, hence the name "Black Cats," shortened from our original moniker, "Black Sea Cats." The engines were fitted with flame arrestors and the cockpit windows darkened, leaving "red light" as our main source of illumination. The red light was preferable for instruments and for reading navigation charts and the like because it didn't affect our night vision afterward like traditional instrument lighting. Red goggles were also helpful in dealing with bright light.

Our introduction to these aircraft was on the airstrip, bringing them and their hundred-foot wingspans in on the tricycle landing gear. At Corpus, our training was entirely in water. How much more fun it was to do both. PBYs had no flaps although the wing floats could be used, depending on the

crosswind, to aid in slowing while landing. Its two overhead engines were used differentially to keep us moving in a straight line for takeoffs or turning in water (a wheel was sometimes lowered into the water as drag to sharpen the turns) and the wing's elevated location afforded us great visibility for searches. We practiced bounce hops and bombing and torpedo work. One member of the squadron received a citation from CinCPac (Commander-in-Chief-Pacific). He so perfectly aimed the little lead missile that it hit the lens of the periscope of a submerged sub during a practice run. He first received a mock bill for $20,000.

Christmas 1942 arrived. We had the day off and headed into Honolulu for some sightseeing. Several of us booked rooms at the old Moana Hotel, famous for its history and huge banyan tree on the patio at Waikiki Beach, and it became a favorite for future liberty weekends. The Navy Survival Museum was nearby, an entertaining place where one could learn skills such as weaving palm fronds and living off the jungle (but, of course, I hoped never to need these new insights).

To get there, Jack Beuttler and I used our thumbs and quickly secured a ride from a gentleman in a Model-A Ford. Jack sat in front and I hopped in the rear rumble seat and the driver wasted no time in putting the little car through its paces. This was the same road that climbed the face of a steep mountain range and over the famous Pali. From the overlook, an almost sheer cliff dropped hundreds of feet to the lowlands stretching eastward to the Pacific waters. It was here that King Kamehameha once backed an invading army over the edge to annihilation. Another story goes that the strong onshore winds and updrafts thwarted a would-be suicide when the jumper merely floated to the rocks below unharmed.

While the Model-A was surprisingly agile on the steep grade, to maintain its momentum the gentleman was now taking the horseshoe type turns full tilt causing me to pitch side-to-side and wonder whether at any moment the whole lot of us would suddenly be airborne as we headed over the unfenced edge of the cliffside. We accelerated over the crest and swung around the curve onto more level ground, where a military security guard was posted at the overlook near a retaining wall, casually staring off at the horizon. As I rose up in the rumble a few inches to take in this magnificent view, a sudden strong gust carried away my officers' hat and it cartwheeled

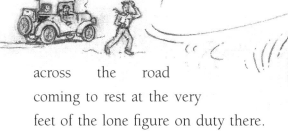

across the road coming to rest at the very feet of the lone figure on duty there. I banged wildly on the car body, Jack got the driver's attention and we quickly squealed to a stop. Sheepishly, I climbed out and headed toward the Army enlisted man who was now eyeing me questioningly. He spotted my ensign's bars and snapped to attention, holding a proper salute. Unlike the Army, in the Navy one does not salute uncovered, so I did not yet acknowledge his gesture and continued my approach, bent down to retrieve my hat and squared it to my head. Then without a word, I smartly returned his salute, did an about face, and marched back to my rumble seat in the Model-A. As we pulled away, the three of us could see the soldier with his hand still on his head, but now he was scratching it trying to decide what had just happened. Jack and I chuckled all the way to the streets of Honolulu.

The next day, the two of us took a cab to Trader Vic's. Jack, a Californian, seemed to find his way around by instinct and we palled around together exploring the city. For some reason, they were having last call for drinks at 3:00 in the afternoon. Sounded good to us. "Bring us a couple of fog cutters, will you? Better bring a couple of standbys, too." They were going down mighty easy, the hospitable waiter later managed another round, and we literally staggered back toward the Moana. It was dark and everything was blacked out. Desperate to eat our way out of some of the stupor, we managed to stumble across a darkened street near the hotel to a small cafe featuring tuna fish sandwiches. Unfortunately, it was hopeless. We awoke with terrible hangovers and were supposed to be back to the base for muster. Jack looked at me through blood shot eyes and said, "Hell with them. Hell with the God damn war!" Hours later, we crawled out of bed and into the sunshine, found our way to the Windward Transit, and made our way back to Kaneohe expecting to be "thrown in the hack." To our amazement, we had not been missed.

Hawaii was a contradiction. This land of almost indescribable beauty, its foaming breakers, lush tropics and mountains, and skies full of vivid sunsets and stars had become our final training ground:

Day after day we would hear the beat of many motors, engines cough and roar as our loaded planes strain at the yoke, and crews readied themselves for another mission. We climb aboard, and outside, exhausts flash blue, the wing lights twinkle, and we taxi out, earphones squawk and then a pause — a roar, a shiver, the sudden pull of unleashed power. We climb and the earth recedes, the trees and hills grow small and insignificant, climbing into ever brightening morning skies and winding through as curious clouds watch us pass. We skirt the jagged coastline and see contrasting beaches and verdant mountains unfold mile after mile before us ... — it was hard to imagine what we were really doing here.

But our time had come.

We were the envy of the entire base. My camera had arrived at the last minute and we had all shipped everything nonessential back home. Jack was part of the first nine-plane contingent that was already well on its way, and our PBY was loaded with gear and a crew of ten. For this trip, Mel Goers and I were to be the navigators, putting our celestial expertise to the test as we winged our way toward Palmyra, a small atoll southwest of Hawaii. We found it and landed within two minutes of our projected arrival time, not bad for an all-day flight. Two sun-tanned officers in shorts arrived, crowded us into a command car, then spun out kicking up clouds of coral dust as they whisked us through grove upon grove of coconut trees. I think the stars shined more brilliantly there than anywhere I had ever been.

The next day, March 4, 1943, the squadron continued on to a surprisingly sandy and dusty Canton Island. There was very little vegetation here and the barracks were named, quite inappropriately, "Waldorf" and "Astoria." As transient officers, we couldn't stay in either, and were given cots in a shack down by a sand dune near the water. I was surprised to find an old Williams classmate, Bill Eaton, as part of the reception group when we landed. I saw him several more times on and off throughout the afternoon and evening.

This place was hot! In an attempt to cool off, we took a short boat ride over to a section once used by Pan American World Airways. Boeing's Pacific Clipper stopped here on its way from California to New Caledonia when Pearl Harbor was attacked.

"Howie, it's hotter than Hell out here, let's beat it," Mel complained. He was right, and we headed back to search for the officer's club. But after a short time, I felt restless and tried a little coaxing.

"Hey, we're leaving early, let's look around some more or take in the show or something," I suggested.

"Nah, I'm worn out. Long day," Mel responded.

"Me, too. Probably seen the movie anyway," another agreed.

I opted to hunt for shells or souvenirs or something indigenous to the island, and after a few minutes of not finding much, decided to see if I could still hit anything with my sidearm, firing a few rounds from my .45 at a tin can and managing to skip it along the beach. My gun now empty, I headed back to my quarters. I was nearly there when a large group of shadowy figures appeared in my path. I continued on nervously and somewhat more slowly, when I was suddenly besieged by the largest several members of the gang and, before I could even blurt out an intelligible "Ugh!" dragged away to a small clearing.

It was King Neptune's Court!

I had heard of this. The hop to Canton had included an equator crossing and because we were almost all "Polywogs" (never crossed before), we had to endure a sacred ritual and were summoned here to face the Royal Barber! With most of my hair now lying at my feet, I was pronounced a true "Son of the Southern Cross" and "Devotee of the Golden Dragon." If you survived this and several even less friendly but time honored physical hardships, you could then officially assume your new status as "Shellback," now an equator crossing veteran.

Bright and early, Bill Eaton gave us a surprise breakfast send off and it was on to Samoa (Wallis Island). This involved crossing the Date Line and becoming "shortsnorters," requiring a rumpled dollar bill that everyone signed. The strip here was embedded in dense jungles, and a transport was waiting to take us to our lodging. There was a small mess tent that prided itself on its cooking and promptly treated us to a wonderful meal, the best I had eaten since leaving home.

After lunch, we shaved and showered for the first time in a while. Then, with the hair on our faces very nearly matching our heads, a few of us decided on a walk, hoping to meet up with some of the natives and maybe even do a little trading. Word had it that sleeveless T-shirts were held in high regard, but all I could come up with was a tennis ball, so I sketched a little native design on it and figured I was set.

Along the way, there were a number of grass huts, and a voice from within one hailed us, "Malolo!" ("How are you?"). Through a big bay window I could see a

white-haired native man motioning to us to come in. He had a sizable family, from adult to toddler, sitting around on elaborately woven mats of Tara leaves. It turned out his white hair was somehow dyed. It was fun talking to him with neither of us understanding anything but all enjoying the attempt. I explained where we were from ("Americano"), and that we were leaving tomorrow ("bongi-bongi"). They seemed interested in our cameras, certainly knowing what they were as they ran outside and lined up for a picture. The cigarettes were a hit; every last one of them helped themselves, except a small two-year-old who later discovered a discarded butt and puffed away, inhaling deeply. Her mother reached over and quickly took it away, long enough to re-light another smoke, then returned it!

> Through a big bay window I could see a white haired native man motioning to us to come in.

They escorted us to another hut where the trading began in earnest. The undershirt netted someone a fan ("eli") colored with white feathers. A bed sheet ("lava lava") was good for a coconut mat with beautifully colored fringe. My tennis ball, on the other hand, was the object of scorn and ridicule, even elders scolding their children for showing any interest in it. This went on for a couple of fascinating hours and then it was time to see what the cooks had come up with back at mess.

Dinner was, again, tough to beat. Afterward, the movie truck passed along the road, tempting us to see what was showing. The venue was carved out of the side of a hill and crowded to capacity. It was "Kisses for Breakfast," but considering where we were, it did seem a little out of place.

The morning of March 7 was upon us, and after managing to get themselves lost for a short time, the navigators (Mel and I) eventually found their way to Fiji (Nadi). Food here would have to be described as a major letdown when compared to the glorious spreads put on by the cooks in Samoa. Here, the Hindu mess boys seemed overwhelmed in the cavernous hall, so after a time we gave up and decided to go look for our quarters.

There was a Quonset hut about a quarter of a mile from the center of things, and although we were looking forward to mingling again with the natives in town, a hard rain had set in, so we just loafed and waited around to see if we fared any better at the mess hall for dinner.

We were nibbling on some kind of stew when Mel piped up, "Hey, I think the rain has stopped. Let's see what's playing."

Several of us stocked up on peanuts, pear juice, and cigarettes and headed over to the show.

"Look at that line!" I exclaimed. Lines were a way of life in the military, but sometimes they even impressed us.

"We'll be over an hour, easy, getting in there." What else was there to do? We finally wound our way in, got seated, and had made it through the first reel when, as punishment, a terrific barrage of thunder and lightning swallowed up the place. I had never seen it rain like that. It could fill your coffee cup in a matter of minutes and quickly turned everything to mud.

"Hell, I can't see a thing," Mel complained.

It was pretty comical, really. Here were 500 Navy guys, most without raincoats, squinting through it all and trying to make out what was going on.

" 'Gentleman Jim'. I think it's called 'Gentleman Jim'!"

By now, I didn't care.

In the morning we came through some rough weather on the way to Espiritu Santo and Base Button in the New Hebrides, where we caught up with the first formation of our squadron. Jack and most of the others were there to greet us. This was in the middle of the jungle with mammoth trees and ankle deep mud. It turned

VP-54 gets rude welcoming. Crew members survey bomb crater on runway. Picture provided by John Bickford whose father, Jack Bickford from PATSU 1-1, is pictured in photo center (see notes).

out to be a brief stay, and a week or so later we finally set down and made camp on the Solomon Island of Guadalcanal. The Marines had secured it about this time and turned it over to the Army for safekeeping. A few of them told us that some of the Japanese prisoners captured during the battle of Guadalcanal were led to believe by their superiors that they had been fighting instead on Catalina Island, just a stone's throw from Los Angeles and the U.S. mainland. That gave us something to think about as we pitched our tents in a grove of Palmolive Peat coconut trees on the edge of the jungle. We were "Home."

The northern coast of the island was chosen by the Japanese as an airstrip primarily for its relatively flat grasslands and proximity, nestled a safe distance from the towering Guadalcanal mountain ridge. Legend had it that Solomon gold was up there, somewhere. Henderson Field, or "Cactus," became our current Allied edition of the airstrip, named for Major Lofton Henderson, the first Marine pilot killed in the battle of Midway.

I was still getting my bearings that day when the squadron tasted their first air raid. Sirens blared and everyone scattered for the slit trenches. It was over quickly, but two of our PBYs were hit and destroyed, an inauspicious beginning to say the least.

The tent encampment was, initially, a crude concoction of salvage materials we found scattered around the area and mosquito netting we propped up with it. The tents themselves were Japanese leftovers and many of us used parts of old parachutes to reinforce the tops against the rain. No more island luxury — our meals were served in a large shed and were primarily C-rations like Spam, dehydrated scrambled eggs, and potatoes. Shower baths were rigged under fifty-gallon drums of water, drinking water was provided in hanging canvas bags with spigots, and heads were constructed over holes in the ground in which there would often be a smoldering flame that emitted a stifling odor of kerosene and hot feces. With every rainfall, sometimes daily, the vicinity became gooey black mud and mosquito habitat, hence our name for it: "The Swamp."

Perforated metal ramps were placed all around camp but often became submerged in the gunk and were slightly better than nothing.

Malaria and dengue fever were a real concern, so we needed to take yellow Atabrine pills daily and wash them down with the local water, which had a curious walnut flavor. In spite of our efforts, there was a significant attrition due to illness. Almost everyone, including me, came down with at least a light case, but many of the guys became seriously ill and had to be shipped stateside.

As it turned out, Jack and I were sick at the same time. We spent a week at the hospital, Jack on one side of me and Major* James Roosevelt, the President's son, on the other. The major commanded the Marine Raider Battalion and had distinguished himself about a year earlier at the raid on Makin and later took part in the Guadalcanal campaign. After all that, here he was in the hospital with a throat infection, among other things, and he and several of our malaria cases were sent back to the states about the same time that Jack and I were returned to duty.

There was very little in the way of equipment, so we set about inventing the various necessities and little indulgences as the need arose. I quickly put together a canvas lounge chair from a few boards and a discarded army cot. Frustratingly, it seemed every time I would return to my tent, someone else would be in it. So I

---

*The Major is better known as Colonel Roosevelt. He was promoted to Colonel in 1944.

built another ... and yet another.

Every gadget and implement in the Navy is given a certain "Mark" according to its modification or the number of other similar articles preceding it. For instance, the second type of mousetrap accepted by the Navy would be a Mark II mousetrap. Since mice were a constant challenge for us around camp, it seemed it was time for a better one. We took turns fashioning them from spare parts. One involved a teeter-totter perched on the edge of a fifty-gallon drum of water to form a critter dunk tank. Another used a ruler, set along its edge with bait, to support an upside down bucket. Within a month, I was sure we were getting closer to a Mark 10. We caught lots, but there were always more.

How time could fly so fast and pass so slowly was puzzling. Our activity for a good part of March was around camp working to improve it and we began to make significant progress. Food began to improve, too. Instead of simply "Spam of the Day," some meat and a few fresh vegetables and even occasional Cokes were finding their way into the mess tent or O.C. It was still primitive, but workable.

Consequently, we weren't spending much time in the air, mostly shuttling back and forth between Henderson and the original camp at Base Buttons. I shared a tent with Richard Jicka (his parents were Czechoslovakian), Whitney Bridges, and Jack. Each of us had covered our dirt floors with floor mats made from coconut palm fronds, some of them eight feet long, and we had learned to construct a whole variety of items to help with the quality of life from this extremely useful plant.

During the day, regardless of the camp, it was often severely hot and mosquitos liked to join us in the shady spots. When an occasionally cooler, cloudy morning happened along, it was an opportunity to catch up on writing or even a little artwork. A couple of us would don our green flying coveralls, also known as Pacific Zoot Suits or "skeeter beaters," that fit snugly about the wrists and ankles. I might see Bridges leaning against a coconut tree, smiling as he read a book, and Jack nearby in one of our homemade chairs, also writing letters. Jicka could regularly be found seated with several of the others at a little square table with a white candle on each corner, engaged in a spirited game of bridge. Pete and Willie, who ran into a little trouble and were a month behind us arriving, were just now getting acclimated as they set up nearby. In the distance, an ambitious someone might just fire up the gasoline washing machine and take on the week's laundry.

At night, along with more mosquitos, we would get regular visits from Japan's

"Washing Machine Charlie" and the annoying sound of his out-of-synch engine slowly chugging overhead before dropping an errant bomb or two. He was hated and the subject of a poem that expressed our feelings:

We turn into our nice, soft cots
To know we're safe sure helps a lot.
As Charlie sows so shall we reap
Now I lay me down to sleep.

Awakened by the siren's wail
For once the damn thing didn't fail.
Half asleep you leap from bed
Jam a helmet of water on your head.

Dammit now I'm soaking wet
Tangled in mosquito net.
Skin your head upon a nail
Step into an empty pail.

Crack your shins, fall with a crash
Arise and make a frantic dash.
Give your head just one more bump
Slide in a foxhole on your rump.

Hell, I didn't have to run
Let's go out and watch the fun.
No reason for my foolish flight
We've got a fighter up tonight.
(continues nine more stanzas)

This biplane or whatever it was became the inspiration for us to respond in kind during our routine night missions. If we didn't find a suitable target that night, then we felt a few hours of leisurely flight above some sleeping Japanese might give them a taste of their own medicine. Hell, we were awake anyway! A bomb, kitchen scraps, beer bottles, whatever we had — delivered every hour or so — made for a far less restful night and I'm sure led to some cranky brass and foot soldiers the next morning.

Initially, we shared flying duties with VP-12, the first squadron to arrive here, and benefitted from their experience at night search and attack operations. Since the middle of December, out of necessity they had been developing what became the early strategy subsequent squadrons would use and spent the winter refining it. They also gave us our name. Our missions were a combination of search, harassment, and bombing at night. We would take off shortly before sundown and proceed up "the Slot" in the middle of the Solomons to arrive near the enemy held islands after dark. Our plane, "Black Magic," generally cruised at around 6,000 to 8,000 feet all night long, searching. Usually, ships could be readily located by their wakes, slightly luminescent from the plankton living in the water. The radioman would key a coded message back to base, giving position, number, and types of ships and other pertinent information. Often an attack force of SBD dive bombers or the new TBF torpedo bombers would be dispatched using our guidance to first hone them in and then illuminate the target by dropping flares. It continued this way for the duration of the night until we finally would drop our own four small bombs and get out as the anti-aircraft guns opened up.

The TBF bombers, which were used a lot around Guadalcanal, had the misplaced honor of being dedicated and shown off to the public about the same time on December 7th that Pearl Harbor was being bombed. The plant was quickly secured to protect this new generation of torpedo bomber. The PBY, on the other hand, was already obsolete and certainly anything but a combat aircraft. It just happened to be around at the outbreak of the war and so it was used. At that time, there were about thirty of them in this part of the world representing almost the entirety of the Naval Air Force here. By February 1942, that number was down to a dozen, only five of which were in flying condition. To survive, night tactics and stealth became essential.

In many ways, it was extremely versatile. Ninety to a hundred knots was the "ball park" speed for its operation, whether climbing, cruising, or descending. It was sturdy enough to land at sea, yet light enough to be able to get off again, sometimes along the crest of a wave or swell, so it was valuable for rescue work. It

PBY cockpit controls - see notes

could carry depth charges, bombs, torpedoes, flares, and spotlights; hence it was used for any mission that the Navy could dream up. Though originally built as a flying boat, it had evolved into an amphibian with thousands of pounds of tricycle landing gear.

Behind the cockpit and pilots were the Navigator and Radioman's stations. The Navigator studied charts and calculations on a large plotting board and could use a variety of techniques to determine our position. The Radioman not only listened to and transmitted messages, he also monitored a ponderous radar unit looking at a few blips on a tiny screen that might give us some hint of what was around us, from planes to mountains. A Galley came next, with a hot plate and two stainless drums of water on one side and a few bunks for sleeping tucked in here and there. Above it in the pylon on a seat between the two engines was the small Flight Engineer's compartment.* Many of the controls for the plane, like for raising and lowering the wing floats or monitoring fuel consumption and other engine instrumentation, were operated from here. In the waist section were the two egg shaped blisters, each housing a flexible .50 caliber machine gun. Flexible guns allowed for movement to better follow a target, as opposed to fixed guns which only pointed straight ahead in

---

*Engineer/ Plane Captain also has aircraft maintenance responsibilities

the direction the plane was flying, as was typical of fighters. The small tail "tunnel" compartment contained a hatch for viewing and allowed for another .50 caliber and gunner. It was also where the life raft was stored because, as on a patrol plane, the tail is the last section to sink. Up in the nose was a bombay hatch and above it, a crude rotating turret accommodating a gunner with twin .30 caliber machine guns. In the early version of the non-amphibious PBY-5, a hatch was located here allowing a crewman to stand up and look around in flight or assist in mooring the plane when back on the water. Each of the various compartments was connected by way of submarine-like bulkhead hatches that could be sealed shut with the spin of an operator wheel.

In truth, our armament was rather minimal. While we could shoot back, we felt fairly naked in the presence of the Japanese Zero fighters. Consequently, our tactics were primarily hit and run. Thanks to the modest cruising airspeed (much slower than conventional fighters) and darkened appearance, our Catalinas were all the more elusive and difficult to locate for the anti-aircraft gunners. We would normally skulk around in the dark, sometimes just above sea level where our black profiles would be undetectable from above. PBY altimeters were an improved radar version, allowing us when discovered to very nearly skim the surface of the sea, presenting a dangerous target for a diving enemy aircraft. If we were spotted when cruising or by day, we would dive for the nearest cloud.

By and large, on these all-night search missions we felt fairly secure. It seemed that the Japanese ships assumed they had not been spotted as long as we did not attack them, so we found ourselves flying around without much interference, even directly above them.

My first search patrol, while exciting, had been a long, tedious thirteen-hour affair all around the Solomon Islands. For many of us in the crew, we had spent months preparing and we were eager to put our training to the test. Our third night out we were off Vella Lavella, a northern island of the New Georgia group, and spotted two destroyers (DDs) and three heavy cruisers (CAs). As dawn approached we made a dive bombing run and things became less simple. The PBYs were frequently used as a glide bomber, swooping down at low power, almost silently out of the darkness in steep dives to present less of a target. The plane could reach nearly 200 knots in one of these dives, far more that the designer of the plane ever intended. Once the missiles whined down, all hell broke loose. We carried 10 million-candlepower bombardment flares that a crewman could heave out the tunnel hatch, effectively blinding the anti-aircraft gunners, as we quickly wrapped the plane into a steeply banked turn and hauled ass while the flak banged all around us.

Then it was homeward bound, back down the Slot, watching the now familiar shapes of the Solomon Islands come to life in the early light of dawn. As the red sun broke the horizon, we slid in low across the shore line of Guadalcanal and down onto the mat, clacking as we rolled over the perforated, heavy duty metal plates that formed our landing strip. Sleepy, but safely back at Black Cat Base, there was nothing like the bite of a very cold beer before bed.

The average duration of one of those flights was ten to twelve hours, but we could stay out fourteen hours or longer. We'd even heard that the Limies down in the Australia-New Zealand area were flying the seaplane versions thirty hours at a time. It seems Australia had lost its connection with Great Britain after the war began so a new route was required. Since Japan controlled the seas between Australia and the mainland, an idea was developed to strip down a Catalina, removing weapons, armor, and any excess weight to make it light enough to handle the additional fuel and three or four passengers. They operated five of these defenseless PBYs, taking a route across the Indian Ocean to Sri Lanka at night and navigating by the stars, some 3,500 miles. The crew and passengers saw the sun rise twice and the formidable flight was dubbed the "Double Sunrise Service." *

Our nights were long enough and once VP-12, the squadron we were replacing, left for the states, we flew every other day or so for a while.

But we did have down time. At first, too much of it. We had to stick close to the tents since the island had only been recently secured, and there were rumors of guerrillas and snipers about, so we practiced our jungle know-how, carving and weaving palm fronds and such. I grew a beard, not too common in those days, but they eventually made me shave it off because they felt an oxygen mask might not fit properly. There was plenty of time for some sketching, mostly pictures of camp life and scenes of planes in action and on Henderson Field.

---

*Dad's story with a few specific details Courtesy of the Library of Australia. Qantas Empire Airways operated the PBYs until July of 1945

Eventually, we moved camp closer to the Henderson airstrip after the Secretary of the Navy made a surprise visit to camp after a heavy rain. He came away convinced something should be done and had a group of Quonset huts built providing much improved living conditions. It was a relief to be out of the "Swamp" where we had wallowed for almost four months. Now, there was even a mess hall, and we soon went to work constructing a screened clubhouse.

Our group of younger guys was rather athletically inclined. Del Fager, soft spoken and instantly likable, was a good 6 feet, 3 inches and had been an accomplished athlete at Illinois State in baseball and basketball. He was a gentle giant until he got in a game. Pete Maravich was an ex-pro ball player — big and powerfully built with a booming voice. His son, "Pistol Pete," became a well-known college and pro player. With credentials like this, it didn't take long for us to erect a basketball backboard, and we had many a frantic scrimmage around that net. I was a little shorter than some of the others, but since there were no referees, I compensated a bit and maybe bent the rules, just a little. It seemed only fair. I found I was able to more than make up for my "shortcomings" on the court by luring a few of the guys over to the "pit." Horseshoes was a passion dating back to my childhood, spawned out of my love of cowboy stories and horses, and the competitions that our family enjoyed at "Woodlands," the family house in northern Georgia. There, the uncles would battle it out at gatherings, playing golf, tennis, and horseshoes on makeshift venues carved out of the fields and woods. So I kind of had a leg up, and the hapless, novice shoe throwers around camp were generally easy prey.

Del Fager

In college, I had barely scratched the surface of some gymnastic activity — a few basics like shoulder stands and "kick-ups" on the parallel bars. That, it seemed, qualified me to try to build a set. With much filing and carving to smooth out a pair of two-by-fours, I mounted them on some supports and gave them a whirl. I quickly regained what little expertise I had in school and polished my routine daily, which soon aroused some curiosity around the camp. Del took a shot, but was taller and gave up in frustration since the bars were not adjustable, "Howie, let's build a higher one. I've always wanted to try 'giants' on the horizontal bar." So we set about rigging up a length of pipe atop a couple of coconut logs. Before long we were a circus act. Del had figured out how to do sensational giants (swings) and nearby I labored along with my meager kick-ups, now looking every bit the straight man.

Even with "all this," time did drag between combat missions, and I found myself searching for entertainment. I always tended toward creative pastimes. Maybe it  was a slight artistic bent, or perhaps it was a desire to leave a tiny mark on a world gone mad. Along with the sketching and painting of jungle and battle scenes, I found myself writing, at first taking notes about what we were seeing and learning, and then compiling a ledger and some anecdotes that seemed like they would be of interest some day.

Of course, mail call was the highlight of every serviceman's day. There were frequent letters from my family back in Indianapolis. My folks and I even numbered our letters in an attempt to better track the time and success of any mail exchange. Dad was meticulous in his correspondence, and of course my mom, unbeknownst to me, was continuing to carefully fashion a scrapbook of all greeting cards, photos, letters, and newspaper clippings that involved me. As time passed, I began composing poems and longer narratives of our actions in the South Pacific.

The Fourth of July was nearing, and unless the Japanese provided them, we weren't expecting to be seeing any fireworks this year. It was just about a year ago, I was passing my "D" check which meant I'd actually have a chance to fly one of those beautiful low wing planes I'd found so captivating. That was probably my greatest ambition — even if it was a single flight and I washed out the next day.

What a complicated affair that little SNV* seemed back then!

It was a day or two before being called out for a mission, so I began a letter to my mom and dad. There were so many things I wanted to share with them:

"Dear Folks,

Thank you for your recent letter, it took it a while to catch up with us. There is much to tell about our new work environment and the changes the missions are going through. But to answer your question, for some reason the flying has not yet become work — maybe it never does. It is always a kick to climb into your plane and begin the procedure of checking everything to prepare for takeoff. Then when you're all set, you energize the engine, and as you engage it, holler 'contact' and flip the switch. As the big prop starts to rotate, the engine whimpers, coughs a bit, and then roars in your ears while you throttle back to a moderate RPM. If it's a multi-engine plane, you then take each engine in turn the same way. Next you begin checking instruments once more — oil pressure up, cylinder head temperature, such and such, and after a few minutes warming up, the engines are ready for a test. That procedure is in itself fascinating, changing the propeller pitch to check its operation, and then as you hold down the brakes, racing the engine while flipping the magneto switches back and forth, and the whole ship quivers. Now a last look around and you taxi toward the takeoff position, in the meantime contacting the tower over your radio for permission to take off. You are at the end of the runway, the tower tells you to stand by as a couple of other planes make landings, then you are cleared, move into position, and pause a moment. Yes, everything is ready. Throttle forward gradually, a little right brake to hold you straight at first until you have enough air speed for the rudder to have effect. You glance at the manifold pressure gauge to see that you are not exceeding the maximum for takeoff.

After that you concentrate between the strip ahead and the airspeed indicator. When the latter rotates to the proper place, you ease back on the stick a bit, and suddenly all tenseness is gone — in its place a sensation of riding on air behind thousands of horses. Then you hit the landing gear control, and up come the wheels to nestle snugly into the smooth lines of a 1944 airplane.

You climb and climb, a watchful eye on that airspeed and swing away into a long arc

---

*SNV was a WWII era trainer built by Vultee. The Navy used these faster, single wing planes for student pilots as they became more advanced.

up into the endless blue. Then the sky is yours from sea level to 29,000 or 30,000 ft. or more and as many hundred or even thousand miles away as your gas will carry you. It's interesting to compare a few hours flight here any day in the week to the days of auto travel we used to put in for a summer vacation. Just think, I can wander out to the plane after breakfast, during the next few hours make the trip we used to drive from Indianapolis to 270 E. Main in North Adams, Mass., eat lunch there, pay a couple of visits, and leave in time to get back for dinner. I only wish I were in a position to actually make the trip.

All this time you've been zooming across the skies, hopping around rain storms like they were mud puddles in the road. If you have gotten away from familiar territory, you've been tracking yourself on your navigation board, estimating the velocity of the wind from the appearance of the white caps and figuring how much that wind will blow you off course. So finally when you are ready to start home, a few quick calculations will give you the proper heading and even your time of arrival. It's a great pleasure to have flown from dawn till dusk all day long out of sight of land, then to return, figuring ahead when you should arrive, and to find the field lying dead ahead and your arrival time correct within a minute — it has happened.

You start circling the field, adjusting your transmitter to the proper frequency, contact the tower and ask permission to land. They give you landing instructions and you start your approach from perhaps a thousand feet. You go down the check list, letting down your wheels and flaps, making the other precautionary adjustments. There is the strip ahead, you're coming down, take off a little more power, sailing over the tree tops, the end of the runway is within reach, you turn into the wind a little more to correct drift, then square away, leveling off with wheels just inches above the ground. You feel them touch and skid and start carrying you down the runway, trees and trucks and men flashing past — the men always stand watching as if they'd never seen a plane before. Then, as you slow down, you begin easing on the brakes alternately and finally turn off into the taxiway. You cut the engine and the old props come to a standstill — you can't help but think to yourself, 'What a beautiful little gadget that is!' And as you walk away with ringing still in your ears, the old question comes to mind, 'If someone had told me, would I have ever believed it?' Can you imagine what the Wright Brothers would think..." There was a sudden interruption — it was chow call and enough for tonight.

VP-54 Howard 5th from left, center and below in "blister hatch"

Future college basketball coach Pete Maravich and "Chet"

Howard in custom chair
after becoming a Shellback

Camp hoops,
Maravich in hat

Shellbacks
("VP-54" shaved in on top)

Guadalcanal

Fantasy Islands

July was shaping up to be an active month for our Black Cat crews, kicking off what was to be a busy winter for those of us in the southern hemisphere. Weather was generally more pleasant this time of year, slightly cooler and drier than when we had first arrived. It was strange to think of the folks back home just hitting the dog days of summer about now.

The islands of the South Pacific were filled with curiosities for an Indiana boy. No matter where I went, there was some aspect of it that was new to me, sometimes puzzling or intriguing, sometimes unexpected or even distressing. Our island of Guadalcanal, for instance, was loaded with land crabs, a creature given to rambling the roadways at night. Unfortunately for them, it was a time when Navy jeeps were also wont to roam, resulting in countless smashed carcasses along the dirt thoroughfares. It made a peculiar contrast to the now rusting hulks of beached Japanese ships, monuments to the American conquest of the island.

The indigenous people were fascinating to learn about and mingle with. Our crew was assigned a flight up to Rennell Island to check on a lost plane and crew. Back in January toward the end of the Guadalcanal campaign, we had retaken Rennell from the Japanese. The island had a rather large inland lake that made a good place for landing Catalinas, but on this trip we chose a beautiful little lagoon and were immediately surrounded by a horde of native outriggers. It was a friendly group, a bit primitive looking with dark black but diseased looking skins, not at all what you are led to believe from Hollywood. The women were mostly clothed in G.I. T-shirts. While we couldn't really understand them, it was obvious that they had items to trade. One fellow showed me a beautiful pogi stick and once again I found myself unprepared. Then I recalled, in my flight bag, an old pair of rather loud South Sea Island swim trunks. A friend had given them to me while I was at Williams College, and the gaudy print, supposedly characteristic of Hawaii where they were purchased, was produced in some Massachusetts cotton mill, sent back and forth before following me again through Hawaii on my way to a real South Sea island. Now this chap was altogether taken with the trunks and I was about to outfit *him* with *them* and the irony was complete.

After this initial "getting to know you" episode concluded, we were gratified to find there were also eight airmen there to recover, all in relatively good condition, and after shuttling them aboard, John got us airborne and safely back to base.

And when some natives up on Sikaiana Island in the Stewarts (island chain) needed medical supplies, once again "Black Magic" was dispatched to deliver them to this tiny island north and east of us. Our flight took us over a towering range of mountains shrouded in a heavy blanket of clouds, creating the illusion of an endless snowfield stretching out as far as the eye could see. Occasionally, the clouds parted revealing craggy green mountaintops. As we broke through the cover, a tiny group of islands appeared in the distance. I was in the copilot seat and could soon see the atoll below, an arrowhead shaped perimeter of coral surrounded by a deep cobalt central lagoon that gradually became reddish brown where the various colored coral rose toward the surface, and jade near the edges in areas that sand had collected over it. A garland of foam surrounded the outside fringe of the island where the incoming waves were split by the jagged reefs. As we drew closer, villagers appeared on the beach, among them, groups of young women prancing about topless, somewhat of a new experience for most of us on board. To our disappointment, by the time the outriggers arrived, the ladies were discreetly re-clad in white blouses and there was nothing more to do than drop anchor and set about unloading the cargo. These were a handsome people with strong physiques, somewhat lighter skinned and with smooth complexions. It seemed the men did not readily mark their bodies or paint their hair, and women were shy and attractive with flowers adorning their long hair and sometimes their necks. Most spoke broken English. They escorted us to the beach in canoes through spectacular coral beds. I would have loved to have shared this experience with my Zoology group at Woods Hole — intriguing masses of red pipe and blue and yellow star coral, white brain coral, sea urchins, giant sea squirts, and colorful protochordates of every kind. This was truly a paradise.

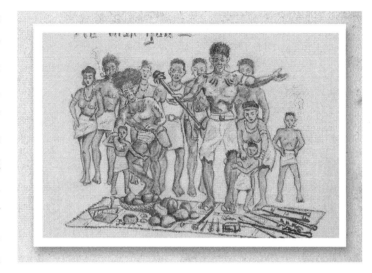

As we walked the short distance to the village, one of the men pointed to the horizon, "There is airplane!" and a moment later, "Is American plane!" I couldn't make out anything yet, but within a few moments, the distinct sound of a multi-engine plane became clearer. The image of the plane took another few moments to reveal itself. It was a USAF B-25.

In the village, the chief greeted us warmly and assigned each of us a guide. Mine was a stoic, rather tall fellow who led me along a group of thatch roofed huts perched on pilings and then, surprisingly, past a sizable gable roofed chapel. Through the doorway, I could see it had an English feel to it, two rows of benches neatly aligned and adorned with mat cushions facing a crudely whitewashed altar covered in flowers. One of the older men inside confided that he was a priest and the mission was where most of them had learned to speak English. Missionaries had built it many years ago, and they now held two services a day in it. My guide then proudly displayed a tattoo spelling "Ambrose" in artistic cursive on his arm, explaining it was his Christian name.

Ambrose and I continued on, ultimately arriving at his family hut and climbing the rickety stairway of the one-room dwelling, the perfect place for an enthusiastic game of barter. This time our crew had come prepared — there would be no repeat of the tennis ball — bringing soap, cigarettes, chocolate, and clothing. In no time, I had exchanged all I had for beautiful shells, baskets, mats, cat's eyes, and all sizes of model outrigger canoes — exact replicas down to the minutest detail. We were both quite satisfied with the whole thing, but not to be outdone, Ambrose insisted

I return with a bounty of additional gifts, pleading with me to do him the honor of taking them specifically to the "King of America" F.D.R. He was so thrilled that he had his boys haul the loot back to the plane, and he instructed his daughter to feed me and show me around. I suddenly found myself surrounded by females, each bearing a different form of refreshment — papaya, pineapple, poi, and some sort of bread, as well as fish, and probably squid or octopus. I decided not to have any part in that last whatever it was, but enjoyed the rest with a coconut milk and fruit juice "shake."

Ambrose's daughter quickly led me on a tour of the village; it was an enchanting place. I kept casting about for glimpses of any of my crew, but wasn't seeing anyone anywhere, and I slowly started to feel a little apprehension about being part of a movie I'd seen somewhere. This girl was lovely enough and becoming increasingly friendly, and this was a paradise and all, but I hadn't a clue about native protocol and had visions of my narrow escape in a full gallop through the surf toward our PBY, the crew urging me on with the engines going full blast, and a band of very angry villagers on my tail. It was time to leave.

After an afternoon of nothing but kindness and hospitality, perhaps it was their simple and beautiful farewell that stayed with me the most. As we prepared to step into the boats, word was given and the children filed past each of us with a timed, "Bye." LaGuardia himself never kissed so many babies. The women then came up to each of us and presented a boutonniere, gently pinning it onto our shirts. These people so well understood the intricacies of true friendship.

Just as we were making our way back into the outriggers, the chief's son gently pulled on my sleeve, speaking to me in broken English, "This war, you still have to fight?" I looked into his eyes and tried to explain that we wished dearly to end it and didn't want things to be this way, but "Yes," we had to. I will always remember the look on his face as he sighed deeply and shook his head, "Too bad."

As we winged our way back toward base, I couldn't help thinking again, like I had so many times since first passing beneath the Golden Gate, just how incongruous this "great war" really was.

I had fully intended to ship those souvenirs to the White House, but once we arrived at Henderson, I was quickly overwhelmed by a herd of eager Black Cats who made short work of not only the extra items, but had me fighting over my own. My apologies, Mr. President.

Back at Guadalcanal, the mail situation had improved. Earlier, in Hawaii, we had a V-Mail system where all letters were written on a one page form that was promptly read and censored. This usually resulted in numerous passages being unceremoniously sliced out with a razor knife. Nothing hinting of a location, equipment, or numbers of personnel could be passed along. The form was photographed on microfilm and reprocessed in the states to be forwarded to families and friends. But by now, letters, newspapers, and packages were getting through O.K. Jack was regularly receiving half pints of Scotch hidden in boxes of cereal.

Before I shipped out, my father and I had devised a plan to communicate my general whereabouts. John Caldow was the Headmaster at Park School, my former school where my dad was a teacher, and we decided to use his name and location as code for the area I was heading into or out of. We first superimposed a map of the United States over a map of the South Pacific area, and then each kept copies. Then periodically, I would mention John in a letter sent home, perhaps indicating a city, like Phoenix, that I had heard he was visiting. Dad could pull out his trusty map, find Phoenix, and underneath it would be the real location where we were currently stationed. Sometimes it would get more creative. "I heard that John Caldow was spending his time again in amongst the rides and bright colors at the Indiana State Fair (the 'Midway')." We had developed our own code, and the censors never seemed to crack it.

Much of the flying these days still centered in and around the Solomon Islands. This rather large chain of longish land masses stretched from the southeast to northwest in a long column off the coast of New Guinea, with a number of tiny island groups dotting the waters in between them. It included places like New Georgia, the Russell Islands, Kolombangara, Bougainville, and of course, Guadalcanal. Both sides were paying considerable attention to the New Georgia area and in particular the Japanese airstrip at Munda. "Black Magic" was at 7,000 feet as the Navy began its saturation shelling of the airstrip prior to the actual landing. What a sight! Our battle ships were throwing everything they had onto the small area, and as the big guns finished up, the dive bombers went in for the final touches. By the time they were through, I doubt if there was a Japanese gun left firing anywhere in Munda.

On a few occasions, we flew with countermeasure equipment to better assess the progress the Japanese were making in their development of radar. The equipment could detect radar emissions that were being broadcast and help us zero

> My younger sister, Marian, would sometimes send me a letter, some with cute sketches, telling me about school, her grades, and catching me up…

in on a station's location. This "intelligence" was then used to evaluate and sometimes eliminated these stations.

Military pay was minimal, especially when you considered the type of job we were doing. Pilots enjoyed an override job "flight pay," but there was almost nothing to spend it on if you didn't gamble, and I didn't. So for the first time in my life, I considered myself independently wealthy. My college debts and the heavy bills for the four different Naval uniforms were long since paid, so I decided to try to help out back home.

My younger sister, Marian, would sometimes send me a letter, some with cute sketches, telling me about school, her grades, and catching me up on life around home. Letters like these were important to us. During my time away, I sometimes felt a little guilty that she was put in the position of maintaining normalcy around the folks at home while both her brothers were overseas. Naturally, I hadn't been home for her birthday, so I sent some money, specifically so she could indulge herself in a nice white evening jacket. I think, as it turned out, she opted for a more functional camel's hair coat — times were still tough and practical was good, I suppose. And wouldn't my dad be surprised if there was a sudden sum of money deposited secretly in his bank account? This one was a total backfire. He always kept careful track of his statements and promptly informed the bank that they had made an error. The resulting confusion was embarrassing to him and he soundly scolded me.

The long months away from girlfriends, wives, or any type of female were telling indeed. We were young men at our sexual peak and took a dim view of the lot we had drawn. I was faithfully corresponding with my lovely Margaret from Wabash, and she religiously responded with carefully composed and artfully drafted letters on sensuous, fragrant blue paper. While we always eagerly anticipated these letters from home, they were little consolation, for by now, we were becoming convinced

John Love (center)

we were not going to return. That modern red convertible was pure fantasy and beautiful women were nothing but a pipe dream.

So searching for diversions was a constant. There was a nightly movie in the Black Cat Bowl, a movie screen set up in a small amphitheater of coconut log seats. We never missed a flick from Laurel and Hardy to romantic stories with Anne Sheridan or Lana Turner. At one point, Bob Hope did a special live show with a host of female celebrities. Sometimes, though, it made matters worse — you could look, but not touch. Our Quonset huts were plastered with tantalizing pinups of the female stars of the day. Occasionally, with the encouragement of a few of the guys, I would try to reproduce in pencil or watercolor the portrait of some gorgeous Hollywood starlet.

In one of my father's letters, he wrote that our family minister, Rev. Alexander, had become a Navy chaplain, and was somewhere in my general area. It was a grey, rainy day at Henderson, so our group was crowded into the Quonset, whiling away the time. In one corner a poker game was in progress, and an argument was gaining momentum amidship. Ultimately one of the group turned to John (Love), and said, "So, what do you think, John?" His response was always tempered and reasonable. "Well, I believe you could look at it this way ..." That was invariably the end of it. He later served five terms as governor of Colorado.

Down at the far end of the building, I was intently sketching a portrait of one of our lovely pinups. Jack happened by, then Del and Ray. Soon all the "Big Seven" were assembled and I was being needled to enhance the drawing with all manner of provocative embellishments. For Pete, a glorious bust was added, and then Art wanted more sensuous hips, and eventually, Del ... well eventually, in explicit detail, all the regions of importance were augmented to the ever increasing approval of the gang.

It was precisely at this point, where the finishing touches were being added, that we heard the screen door slam. I casually glanced up to see a familiar figure enter and make his way down the aisle between the bunks. At first, I was overjoyed. It was Reverend Alexander! Then a moment passed. "Holy shit, it's Reverend Alexander!!"

I frantically scrambled for paper, books, anything, and just managed to conceal the thing in time to thrust out my hand and greet him. As it turned out, the good reverend was so happy about making contact with one of his parishioners, he set up a weekly Communion at the Black Cat Bowl. It proved to be very popular.

Native children on wing

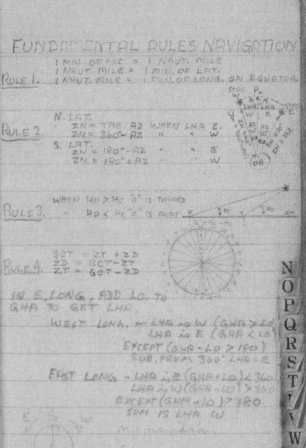

FUNDAMENTAL RULES NAVIGATION

1 MIN. OF ARC = 1 NAUT. MILE
1 NAUT. MILE = 1 MIN. OF LAT.
Rule 1. 1 NAUT. MILE = 1 MIN. OF LONG. ON EQUATOR

Rule 2.
N. LAT.
$Z_N = TRS\ AZ$ WHEN LHA E.
$Z_N = 360° - AZ$ " " W
S. LAT.
$Z_N = 180° - AZ$ " " E
$Z_N = 180° + AZ$ " " W

Rule 3. WHEN $H_O > H_C$ "a" IS TOWARD
" $H_O < H_C$ "a" IS AWAY

Rule 4.
$GCT = ZT + ZD$
$ZD = GCT - ZT$
$ZT = GCT - ZD$

IN E. LONG, ADD LO TO GHA TO GET LHA.

WEST LONG. — LHA IS W (GHA > LO)
LHA IS E (GHA < LO)
EXCEPT (GHA - LO > 180)
SUB. FROM 360° LHA = E

EAST LONG — LHA IS E (GHA + LO) < 360
LHA IS W (GHA + LO) > 360
EXCEPT (GHA + LO) > 180
SUM IS LHA W

US Highway 1, Guadalcanal

Howard teaching the squad "cowboy" style roping

Natives and crew swap gifts

Give me a break

It's hard to describe the feeling I had the day one of our planes did not roll down the mat, as expected. It had quite evaporated with all its crew and was never heard from again. A few weeks later, another one crashed on the runway with no injuries, but a totaled airplane, this time the victim of a nose wheel collapse. The missions continued but the war was becoming much more personal and morale was starting to suffer.

Our skipper realized something had to give, and suddenly, there were rumors of "R&R." Sure enough, planes and crews were slowly being dispatched to Nouméa in New Caledonia. The crews returned, not only revitalized, but laden with canned beer to restock the club supply. One flight was returning with some 150 cases stowed on the catwalk the length of the ship when one of the lookouts spotted a yellow dingy tossing on the waves below. They circled down and could see a lonely figure waving from a life raft. The sea was choppy and this would be tricky. The PPC (Patrol Plane Commander) had to make a command decision and tersely ordered, "OK boys, we're gonna set her down. Jettison the beer!" The reluctant crew began heaving the precious brew overboard until a crew member made one last appeal, "Please sir, can't we just keep a couple of cases?"

"Request granted, but only two. T-W-O," came the reply.

The open sea landing accomplished, the aircraft returned with the pathetic Army Air Force P-40 pilot in tow and deposited him safely at the Black Cat Base.

His plight grew even more serious when the word spread that this "dogface" had been traded for 148 cases of beer.

Before long, my turn for R&R rolled around, and what a welcome experience it was. In Nouméa, we were billeted at an old mansion on a point of land. The clean, white bed linens were a forgotten luxury. The feel of three warm showers combined with almost chilly daytime temperatures (I actually caught a cold!) made this first visit to a French speaking community seem all the more extravagant. It was certainly a welcome change from a muddy camp in the tropics. A Frenchman named Jean took us out dynamite fishing early in the morning. He would toss a stick into the water and the concussion would kill or stun all the sea creatures nearby. Then he instructed us to dive into the icy morning waters and retrieve everything we could. It didn't seem a particularly sporting way to go, but considering the seafood feast that evening, we managed to justify it.

Later on, we searched out the neighborhood pubs and did the town. Nouméa was a smallish place and showed some signs of wear with many storefronts bare or boarded up. Occasional shops still provided food and essentials — an attractive young French gal served us a toasted onion-omelet sandwich for ten francs.

Unfortunately, the only other few females around were at the "Pink House," the local bordello. This place had long lines, but I didn't pay them a visit. In retrospect, I'm not sure why, maybe a few too many G.I. films on V. D. Anyhow, I took a pass. I did have an opportunity to "check out" in a Navy seaplane version of the OS2 Kingfisher, doing spot landings in the bay. It was also entertaining to scope out the well stocked Navy Supply store. It seemed to have every conceivable piece of issue flight gear. Before shore leave ended, there was time for a train ride on flat cars up into the mountains, slapping monstrous mosquitoes along the way. Our friend Jean organized a deer hunt, not terribly successful, but we did manage one boar and returned with it to camp and the mess tent.

Relaxed and rejuvenated, I ran smack into my turn as squadron duty officer the minute I stepped out of our PBY. This was a 192 hour marathon handling all squadron business, telephone calls and messages, and a hundred other odd jobs that keep the officer in charge busy and nearly sleepless for almost the entire time. By the end of the week, I was relieved to break in the new man and return to flying status, but I had to admit it was an interesting study in how the system worked and what kept it ticking.

Our routine at Guadalcanal took a new twist. For months now, the Japs, desperate to retake the Solomons, moved their troops and other necessities throughout the area under cover of darkness.* Any successful military action would require equipment, fuel, ammo, concrete, and steel, as well as troops in massive numbers, so they began using smaller, more mobile barges to move along the shorelines at night to avoid the heavy losses they had been suffering using larger vessels. We knew even one sunken barge could send down as much in tons of cargo and supplies as a score of bombing runs on their supply docks, and we countered by contacting our rejuvenated fleet of P.T. boats to overwhelm many of the barges. Of course, our dumbos flew at night too, and we took turns at the blister guns, strafing the convoys. It was a strange sensation triggering this long arching finger of tracer bullets (every fifth shell), like a mile long pole. I merely manipulated it into one of the barges until the tracers started bouncing around and knew I had a hit. One September evening alone along Moli Island we made run after run strafing ten barges in the darkness below us. I have often wondered how many I killed — kind of an unsettling feeling, but an impossible situation.

There was still heavy fighting going on to the north of Henderson in the New Georgia Islands group, just below our routine patrol area in the "Slot." Tiny Arundel Island was still in doubt and a struggle to gain an advantage there had lasted a month. Returning from a mission, a developing air attack forced us to land at the American outpost there. We hunkered down as the air raid intensified and our guns opened up, and one of the Japanese aircraft was hit. It glided into an adjacent field where it crashed but didn't burn, and when the shooting finally ended, what seemed like the entire population of the island raced out to see the plane. The unfortunate Japanese pilot did not survive the landing and was still swaddled in something that I recognized.

The "Belt of a Thousand Stitches" was considered a good luck charm for a Japanese flier, although not so much so for this particular one. In the early days of the war, 500

---

*This became known as the Tokyo Express. Usually completing an entire resupply run at night, the Japanese were proficient in the use of this tactic and found their movements nearly undetectable in the darkness until the Black Cat squadrons began their own night missions.

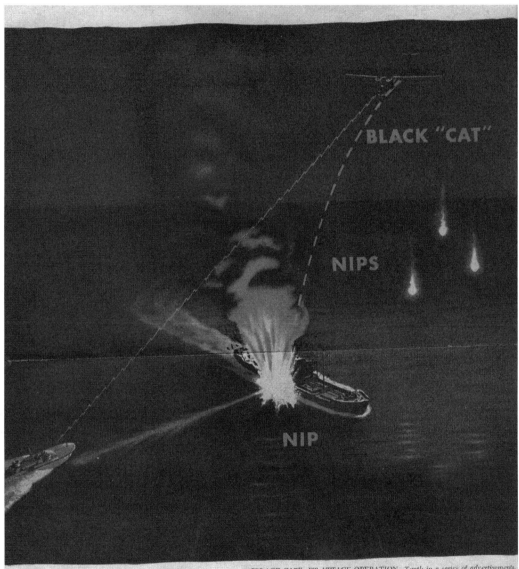

Night bombing and strafing runs were carried out against the Tokyo Express, as depicted in this 1943 Look Magazine Military Ad and the photo to the right.

Military map of Arundel Island (on right)

Howard pictured with "Belt of 1000 Stitches"

friends would make two stitches each in the belt as a wish for safekeeping and good health for the airman. As the war progressed and the air force grew, it became impractical to continue this painstaking approach to the belts and so the task was put on an assembly line like everything else in the war effort. Now, Japanese women, 500 of them in a line, were given two slips of paper with the proper wishes for the two stitches they would sew into each belt for a specified flier. In this way, many more of them would be protected from harm.

Interestingly, during the attack on Pearl Harbor, a Japanese fighter was shot down at Kaneohe (where I was based) and the pilot was found to be wearing one of the belts. He was very, very dead. A Lt. Commander who was investigating the wreckage found this intriguing. He mentioned the incident to his wife when he returned home and his Korean housemaid, Mai Su, overheard the conversation and interrupted with an explanation.

Mai-Su had lived in Korea as a young girl. Early in the war with China, her mother told her about the story of the famous "Belts of a Thousand Stitches" and the powerful "juju" that would turn back bullets better than armor and always worked. All the Japanese women in Japan and Korea were making the belts for the army, but they needed more, so the Korean women were ordered into factories to make them. These women resented the work and had no interest in saving these pilots, but were severely punished if they refused — until one of them realized they didn't have to sew stitches that represented the wishes that were written for them. As Mai Su put it, "May the dog that wears this go down out of the sky in flames, and may other dogs refuse to eat him! Now the belts are all mixed up and no one knows why the juju is failing, except the Korean women. It is powerful talisman and always works!"

It seems my belt must have included that Korean touch.

Bombing a ship, sub, or other target from a PBY was challenging. Generally, the Nordon bombsight wasn't practical when making a glide run. In fact, when it was possible, we preferred dropping our 500 pounders by eye in a timed series from around 1,000 feet. Much lower than that at our airspeed and we risked damage to our own plane from the blast of the bombs we were dropping. Earlier in the campaign, a Cat using instantaneous fuse bombs scored hits on a cruiser from extremely low altitude, blowing it up and shredding itself with shrapnel holes. The tunnel gun hatch, which was manned, was sloshed with salt water.

Sometimes things that could go wrong *went* wrong. Back in August, we were north of Black Cat Base off the Island of Tulagi and the Florida Islands on a night search. We did everything by the book, started our run, descended to the proper altitude, and timed the release. John called for the drop — nothing happened. The micro switch had malfunctioned and we went sailing over our suddenly reprieved target, clearly in view below. What a feeling of frustration. By the time we circled back, the sub had disappeared beneath the waves.

On another occasion while on patrol, we happened upon a rather large Japanese task force. After looking over the situation, we selected the largest vessel as our target and made a diagonal run across it. Our four 500 pound bombs were armed to explode on contact, but only after falling 4,000 feet. John leveled off at 4,000 feet and we let them go. The first and last bombs exploded on either side of the cruiser, but the middle two did not go off. Could it be that they had landed on the deck before falling quite the full 4,000 feet?

More recently, a Sea Cat was flying over Palau during a night raid and found the clouds so thick his bombardier couldn't see anything. After struggling with the conditions for an hour or so it appeared hopeless, so they dropped their eggs and left for home. The next morning, reconnaissance photos showed that a Japanese freighter had been sunk in the harbor — in this case, something that could go wrong went right.

Then at times the missions seemed to border on the ridiculous. We had been ordered to drop thousands of leaflets over Jap positions and had composed a propaganda message translated into Japanese. On the back of some of the sheets, we added our own thoughts in English. To heighten the impact, we still liked to include a few empty beer bottles, which supposedly created a loud, creepy whining noise as they spun in, a little like a bomb that never went off.

Much of the year had come and gone and once again morale was becoming a problem. The last few months had been tough on personnel and planes. Now, Bill Anderson, a PPC from Georgia, had an engine catch fire and they were forced to crash land at sea. They managed to get everyone out of the burning plane and secured two life rafts, putting some distance between them and the sinking plane before an enemy vessel arrived. They made their way to shore, narrowly avoiding discovery, and eventually managed to escape with the assistance of the friendly "coast watchers." Their Plane Captain became separated from the group and was captured and killed just a short distance away from the rest of the fleeing crew.

The war seemed endless and we had now been overseas for nine months and counting, nearly twice the typical tour of our Navy crews. Somehow, another shot of R&R was arranged, this time in Sydney. An R4D * transport took the first group of fliers down, including most of my close friends. I was assigned to the second plane a day later, in charge of a large group of enlisted personnel. Jack and another buddy, Dick, had said as they left, "Don't worry, Howie, we'll have you all fixed up with a hot date when you get in!"

So I was not surprised to find the bunch of them at the airport as we landed the following afternoon, each with a fancy Australian gal on his arm. "Let's phone your date," they said, and one of the girls and I squeezed into the phone booth. She dialed up her roommate and in a moment, announced, "I am so sorry, she was thinking it was tomorrow night and can't make it this evening." The whole episode had taken maybe thirty-seconds and I was already shot down.

I decided to have a good time in Sydney anyhow. For some reason, it reminded me of San Francisco, perhaps just the buildings, taxis, and crowds. Of course, traffic was now on the left, catching me by surprise more than once as we stepped down off a curb. You do everything you can to survive for months in enemy territory, only to get mowed down by a cabbie on your first day of R&R. But there was so much to see. Some of the vehicles were outfitted with giant charcoal burners attached to the rear of them, and here and there were delivery vehicles with large, ungainly gas filled balloons strapped to their tops. "No petrol, mate? How about some coal?"

After exchanging our money for pounds, florins, shillings, and pence, Jack, Dick, and I grabbed a cab and set about finding our appointed flat. It was a wild ride.

"This is it. On the right," Jack gestured at the two story brick building. "It looks swell! Whose got the fare?"

We settled up and the cab drove away. "Hey, I'm two Bob short!"

"Too late now. He's already halfway to Rushcutters Bay by now. Let's get cleaned up and look around."

> So I was not surprised to find the bunch of them at the airport as we landed the following afternoon, each with a fancy Australian girl on his arm.

---

*R4D was the Navy's version of a DC-3 similar those used for passengers on commercial airlines throughout the US. The army designation was C-47.

Yes, it was a wonderful city. The folks were friendly, the food good, a great zoo, high surf, and plenty of booze. Beer was served warm and stout and was a strong, midday libation. Oyster bars were everywhere, and I found after a few Scotch and sodas, that I could learn to love the things. And to my surprise, I quickly forgot about the unfortunate outcome of my first attempt at a date in Australia, thanks to one beautiful and enticing lady named Nadia.

It is a great thrill to meet a new girl and say to yourself, "This may be the one," especially if, as you get acquainted, you begin to see her personality assume the very lines you had always imagined as your ideal, with an occasional novel "twist" that you would never have seen coming, just for spice. It then becomes tragic when, all along, you know that due to impractical circumstances for both of you, this "relationship" will never really be able to take root.

On my second night "down under," I had survived a long and uneventful date, so the next morning when Dick suggested I come along on a double with him, my enthusiasm really wasn't there. I had a change of heart after he reminded me of our vow, made back in the Solomons where it seemed you were either bored to tears or scared to death, that we would never waste a day. So it was off to the races, literally. He had planned a day for us at the track.

My first glimpse of her was beyond reassuring. Her eyes were large and sort of a mixture of colors, her hair shining blonde and turned under at the ends. Her simple cotton frock accented her figure beautifully and her smile was warm. In a word, she was stunning. "And this is Nadia," I heard him saying, and I thought, "Nadia — how pretty."

"So you are the artist," she said, smiling. I clumsily answered, "Huh?" This is where it often went wrong for me, during that initial introduction I either forgot names or just blurted out nervous nonsense. But this time it was different. Gathering myself, I said, "Oh, Dick probably told you that. I'm really no artist. He's just fascinated when I hold pencils and things." Dick again seized the opportunity to elaborate, building a resume I didn't deserve, but entertaining her and his date as we quickly became more comfortable together. We decided to hail a cab, crowded in, and I was impressed by how at ease this girl was on a blind date with a military guy. She told me she was eighteen and lived with her mother who was otherwise alone. She loved art and dabbled a bit.

It was a marvelous afternoon at the races. I let Nadia make all the picks and then would quite naturally agree with her selections. She managed to nab winners in several races, then after losing a couple, was considerate of my pocketbook and quit while we were still ahead. Of course, we needed to celebrate and left in search of shakes and sundaes. The afternoon wound down and to my disappointment, I discovered she already had a birthday party commitment for the evening. However, she quickly suggested we meet again the following day for a trip to the zoo, and so our date was set.

The zoo was fun, but it didn't even matter. We were enjoying every moment together and watching her as she walked along in the brilliant sunshine, I couldn't believe how lucky I was to have reconsidered that first double date. After lunch at Oriano's, she cuddled up to me in the cool breezes on the ferry as we headed back to King's Cross, where I dropped her at her flat for an hour while I scurried home to get cleaned up for the evening.

Over on Elizabeth Bay Road there was an Officer's Club, and I was surprised to see a large gathering and a dance in progress. Moving onto the floor for our first dance together, we were actually both trembling. I drew her closer, and it seemed we fit together perfectly and the floor just dropped away, like we had been dancing our whole lives together. The piece ended and we lingered together for a long while, now both knowing we were in love. "L-let's go for a drink," she said.

We sipped our cocktails slowly and conversed easily. After about an hour I suggested, "Would you like to take a walk?"

"Yes, let's do," she replied and quickly took my arm.

"Well, you'll have to lead me around," I said, "after all, I'm pretty new here."

"Let's go sit in the park."

Our walk took us through an alley, darker than any place I had ever walked with a girl. It finally opened up into the park and a variety of small benches lay ahead. I quickly made for the darkest one, way over by an air raid shelter. We sat down and she looked at me, and then surprised me by saying, "If you're going to kiss me, let me take off some lipstick first." That first kiss was the biggest thrill of all. I remember thinking, "This is worth spending eight years, much less eight months in Guadalcanal. Think about it; remember every detail, Howie. In a week, that's all you'll have." Her lips were soft, cool, and sweet, and the kiss sent chills up my spine. I didn't want it to end. Finally separating, she said, "I hoped it would be like that." I couldn't help thinking of the boys in the outfit who had wives they loved back home, that this is what they must feel like. I was sure we both knew that we would never be married. Assuming I lived through the war, she knew I would have to return to America, my home — that Australia could never replace it. And I saw that she would never leave her mother alone. They were closer than sisters, and her mom would never leave Australia for the states. Yet, we were not afraid of love. We were content to live out this dream, even knowing it would before long vanish, leaving us with only the memories of our short time together.

We spent another two days enjoying everything this Australian town had to offer, the sights by day, the dancing at night. We now had pet names. She called me "Happy" and I surely was, and to me, she was "Lucky" from our glorious afternoon at the races. Our final time together needed to be special, and we spent it at the beach on that lovely sunny day. She had a perfect complexion, smooth skin that had not yet seen much sun, contrasting to my ruddier tanned body from months in and around a tropical jungle. I gave her two yellow roses for her hair, and we sat and talked and enjoyed a picnic lunch. I shall always think of her when I smell a yellow rose. Our final day was drawing to a close. It was one of those times when she caught me looking that she quickly said, "Happy, you love me, don't you?"

"Yes, Lucky, I guess it's no secret to you. I love you and I'm glad I do."

"I love you too, darling," she said sweetly as she leaned over. "You Yanks seem so much more well mannered than Australian fellows. I wish I could visit America and see what it's like. I'd probably love it and want to live there. But you see how it is now. Tomorrow you go back to the Islands and I'll probably never see you again. Why is it that someone I love has to go up there where they could be killed or injured, when they could have jobs right here?"

"I don't know, Lucky. I'd give anything to trade with one of these guys, but that's just the way it is," I said helplessly.

"Do take care of yourself and think of me — and I promise I'll write every week. Just now it's ten minutes to eleven. Every Thursday at ten till eleven, I'll throw you a kiss."

Our final embrace was tender, loving, and final. Some five years later I received a letter from Nadia. She had not forgotten me and was planning a trip to the states and wanted very much to get together. As luck would have it, a week earlier I had met my future wife-to-be, Dorothy Dale, and we were about to embark on a new adventure of our own. I chose not to answer the letter, and Nadia and I never saw each other again.

PBY on patrol

Volcano visible through cloud cover below wingtip

Howard and Art Bonnet check weapons and prepare for a hop in SBD bombers

Leaflets thrown from BlackCats

> BLACK CAT MESSAGE TO JAPS—
>
> (A TRANSLATION OF THE LEAFLETS DROPPED ON VILA BY BLACK CATS ON THE NIGHT OF AUGUST 31ST–SEPTEMBER 1ST FOLLOWS:)
>
> "TODAY THE AMERICAN HEAVY ARTILLERY BEGAN THE SHELLING OF KOLOMBANGARA ISLAND. HOWEVER, THIS IS ONLY THE BEGINNING.
>
> "YOU WILL NOT BE ABLE TO STAY OUTSIDE OF YOUR DUGOUTS AND AS A RESULT YOU WILL SUFFER FROM MANY CASES OF MALARIA AND DYSENTERY.
>
> "WHILE YOU ARE ENGAGED IN A PAINFUL STRUGGLE THE JAPANESE NAVY, WHICH IS LIVING IN COMFORT AND PLENTY OUTSIDE OF THE BATTLE ZONE IS ABSOLUTELY HELPLESS TO AID YOU.
>
> "BY OUR UNCEASING ATTACK YOUR FOOD AND SHELTER, EVEN YOUR DUGOUTS WILL BE DESTROYED, AND SOME OF YOU, NO DOUBT, WILL BE BURIED ALIVE.
>
> "ASK THE SURVIVORS OF THE 229TH REGT., ABOUT THEIR EXPERIENCES ON BATEIZAN."

Group on R&R in Noumea. Squadron members pictured from left: Skip Marsh, Jack Beuttler, Gewin McCracken, Elliot Schreider, Bob Pinckney. Kneeling: Richard Jicka, and unknown crewmember.

Australian Koala Bears

Australian Kookaburras

First at something

We all flew back, sorrowfully, to the combat zone, wondering what surprises might be in store for us. I didn't have long to wait. Within another few days, I developed a severe sore throat and my neck began to swell. I felt awful. The doctor sent me over to the MOB-8 Naval Hospital where my condition was diagnosed. "You have made history, Ensign," he said. "You have the only case of mumps on record on the island of Guadalcanal! Where the Hell did you get it?"

"We don't have an isolation ward here," the pharmacist's mate explained to me. "We are confining you to this end of the Quonset hut, and will put a screen across here. You keep your ass away from those other 26 patients. You're here for three weeks, not a day less!"

Later, a couple of my buddies from the "Black Cats" showed up with a watermelon. (Seemingly, they had already dealt with mumps as kids). According to them, Del's girl in Sydney, the one I had squeezed into the phone booth with, had written him that she was laid up with mumps. "What the Christ did you do to her in there, you hard up shit-head?"

"Hell, I was only in there thirty-seconds. Never even touched her!" I never was able to convince them.

The days dragged on. Fortunately for me, it was a "light" case, with no "serious" repercussions. Unfortunately for me, I was startled awake in the morning by a loud, crackling sound, like small arms fire. Already a bit cranky and totally tired of the whole thing, I bellowed for someone on duty. In situations like this, it is not uncommon for an "officer" to search for an appropriate pejorative when addressing an enlisted man.

"So I've got two questions for you, you sorry son of a bitch!" I announced when the corpsman looked in on me. "First, don't you have any female nurses around here? And second, have the Marines landed again out there?"

"And I've got two answers for you, SIR!" he sarcastically drawled. "First, what are female nurses? And second, that's an ammo dump blowing up out there and I'm betting we're all going to be hitting the dugouts!"

When he returned a short time later, he was carrying a helmet and gas mask. "You'll note the conflagration has now progressed into the artillery shells. Next it will be the 'big stuff'! The Old Man has ordered us all into the bomb shelters — that is, all except you. You are in isolation!" His drawl couldn't conceal his wry smile.

At that moment, there was a huge explosion and I was literally knocked off the bed, and he simultaneously disappeared, doing some kind of crouching "duck run." I picked myself up, closed the screen door that had been blown open, rehung the fire extinguisher that had been dislodged from the wall, and climbed back into the sack. On the one hand, I felt I had been unfairly discriminated against: I was sure I was well past any infectious stage of this disease. On the other hand, the rest of the hospital was crowded into a dark, smelly, underground shelter sweating it out. I was reclining, nice ocean breeze, white sheets, not so bad.

Wham! Another thunderous concussion and again I was on the floor along with the fire extinguisher, looking through the screen-less door, as bits and pieces of something rained down all around. Once more I secured the area and returned to my bed, much less confident now. I began to think things were really going south. I guess you hope that when your time finally comes, you go out in some glorious way and are not found under a pile of debris from explosions your own side had set off, sporting a case of the mumps. The chaos continued throughout most of the afternoon, and then, thankfully, subsided, as it had apparently used up all of the "big stuff."

Shortly, my hospital mates reappeared, an exhausted and motley looking bunch of wet and dirty outcasts. "Must have been pretty nasty down there," I said as I gave my pillow an unnecessary pat.

Elliot Schreider, 3rd from left. Del Fager, 2nd from left

We received word that another plane, this one with the crew that had earlier traveled with Reverend Alexander for the R&R in Nouméa, was missing. He was taking it particularly hard and flew with us in "Black Magic" as we spent an entire Sunday searching in vain for them. The pilot, Lt. Merle Schall of our squadron, had endured one of the worst cases of malaria any of us had experienced here and had been sent to a Navy hospital in New Zealand to recuperate. He was there a good month and should have gone stateside, but he refused, wanting desperately to rejoin his crew. By then, the Skipper was sending us all off to Sidney in the same precise order as our initial arrival times in Guadalcanal, and both Merle and his copilot, Elliot Schreider, had been among the first. Elliot later told us that it was decided that Schall, having spent a month already in New Zealand, albeit in the hospital, would need to continue duty while Elliot went ahead and took his designated R&R time in Australia. That night, Schall's plane went down in Empress Augusta Bay. Merle was a fine pilot and, back in August, he, Elliot, and the crew had been the victim of a friendly fire incident, shot down by a radar firing from one of our own ships in the Blackett Straight. With one engine out from the attack and only 800 feet of altitude, he managed a frantic emergency open sea landing at night without benefit of knowing about wind direction, submerged reefs or other obstacles, or even the very state of the waters below them. They came to rest in between two large swells and watched as the fleet steamed away from them having chalked up another "bogey." The PBY remained afloat for the remainder of the night, some seven hours, very near the spot where John Kennedy's PT boat was cut in half by a Japanese destroyer two weeks earlier. One of those PT boats managed to find them and brought the crew back to their base at Rendova where a Black Cat crew later picked them up.

This time things were much different. There was a hopeful report the next morning and finally another PBY was able to locate two survivors who had been thrown out of one of the blisters. They were badly shaken, but recalled a serious downdraft plunging them toward the ocean surface and forcing a wingtip into the water. The plane cartwheeled, throwing them clear before crashing and burning. I was stunned to learn that Bridges and Jicka, two of my roommates in Guadalcanal, were part of the remaining crew that had perished. Richard Jicka had just returned from Sidney and replaced Elliot as First Officer.* We had lost another plane and another part of our family.

I was surprised one day to find a training schedule posted and equally excited to see we were all to be qualified as PPCs (Patrol Plane Commanders). One by one, we were all put in the left seat and practiced takeoffs and landings "in command" of

---

*First Officer is another designation for copilot

our aircraft. By Dec. 4, it was official, and a pay raise and promotion to lieutenant junior grade (Lt.jg) was in order. The gold bar now became silver.

Almost immediately, there was a stunning announcement that we were to be shipped stateside. The ensuing missions were interminable. We were sure we would be shot down before we could make it back. As the day approached, several in the squadron prevailed upon the local Seabees, the Navy's answer to the Army engineers, to build us sea chests to ship home our personal gear and souvenirs. Over time, I seemed to have gained status as the squadron artist. I had designed our Black Cat insignia, a snarling cat riding a bomb, and applied it with colored lacquers to a number of leather flight jackets. Now everyone was approaching me to stencil and otherwise adorn their sea chests. I was busying myself on the one belonging to our intelligence officer as he happened in. He seemed to be admiring the work and casually picked up the gin bottle containing the lacquer thinner, and before I could say anything, swigged a mouthful before screaming and running from the tent spewing thinner everywhere. It seemed a perfect end to our last day in this beautiful place, where what you did so often failed to make any sense.

The squadron was replaced by VP-81 and started home Dec. 10, 1943, Henderson to Espiritu Santos. We were aboard a big four engine Coronado PB2Y2 flying boat operated by Pan Am.

By chance, H. V. Kaltenborn the radio commentator was aboard and we explained the details of the Short Snorters club to him. We had him signed up in short order, three of us relieving him of a dollar bill in return for endorsing another one for him.

After a refueling stop at Canton Island, we continued on to Honolulu. By now we were all dying to get our hands on a more advanced aircraft, and I was able to persuade the captain to give me some "stick time" in the PB2Y2. It was wonderful and seemed luxurious compared to our GI equipment.

Bright and early, the squad boarded a troop ship bound for the West Coast and San Francisco, and passed under the Golden Gate on New Year's Eve, 1943. The Sir Francis Drake Hotel was the place to be that night, and we celebrated the New Year with some ladies at the Starlight Ballroom. We had rolls of worthless Japanese Yen and delighted the girls by using them to light cigarettes. Great food, drink, and company, it was an all out party till they closed the place. It was 1944 and we were loving it!

Our orders directed us to report to Alameda NAS the following day for flight physicals, which would qualify or disqualify us to return to active duty. We reasoned the more indulgent our New Year's Eve became, the stronger our chances of blowing the physicals and ending up with the coveted stateside duty. So with major hangovers, we boarded the bus to Alameda. We had to carry Pete, who had really set the tempo the night before. Maybe all the alcohol relaxed us too much because we sailed through our dreaded Schneider tests with perfect blood pressure, etc., and quickly found ourselves all reassigned to active duty. It was kind of a shock, so our next angle was to try to improve our lot by putting in for F7Fs (Tigercat fighter) or PV-1s (Venturas), anything more modern than those lumbering PBYs of our first tour.

> Coincidently, I found that my younger brother, Mac, was also there, and that he would soon be leaving to become an Army medic somewhere in the Pacific Theater.

Since my closest friend Jack lived in San Francisco, I spent a few days with him taking in the town. We hit Fisherman's Wharf, the International Settlement, and put away our share of Scotch and sodas. A few more of the Seven joined us for dinner with his parents one night, and I became acquainted with his sister. Soon she and I were dating. The two of us visited Golden Gate Park and the Redwoods, and at one point, even discussed marriage. We would keep in touch with each other for the duration of the war, and even got to see each other on a number of occasions. But somehow, the chemistry wasn't quite there, maybe it felt a little like a "rebound," maybe the fact that I knew Jack a little too well played into it, I'm not sure.

I soon found myself climbing aboard the Super Chief, two days and a night heading home to Indianapolis for leave. I wondered how things would seem and what changes our town had been through in my absence.

I knew my being away in a war zone was rough on my parents and hoped they were both holding up well and that the adjustments in their life's daily routines since the war began hadn't been too hard on them. They had been through rationing of gas, tires, and anything rubber and had been allowed only four gallons a week while abiding by the national speed limit of 35 MPH. They had endured Indiana winters with modest amounts of heating supplies. They picked up and used prescribed Ration Books that allowed only limited amounts of many foods we had always taken for granted like sugar or meat. Clothing items including shoes were in short supply and nylons weren't available until after the war. They watched as railroads tracks were stripped of their rails and bumpers removed from cars for the metal they contained. Victory gardens were all over town, and the folks grew fruits and vegetables and everything they could in the yard and canned it. Like many Americans, they even returned grease and fats from cooking to the butcher shop so they could be collected and then later processed into explosives. The family had been living with less so we could have more.

I wondered how much my little sister had grown up.

Suddenly, I opened the door and we were again a family. I savored the home life with them all and caught up with old friends. Coincidently, I found that my younger brother, Mac, was also there, and that he would soon be leaving to become an Army medic somewhere in the Pacific Theater.

While I was home, I was recruited to speak at my former high school and again confront that always distressing podium. This time, it was made a little easier by the fact that there was so much to share, so many stories to tell. I even spoke to two shifts at the Goodyear Tire and Rubber Plant, letting them know how their dedication to their jobs was sincerely appreciated by our fighting men. Everyone needed to do their part.

Those precious days flew by, and before I knew it, I was back on the Super Chief, two nights and a day to San Francisco.

Guadalcanal with perforated steel plates that formed paths and runways

Squadron logo that Howard designed

The Seven
Del Fager, Howard Miner, Jack Beuttler, Gewin McCracken,
Ray Peckham, Art Bonnet, Pete Maravich

Battle-scarred Munda airstrip

Quonset hut

PBY night patrol

Beach on approach for sea landing

Jack Beuttler, Art Bonnet with "Chet," and Ray (Peck) Peckham

The Second Tour

It was on to the famous North Island (N.I.) NAS. I had hit a snag coming down from San Francisco and was almost six days late when I arrived at the San Diego base, but the rest of the Big Seven were there waiting for me in our new quarters. In the morning, the group of us was all together looking over our orders when Peckham spoke up.

"Aw, no! Look at this!"

"We're slap bang back in the 'Black Cats' again," I said in disbelief.

"What happened to the F7Fs? A seagull can outrun those PBYs!"

It was true. Our dream of dashing around the skies in a fighter or dive bomber was history, but at least we were all PPCs now with our own planes and crews and were still together along with about ten other members of the old squadron. Maybe this was the best thing for us, becoming the nucleus of the new version, the new "54." It seemed an awesome responsibility to be assigned to the left seat, but we felt battle trained and confident, refreshed from our time off, and feeling a mixture of excitement, nerves, and curiosity. We were to be now known as "VPB-54," the "B" stood for bombing.

Suddenly, there was a different ingredient in the mix. We had a new skipper, a young lieutenant commander, the son of an admiral, a former destroyer man, and fresh out of Navy flight school. It quickly became apparent that, as an old line officer, he was determined to make a name for himself — everything was now by the book but with more or less a "destroyer" flavor. We were to use theoretical practice instead of our battle proven techniques and we could already see the fallacies of it and where it was heading. Training missions now lasted far into the night. I can hear him still, "Stand by to execute! ... Execute!"

During our five months in San Diego, there was considerable emphasis on our physical fitness, especially in the Olympic pool. It was a requirement to pass a triple-A test involving four different strokes: side, back, breast, and crawl; an endurance swim of over a mile; five minutes of treading water; and finally a jump off the high dive with an underwater swim the length of the pool. I had done enough swimming in college to get by the four strokes in good shape, but I struggled with the distance and the high dive. I discovered I could side stroke until tired, recover by doing a back float and kick along almost indefinitely by keeping my lungs partly filled with air, then swim a side stroke into my "second wind" and on for a mile or more. My first effort at a feet first dive off of the high board was a pitiful failure. It was supposed to simulate jumping off the deck of a sinking ship and escaping by swimming below any burning oil. Our coach continued to patiently give us instruction and, before long, I was able to pass the entire test.

On the other hand, Roger, my navigator, was skinny and when those "skin and bones" mixed with water he had a habit of sinking like a stone. He finally came up to me almost in tears and said, "I'll never make your crew!" Yet he went back in, again and again, swallowing pool water all the while, and somehow, he eventually got through it. And what a fine navigator he was!

Soon, my crew began to take shape. Robert (Bob) White, our copilot, was a good flier and I knew I could trust him to handle things if my attention was required elsewhere. He was eager and absorbed information quickly. Roger was conscientious and a crack navigator. He sported a Texas drawl and was married — I sketched a picture of his baby from a photo for him.

Our plane captain, Norris Townsley, knew what made the plane tick, and my second mechanic, Machinist Mate Keene, was ambitious and also knew his beans. He had a way of anticipating me. First Radioman Lambert kept the complicated radio gear in operation and had been in our first squadron. Very experienced. His Second Radioman, Synan, was a fast learner and very diligent. My two gunners, Combs and Richardson, were wicked behind the .50 calibers and doubled on the camera and bombsight. It was a solid group and I would have stacked them up against any in the squadron.

It was something flying over the United States for a change. We balanced doing takeoffs and landings with time in the link trainer and classes in navigation and recognition. Ray Peckham and I took a short instrument hop up the coast, flying past Santa Anna, Long Beach, and up to L.A., circling over the town and eventually heading over to Catalina Island, the famous resort. It was our aircraft's namesake.

The terrain from the air was so different from the jungles we had become accustomed to — deep gullies and irregular valleys with sides cut and streaked from erosion. As we swung over the border, the little Mexican towns appeared contrived by a designer gracing them with very wide streets, carefully spaced but unpaved so that grass filled the open spaces, save two winding sets of ruts.

When flying around a big air field like N.I., I was constantly impressed with the miracle of radio, listening to the control tower directing countless planes as they circled, landed, taxied, took off. I found myself surprised every time I spoke and actually got an answer. "North Island Tower from one victor three, on final approach and request permission to land on two ball* runway, over."

"One victor three, this is North Island Tower. You are cleared to land. Wilco."

Our PBYs may have had their drawbacks, but their GO9-transmitter radios were not one of them. It was one of the best radios ever made. This device was big and hot with foot-long tubes glowing inside. It seemed you could pick up signals from almost anywhere in the world and sometimes it was fun to try. A long cable with a heavy steel weight at its end, towed behind the plane, provided an antenna and while it was easy enough to extend, retrieving it required a lot of hand cranking effort and some discussion about whose job it would be.

We still did a considerable amount of training after dark and could use that cable as an indicator of our altitude when making night landings on water. In the South Pacific, a moonless night meant almost total darkness below, and while altimeters helped they weren't accurate down to the surface and you never were sure about high swells and waves. At about fifty feet, the bob on the end would hit the water and sometimes snap off. The pilot slowed as much as he dared and then

---

*Two Ball runway allows landing from east to west. One Ball from west to east — Dad's flight notebook

cut throttles to full stall in, a landing that frequently had consequences, popping rivets and scattering things about the cabin. We always carried golf tees and pencils to plug holes and stop the water leakage.

Returning to the combat zone, a place you felt lucky to survive the first time, was a real motivator, at least as far as R&R was concerned. The point now was to squeeze as much into our remaining time in San Diego as we could. We wanted wine, women, and song, and the song wasn't all that important. Most of the bars closed at midnight, and our nightly torpedo and bombing run training lasted until 10 p.m. most nights. It was a predicament, requiring a quick shower and shave, and then a boat ride into town, leaving barely an hour to get caught up. We switched to drinks that packed more punch, like Zombies, for a while and Jack introduced me to Nickolovski's, a brandy laced with absinthe. In fact, there was a game based on this drink that seemed to get the crowd going. It was great sport and the ladies seemed to find it particularly appealing.

Del and I and a few of the others decided to chip in and buy a car, a 1940 Studebaker for $950 with good tires and a radio. It was time to widen our range and we drove the sixteen miles to Tijuana to see how it stacked up with what we had observed from the air. It was a crazy little town, mostly souvenir stands and trinkets. The senoritas ... well, none of us spoke Spanish, but apparently we didn't make much of an impression. They did have the best steaks I've ever eaten with a portion measuring over twelve inches and an inch thick. We resolved to head to L.A. for a weekend, a challenging test for our new jalopy, but first had a work session away from North Island for a week.

Howard at controls

The training was strenuous, but grew more interesting by the day. Across the Laguna Mountains inland from San Diego is a sizable salt water lake called the Salton Sea. A modest-sized group of us traveled there, a week at a time, and stayed at the smallish base nearby. The lake's considerable size provided a perfect setting for water work. It was some forty miles long and ten wide, allowing a half dozen or more takeoffs and landings in a single pass, and an adjacent runway allowed us to put the tricycle gear down for land work.

This desert landscape hadn't a hint of trees — only occasional cactus and sagebrush — and was reminiscent of our visit to little Canton Island in the South Pacific. The sand dunes and desert-scape gave way to stunning vistas of craggy mountains beyond the lake, a few with snow lines mirroring the white clouds above their peaks. Depending on the time of day, the colors would be blues, browns, purples, or all of them. They seemed so very far away from the lake, but as you climbed into the sky they quickly grew in stature. In the valleys below them, the irrigating systems were remarkable, a network of waterways converting desert into green fields for agriculture.

Most of our group had made the trip — Jack, Mac, Del, Pete, Bonnie, and I — and it was the first time we had been able to work together, several of us taking planes out and sometimes flying in formation. We were becoming more excited about "54" and the possibilities. A cross country run took us, one at a time, on a circuit of four towns — Indio, Blythe, Yuma (Arizona), and El Centro — flying blind on radio beams the entire way. I had gone first and now watched with the group as each of the others took their turn.

"So how did it go, Howie?" Mac asked curiously. He hadn't been up yet.

"Smooth air most of the way, a few bounces between Blythe and Yuma. But you know how it is, kind of a scavenger hunt. I wasn't sure about the Yuma leg, but we hit it on the money."

Del changed the subject. "Bonnet wants to head into Palm Springs tonight after we all finish our hops. Ever been before? He says there's a barn dance at one of the ranches and they love having Navy guys stop by."

"Nope. Sounds swell, though."

"Count me in," Pete added. He had heard there were even costumes at some of these places and everything from ten-gallon hats to bathing suits. We watched as Bonnie touched down smoothly, sending plumes of white spray up and onto the fuselage where it was quickly scattered by the props. "Jack, you've been there. I hear the houses are amazing!"

"A lot of them are built around swimming pools — beautiful lawns, big driveways. But I don't know about this ranch," he replied.

"Simple folks, scrimping and doing without. It's a war you know."

"You'd switch places in a second. So whose up next?" I asked.

"That would be me." Pete checked his charts again.

Before long he had completed his loop and we could see him making his approach, when Del and I had an idea that we thought might make this more interesting. To aid in getting a PBY out of the water, there were ramps constructed and, in many locations, a crew member or two would hop up on the opposite wing causing it to tip enough for the other wing to clear the ramp as it swung around in a 180-degree spin. A line could then be attached to the tail and the plane would be hauled up the ramp. Here, the ramp was shallow enough that one of the field personnel guided the pilot, nose first, carefully up it and onto dry land.

As Pete approached, looking for instructions, that individual was nowhere to be seen, and Del seized the opportunity and pulled his knit cap down low, largely concealing his face. He then proceeded to wave wildly but convincingly at the ever approaching PBY. Once Pete started up the slope, he could no longer see anything in front of him other than Del's flailing arms and he was slowly but deliberately directed to one side of the ramp and into the ditch along its edge. As the starboard wheel started to sink into the mud and bog down, Pete added power, Del waved more furiously and the plane buried itself deeper and deeper. The "Black Swan" was at nearly full throttle and not moving when Del popped off his cap, revealing his true identity. With the duty officer now speeding toward us in his jeep and Pete cussing loudly enough that we could still hear him over the roar of 3,000 RPMs, Del and I decided it was about time to slowly fade out of there and leave it to the "Swan's" crew to explain how they managed to get stuck in the mud. I'd have to say it took several days for them to forgive us for this indiscretion.

Maybe I was just in a good mood from completing a successful flight, watching Del toy with Pete, or even just giddy about seeing Palm Springs and the dance later. "You know, these old PBYs really aren't so bad. I guess they're growing on me."

The week ended and we were ready to get out of San Diego again and see what L.A. had to offer. Gas was rationed, but getting chits (tokens) was no problem, so we headed out, eventually arriving in Beverly Hills. It seems we raised the appropriate amount of cane, then filled up and headed for home, driving in shifts to allow enough time to make it for Gewin's 8:00 a.m. link trainer period. All of a sudden, the water pump began to howl and we limped along into the morning fog, not arriving until after 10:00 a.m. Missing training periods hadn't been a big deal in the past, but they had decided to clamp down on missed appointments, so it was a shock to find that we were to report to the executive officer. He read us the riot act. "Your skipper is away on a cross-country flight for a few days and left word that you should all be thrown in the hack until he returns." In our case, this meant being confined to the hangar and then marched to and from mess under armed guard. Pete responded, "You can't do that!" to which the exec replied, "Of course I can, and as a matter of fact, YOU will be the armed guard." So Pete reluctantly marched us at gunpoint to mess and back, and in four days, when the skipper returned, we were lined up for a good tongue lashing.

"I suppose you have all learned your lesson," he said. I sensed Gewin was having blood pressure problems and was about to "blow his cool," and quickly chimed in, "Yes, sir. I'm sure we have." We only had two days left and didn't want to spend them marching at gunpoint.

"Then you are returned to duty." Actually, it was Friday, so we returned to San Diego.

Two days later, May 20, the squadron received orders to fly out and the entire group was packed aboard our new flock of PBY-5As, flying in small groups of three. Each plane, with some eleven personnel and all their gear and equipment, was loaded to more than maximum gross. In addition, the planes had landing gear weight to bear (all previous flights arranged to have the gear shipped over), some 1,100 pounds or more on its own. A couple of hundred people — family, wives, girlfriends, and members of other outfits — were on hand for an unforgettable send off. Crying, waving, whooping, and the suspense that comes with watching an overloaded aircraft takeoff surrounded our planes as they warmed up. We revved the engines and rolled down the west runway of North Island, clodhopping our way off the end of it and out across the water with fingers crossed that we could stay in the air. The first half hour was touch and go, as we played with METO (maximum except takeoff power) and climb power trying to inch up to some sort of cruising altitude. What a long night. Early on, the drop-off fuel pods were jettisoned into the ocean, and as the plane slowly burned fuel, we became lighter, ultimately managing a climb to 10,000 feet. I was an occasional smoker in those days and had supplied myself with cigars to help keep me awake. About that time, a little front persuaded us to take it up another 3,000 feet to get over it and between the cigars and the unpressurized cabin, I started to get woozy and nearly blacked out. My copilot, Bob, quickly grabbed the controls and yelled over the engine roar, "Howard! You there?" I came back around and we quickly lowered our altitude for the balance of the trip. Weather and winds became more of a factor as the flight continued and staying on course became a continual challenge, so I had Roger take star sightings all night long. As dawn finally broke, I was thinking we must almost be there, but the morning plodded along unendingly. Then, thank God, Land! Roger had guided us right into the Hawaiian chain. Twenty hours had come and gone before our plane finally made landfall, and when we set her down at Kaneohe, we were on fumes.

Here, VPB-54 set up housekeeping. The officers moved into a cluster of small apartments on the base and soon received our new assignments, primarily patrol and more training. Jack and I sat in his apartment enjoying a Coke and listening to the radio with the latest news from Rome and New Guinea, when an announcer read a flash that was handed to him. His manner was so casual that the two of us didn't immediately grasp the importance of the actual text he was reading from. For the next several hours, we tried not to allow ourselves to get too excited as brief reports on the events in Normandy continued to be broadcast. The morning papers confirmed the rumors, and it seemed these opening hours of the invasion were very encouraging. It was a hugely critical day of the century, and the men out here in this theater were as anxious for the latest developments as the folks back in the states.

The squadron had grown to fifteen planes and eighteen crews. Kaneohe boasted a considerable history with PBYs, dating back even before the Dec. 7 attack where thirty-three were hit and destroyed here by bombs and fire. But seaplanes attacked on land were a different matter than those in the water, where almost any damage to the fuselage could quickly send them to the bottom. Those thirty-three planes were salvaged and stripped of parts and in just ten days fashioned into another ten flyable aircraft. The repair crews were truly remarkable.

Compared to the hard push of the training in San Diego, this phase involved longer hours and fewer sessions. We still did our share of flying, but it was far less taxing than it had been a month ago. Someone came up with the idea that our Catalinas were suitable for carrier duty, and soon we found ourselves practicing takeoffs and landings on a small, carefully marked landing strip that was supposed to represent a carrier deck. We labored through a few training sessions but, of course, patrol continued to be the norm, as it was during the first tour. The many hours of searching limited our usefulness in other ways, but there was no questioning the level of security it had provided in the Solomons. It was essential to anticipate and observe enemy movements over a huge area.

Our patrols now required us to cover a triangular segment of however many hundred miles out, then across, and return. This patrol tactic was common for PBYs and was already used a little northwest of here before the battle of Midway as our intelligence people were frantically trying to figure out the "where and when" of the attack they knew was coming. The Cats fanned out daily and finally sighted part of the transport group. Ensign Jack Reid of VP-44 quickly sent a message that prompted a B-17 attack, the first of the encounter. Early the following morning, Howard Ady from VP-23 spotted the main carrier group and a short time later, another PBY flying closer to Midway, reported carrier aircraft heading toward the island. Because of the sightings, our planes were able to get in the air and four Japanese carriers were sunk along with the loss of hundreds of planes and thousands of Japanese military personnel. It was the turning point that American forces had been waiting for.

Frequently, this pattern would involve a little piece of Pacific rock called French Frigate. Nearby were some reefs, and we could see the Seabees scooping up the coral into an airstrip that had the look of an elongated carrier deck. Apparently, it was going to be used as a refueling stop for fighter aircraft being ferried out to the war zone. Whenever passing over this white rectangle, we made an effort to drop a bundle or two of current newspapers, cigarettes, and chocolate into the waiting arms of the construction guys below. Some time later, I was checking the operations board for my assignment and saw the chalked inscription:

"Land French Frigate Shoals with supplies." We were to be the first aircraft to land on the new man-made island. It was kind of exciting as we swooped in, dodging a couple of cranes and touching down on the not-too-long runway. I braked to stop in the middle of a swarm of cheering Seabees, and it was great to finally get to shake the hands of some of the men we had only known before as unreadable pinpoints. I happened to look around as several of them were already busy loading a huge crate marked, "To VPB-54." It was crammed full of fresh fish that they had caught that morning. Back at the base, we distributed the bounty to all our personnel, and for weeks we had the fridge stocked with seafood.

We had managed to sell the Studebaker for $250 more than we paid for it right before we left the mainland, thinking that would give us a little cash to spread around on the islands, but most of our down time was spent entertaining ourselves with tennis and sometimes golf. Unlike San Diego, the women were relatively scarce anywhere around the base, so we made do with Navy-type parties and enjoying the food and drink between missions. Those missions began changing as well. A task force of several planes, including ours, was now dispatched out to Midway for a brief tour, and we were again back in Quonset huts, this time near the beach. The schedule was supposed to be a three day turn — one day off, one day standby, and one day patrol. So sometimes we would have two days to kill. We would break it up with long junkets along the beaches getting acquainted with the multitude of native birds. The scruffy young gooney birds, rocking on their elbows on the sand dunes where they had just hatched, were hilarious. The adults were marvelous, soaring with grace and flicking the waves with their wing tips. The lovely terns were fast learners, and we found we could teach them to eat from our hands. There were thousands of these ocean birds to mingle with by day and gently croon us to sleep by night.

> An SBD went into a dive and the unsuspecting rear gunner found himself being launched out of the cockpit.

During one of these lulls, I was walking toward the pier contemplating the curious way things often play out in wartime and I found myself imagining the raging Battle of Midway. It had included the loss of Torpedo Eight and Bob Evans, the saluting soldier that had so inspired me during that football game at Wabash.

And would things have gone differently if VP-44's Jack Reid and his PBY crew hadn't discovered the approaching fleet? Our own Elliot Schreider, now flying Liberators with VP-116, was originally with VP-44 when he first arrived in Hawaii before our first tour and was briefly acquainted with Reid. Reid's crew flew some 650 miles daily for several days searching for the battle group and each day just at the turn around point, a pesky and persistent Nell 96 (Mitsubishi bomber) would open up on them, putting a few holes in their PBY. They fired back from the blisters, but were unable to damage the attacker enough to deter it. When they returned to Midway, Reid's Plane Captain, R.J. Deroin, managed to rustle up a few rounds of a new type of .50 caliber bullet used in the Army B-17s stationed there. It was specifically designed to explode on impact causing more damage than conventional ammo. They divided these cartridges between their blister guns and felt ready to take some measure of revenge on the Nell 96.

DeRoin had a wife and two children. On this particular day, he loaded an additional 50 gallons of fuel for each of them for luck, and with that extra 150 gallons the PBY lifted off and again began its routine. However, when they reached the appointed turn around, there was no sign of the Japanese aircraft. Disappointed, copilot Bob Swan persuaded Reid to continue on a few minutes more, and with DeRoin's assurances about the extra fuel in reserve, he agreed. Another ten minutes and below them, visible on the horizon, were the first of the Japanese attacking forces. With this fortunate sighting, Reid's crew had more than evened the score with the Japanese Nell 96.*

As I continued toward the pier, I noticed a submarine tied up to a massive piling and intrigued, ambled over for a look. There was a navy chief on deck. I struck up a conversation, and he soon invited me aboard for the cook's tour of the ship.

Somewhere down in the bilges, we were both startled to hear the engines fire. "We better get topside," he shouted as he hurried up the ladders with me in hot pursuit. We burst out on deck just as the gangplank was lifted aboard and I made for the beach. He had told me the sub was sailing under sealed orders for who knows where. I wondered what the ramifications would have been had I not made it off her. I presumed I would've been AWOL, but was it really my fault? Would I have gotten any pay? Flight or Sub? Court-marshaled?

While at Midway Airfield, an interesting piece of good fortune occurred. An SBD went into a dive and the unsuspecting rear gunner found himself being launched out of the cockpit. He somehow caught the edge of one foot and hung on that way all through the dive. The pullout reinserted him back into the cockpit, leaving the poor gunner unable to talk or even walk when they safely got him back down. He made a reasonably full recovery and when we returned to Hawaii, we all had a top notch story to tell over drinks.

---

* Nell 96 was a Japanese bomber made by Mitsubishi

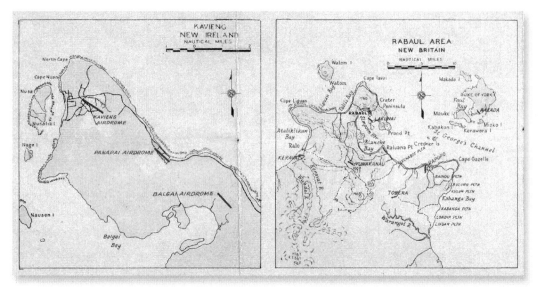

Military map of Kavieng (on left)

Our new skipper continued to feel like a bad fit. A few members of the squadron were still suspicious of his motives and most of his approach to training continued to fly in the face of the reason and expertise we felt we had secured during the first tour. Everything he did since arriving at North Island just rankled us, so much so, that several of us arranged an audience with the base commander. He listened to our story and explained in detail the precarious steps we would have to undertake to accomplish a change. After mulling it over a few days, we had just about decided to take the shot when we were, perhaps mercifully, ordered back to combat. It was July of '44 and the squadron was heading south.

Our path from Kaneohe through Espiritu Santo to Guadalcanal included Funafuti instead of Samoa and Fiji this time around. After a few days, we returned to Espiritu and made camp in a huge grove of palms, holed up in the Quonsets near the Buttons airstrip. We began regular search patrols from here, sometimes for enemy activity, once unsuccessfully over the mountains for several hours in hopes of locating a downed plane. In between flights, I set up a drawing board and fiddled with artwork, eventually christening my plane "Frisco Gal," with paintings of a startling, negatively clad blonde on either side of the bow, including front and backside views. Off-duty afternoons were usually spent at the 'O' Club, taking advantage of the facilities and singing a few profane bars of "The Long, the Short, and the Tall."

There was now another story making the rounds down at the club. Earlier in the year, one of the squads working a little north of us had sent a Cat along with an army bomber group for an attack of Kavieng, a Japanese stronghold on the Island of North Ireland. The pilot, an Arkansas boy, was making his way down the elongated coastline when he received word that a plane was down and fliers were in the water. It was apparently one of those days when seas were uncooperative, swells too large for a safe landing, and tough choices would have to be made. When they arrived at the designated location, a B-25 passing by radioed that a plane was spotted down nearer Kavieng and led them toward the harbor. In they went, popping rivets and shaking the old girl violently. But things were so rough that they couldn't bring the raft alongside with the engines running, so he gave orders to shut them down and hoped they would restart again in the splash and spray. The good news was the rough sea was making them a difficult target. They got the six airmen aboard and the engines restarted just as enemy fire, which had been a little short up until then, began straddling the plane. Once airborne, his escort radioed that more fliers were in the drink. They climbed and headed about, this time closer to Kavieng. The landing was good, but the Japanese were watching and had their guns trained by now. Again he had to kill the engines to load the three survivors, and on restart, the port engine flooded. They circled with one engine to create a moving target until it had a few minutes to dry out. Mercifully, the engine kicked and they were quickly in the sky.

At least long enough to get a new call that there was yet another one down much closer to shore. Against his better judgment, the pilot continued on and again landed where an oil and dye sheen were visible. Here the plane and raft were already gone and there were no survivors in sight, and they immediately got out of there just as another message came across the radio. A fourth raft! Actually two. He wondered if it would be possible to land a fourth time with the PBY's weakened hull in seas that really weren't safe for a single landing. He tried not to think about it as they went in yet again, this time flying over gun positions and taking heavy fire. They landed barely a quarter mile from shore and of course the engines had to be shut down. The strafing was all around them now. It must have seemed a lifetime as they watched each of the six crewmen slowly hauled on board. The engines caught and the overloaded PBY climbed as the tracers pummeled the very water they had been sitting in. They got all the injured back safely, all survived, and Lt. (jg) Gordon was later awarded a Medal of Honor.*

Espiritu continued to be our primary base for a few months. The flying in and around the Solomons and the New Hebrides was a far cry from the stateside work we had been accustomed to and it began to look like our focus would involve much more daytime flying. Patrols often included searching for lost planes as well as subs and shipping. During the first tour, we would typically meet in a tent before missions. I always found it strange that as I looked around that tent, I was surrounded by not just Navy guys, but teachers, salesmen, lawyers, store owners, even students, and all of us were sitting there discussing how to inflict the most damage and kill the most people. There was never a doubt in any of our minds who the enemy was and that they needed to be stopped, but there was a certain relief for some of us seeing action for the second time to find more of our effort would be spent on rescue work. Saving lives, our own countrymen's lives, was a hugely satisfying experience.

Not only were rescue missions becoming more common, the chances of successfully locating a downed flier were becoming more promising. Information came in from coast watchers and as the war pushed northward, friendlies among the islanders and guerrilla fighters were increasingly helpful. Searches began more quickly and rafts were better equipped with markers. Some even had broadcast transmitters with a small hydrogen filled balloon attached to antenna wire to enhance the chances of being spotted by one of our planes.** Dumbos were now

---

* This account differs from the contemporary account and Lt. Gordon's own retelling of the story of the rescues. It was reported in an interview with Gordon by Charles Rawlins in the Saturday Evening Post in Dec of 1944 and corroborated in an article by Don Wharton, Look Magazine, (Feb 1945). Both of these articles were part of my father's collection of memorabilia.

** Gibson Girl hand cranked transmitters involved an H2 generator, a metal cylinder containing granular material that when mixed with sea water would produce hydrogen gas. It was part of a kit that included a box kite, the hydrogen generator, and even a small light that was strapped to either the kite or balloon. The gas was used to pressurize the balloon if there wasn't enough wind to fly the box kite. courtesy Henry Rogers - WHRM

used routinely as escorts during attack missions, greatly reducing the size of search areas. We had just returned from a search involving six of our planes, but in this case we were unsuccessful. Downed airmen still found themselves in a perilous situation, although compared to the first tour, that situation was much improved.

Flying by day could provide as much drama as our night time missions. For instance, during one of the frequent shuttles between Espiritu and Guadalcanal, our flight path took us near an awe inspiring sight — a very active volcano. Taking care not to fly directly over the pit of the volcano itself and steer clear of the scorching temperatures and volatile air currents, we skirted around its flanks to what appeared to be a more stable situation. The slopes turned out to be newly created lava beds producing much the same conditions we had tried to avoid. At that moment, my first thought was that one of our crewmen had been taking pictures from the port side waist blister through the open slide and might still have it open. The plane hit a monster updraft and was lurched some 500 hundred feet upward in an instant. I struggled to regain control and shouted into the intercom as we reached a safe distance. The crewman had apparently closed the slide moments before we bounced in the rough air and received a nasty thump on the noggin to remember the volcano by.

Although night flights were less typical than during the first tour, routine night patrols still occurred and were not always routine. We had an evening encounter with a Japanese task force, which surprised us by sending a blistering hail of anti-aircraft fire our way. Roger, our navigator, was cooped up in the center of the plane and unable to see what was going on, but heard the gunfire over the engine noise.

"Navigator to pilot, what are we shooting at?"

I hesitated a moment, trying to figure out the right words to explain our situation, and before I could answer several crew members took the lead.

"Waist gunner to Navigator, I'm not shooting."

Then another voice, "This is Combs, I haven't fired a round."

"Nose gunner, I'm not shooting either." With all the gunners accounted for, Roger paused then replied somewhat timidly over the intercom, "Navigator to pilot — Well then, why aren't we?"

"Frisco Gal" and her crew touched down at Buttons after a long flight and we suddenly found we had several days off. Mail back and forth to the states was now happening in remarkable time. Some of the guys even held competitions and reported getting letters from as far away as New Jersey in a matter of a few days, a huge change from the early days of the war. There were rumors circulating that something big was brewing, and the group was killing time at home in the Quonset until we could learn a little more about it. I was writing a letter thanking my folks for a package they had sent. In the attached note, they wrote that during a family trip to Georgia, they had passed through Atlanta and had seen one of the new B-29s, America's Superfortress high altitude bomber. They couldn't wait to tell me about it.

I paused a moment to look around the hut at the cast of characters I had fallen in with. Pete was a Serbian fellow, a Pittsburg native who had earned All-American honors playing basketball at a small West Virginia college. He loved his cigars and could frequently be seen chewing them down to stubs. Pete dated quite a number of girls back in San Diego and Hawaii and, somewhere along the way, had gone out with Miss Hawaii. They hit it off and she decided to make him a present of a small German Shepherd puppy, Chet. When we headed overseas, Chet went with us and the two of them were constant companions.

Pete had a passion for the news and I had suggested the idea of posting a big chart on the wall and coloring in the daily progress of the allies as they advanced across Europe. He was excited at the prospect and was now hovering over the map, filling us all in on the latest developments. He'd come a long way since our first tour days when he could be found banging his head on the wall in frustration over the early, sweeping successes the Japanese enjoyed around these islands.

Jack, on the other hand, had struggled for three hours with a wringer-less washing machine, and swore he would run around naked from now on. There was now an enlisted gent, who for a few cents per item, would do the wash. This fellow made a little money and remained valuable enough around the camp to manage to get out of most of his other work, and that suited him fine. Jack had an opportunity to use our "laundry service," but wouldn't part with the money. Instead, he has decided to invest it and is playing poker with Gewin McCracken.

Mac, a pretty fair poker player, managed to fall on his face yesterday and now looks like he fell asleep in the sun for an afternoon with all the merthiolate he has spread around on it. You would have expected better from an Alabama farm boy, and we'd been giving him a hard time. He joined the Navy right out of Jackson State Teachers College.

Del and Art Bonnet have taken to playing duets on clarinet and sax and sound good together. The trouble is that Del only knows one song and we've heard it now a thousand times! Sometimes he'd practice while we were all airborne, piping it between us through the intercoms, until we threatened to throw him out and leave him to the Japanese. The two of them dated a couple of girls a week or two ago when we were back in Guadalcanal. Henderson had become a big and very busy place and there was even a donut shop down near the strip. They were heading out for a hop at about the same time and while looking around to find where the ground crews put their planes, they wandered over for a bite. Bonnie was from Evanston, Ill., and it turned out one of the girls behind the counter was, too. She had a friend, both staying at the nurse's compound, and the four of them went out for the evening, barely managing to get the girls back before it was locked up for the night.

We all loved Bonnie. Back in San Francisco, when we all first arrived at our hotel to get cleaned up, they didn't have our reservation. His mother had owned a string of hotels in Evanston, and after a few minutes of small talk with the manager, he walked over to us and announced, "We'll have a room in an hour!" Somehow he had gotten them to take a conference room and outfit it with extra beds and wall dividers so we could all share it. He was our hero.

The whole group of them had joined in on the poker game by now, and I couldn't help thinking to myself what a remarkable bunch this was. We came from all over the country and from all walks of life. Here we were, each of us gathered for this common purpose, doing things in an aircraft invented a dozen years ago and before most of us had entered high school that would have surprised even its designers.

About this time, someone laid down a beer and Chet knocked it over and lapped up the puddle. Poor Chet loved beer, but Pete's convinced it's stunted his growth. He's only about the size of a beagle.

"That's the last beer anyone gives that dog!" And with that, there was never another beer on the floor of the Quonset.

Ray Peckham? He's asleep. Again.

Del (left) in blister

PBY over reefs

Art, Del, and Howard "playing" instruments

"Frisco Gal" from "front" and "rear"

"Frisco Gal" and her officer crew "Dog 65" - Ensign Roger George, Lt. Howard Miner, Ensign Robert White

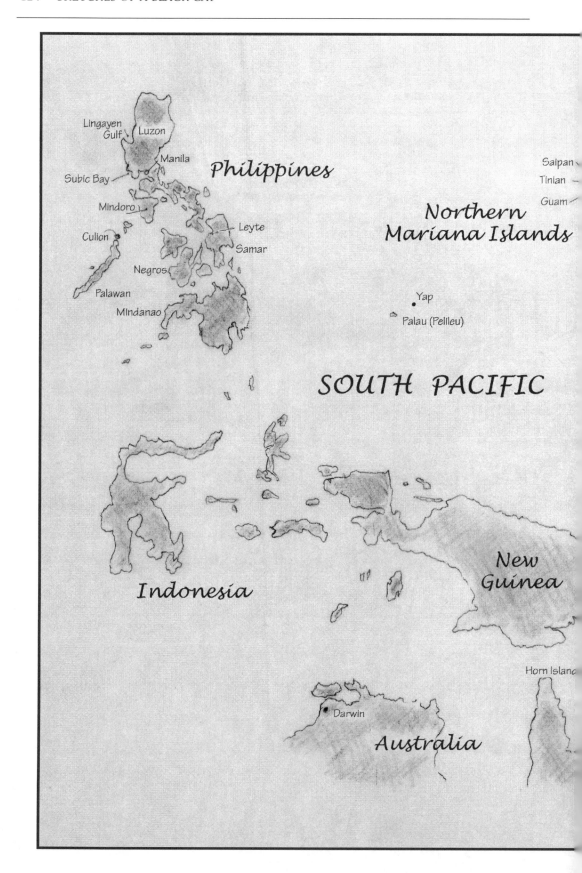

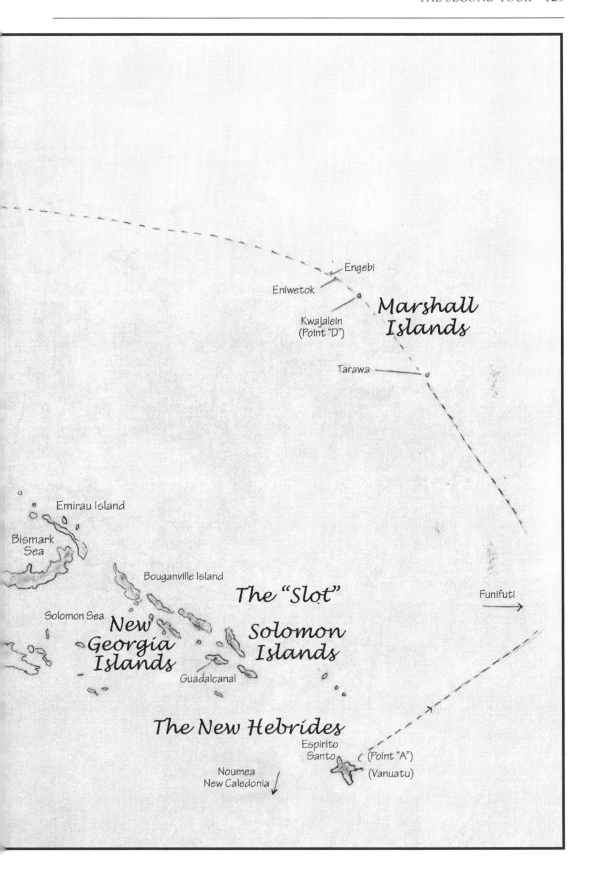

A Special Task

It had been about seven weeks since D-Day on the opposite side of the world. Germany had lost at Normandy and 9,000 brave servicemen gave their lives to make it happen. It was an effort made all the more remarkable by an unspeakable and lesser known tragedy that occurred about six weeks earlier during training exercises for the invasion. Some 30,000 troops and a host of vessels conducting mock beach landings in British waters were victims of a surprise attack during their training, causing another nearly 1,000 men to lose their lives. Although there was to be much finger pointing, the entire episode needed to remain secret so as not to jeopardize the pending invasion, and the fate of those unfortunate servicemen was not revealed until much later.

Over here, we were getting ready to move north toward Guam and Saipan. Our speculation about "something brewing" turned out to be correct as a sizable task force was being organized in an attempt to move a great number of Marine single-engine fighter planes over several successive days to a forward area across some 3,500 miles of water. For us this was a special mission, and while we had a potentially grim part in it, it was certainly a determined and vital part. It was to be a history making operation. The move would only make four stops, and some doubted whether it was possible to safely move such a large number of small aircraft under their own power over that great expanse of ocean. Since our more primitive

"Dumbos" worked quite well in both fluids, our primary mission was to bolster the confidence of members of this "wagon train" by being a constant presence in the event of a mishap.

Our part of the flight was to consist of two waves on two consecutive days. Each wave would be comprised of nine transports, twenty-two of the small planes, and three PBYs. Since we were much slower, we took off in intervals ahead of the other aircraft so as to be dispersed along the route as the speedier fighters caught up. Should any go down, the nearest PBY would be directed to the scene to attempt a rescue.

The crews were selected over a week before our departure. Our skipper was to go on the first day, and Ray Peckham and I were to accompany him. In the second section were John Love, Harry Shaw, and Ralph Badge. Our squadron had acquired several of the purely seaplane type of PBY that could only land on water. These "sea cats" were lighter and considered somewhat better for open sea rescue work, and it was decided to have one sea cat in each section. Peck and I were relieved that the skipper had selected the Seacat for himself, as we much preferred landing on the strips than in the bays.

Our buddies took it upon themselves to prepare our souls for the trek into the forward territory, recounting tales of unfortunates who had confronted every kind of wind and swell condition with unspeakable outcomes. In turn, we promised to arrange for the entire squadron to be transferred up there for permanent duty and boasted that we expected to return laden with Jap souvenirs — especially since we were taking all our liquor for trading purposes.

Day after day, the seventy or so pilots were briefed on flight plans, weather, ranges, and other navigational aids. Each day we expected to head out, but a streak of very bad weather persisted. Finally, I awoke before daylight to peer out into more heavy rains, and learned I had drawn the early hop and needed to takeoff an hour ahead of the others so we would arrive into the last third of the journey as the procession passed us. My crew and I gathered at the mess hall for early chow served by sleepy eyed stewards. To his credit, the skipper had somehow lined up several dozen fresh eggs for us to cook en route, so with my poncho over my head, I joined the others and we all made way to the waiting truck and headed for the mat.

Aerology had predicted a weak front stretching all along our flight path, and we ran into heavy overcast at about 800 feet. We held at 500 feet for about fifty miles, dodging a few lofty islands along the way, but then it became obvious a greater intensity front and a line of squalls would force us up or around to avoid flying into the monsoon on instruments. Clouds were an interesting contradiction. They represented turbulence and poor or worse visibility and sometimes could pose a real threat to a plane, but they were also our preferred hiding place when we were unfortunate enough to stumble upon an enemy fighter, a rabbit buried in the briar patch. After poking around at 9,000 feet, we judged the buildups too high and too solid ahead, so we decided to instead head left and around for some sixty miles off course.

We made good time at that altitude and listened in as the other planes took off and joined in. As the hours passed, the group closed in — until there was a sudden report of engine trouble, an oil leak. After some debate, the pilot decided to remain on course and I wondered if we would get our first taste of the conditions down below. Our last good look at the sea told us there was a moderate swell with at least a fifteen knot wind, about the roughest conditions that would allow a rescue attempt. We sweated a little, but I'm sure the pilot was far more uneasy. He surely knew what a rough sea meant, and he had no power of decision, the plane either stayed up or it didn't. The burden of determining whether to leave that man floating in the foam or attempt a rough landing — and conceivably an impossible takeoff risking nine more lives — was left to us. So, yes, we sweated. And listened to the radio.

Another hour passed, then another, and finally we were starting letdown toward our destination. The plane picked up speed, hitting the stratus layer where we went on instruments for about ten minutes, then popped out at 2,000 feet where dead ahead was the broken silhouette of an atoll. On flights over the Pacific, it could be hours between any glimpses of land or even the tiniest speck of an island. There was so much vast, sheer blue openness, sometimes at least partially obscured by thick clouds, that locating that particular "speck" you were looking for was a remarkable feat in itself. Roger, our navigator, had led us straight and true above the clouds and we were about to split our target. An experience like that was always gratifying for me, but for a navigator it's a moment of indescribable pride.

The sun was shining ahead and the shallow waters of brilliant blues and greens were dappled with the white rolling coils of spray across the reef. These tiny green isles were separated by small interludes of water forming almost an unbroken chain around the lagoon. On the far side, a number of ships were anchored and beyond we could now distinguish the coral mat and taxi-ways of the air base against the trees.

Bob still could not raise the tower on voice, so we "broadcast blind" that we were coming in for a "one ball" landing. There are only two choices on a single strip, and there was a thirty-knot wind nearly abeam of the runway. To make matters worse, communication between an approaching aircraft and someone down below gave us assurance that we were recognized as "friendly" and would not end up in tatters before we could make our way down — so there was a sense that gun sights might be trained on us if we were in truth arriving unannounced. I circled in a right hand turn, dropped wheels and watched for the green light from the tower as we came in. It was on. This was the worst crosswind I'd ever experienced and it quickly became necessary to crab into the wind nearly forty-five degrees to keep from being blown off the strip. We came in over the beach between some coconut trees lining the mat and eased back the throttle. The ship settled near the deck, still in a nearly sideways, violent crab. As we skimmed over the surface, her nose swung back and the wheels touched and clung. "Frisco Gal" was down at Funifuti, and there, we were greeted by a group of brown-skinned natives and sun tanned island personnel.

On my headset, I could hear Peck requesting direct approach for himself and two of the small planes. I learned later that in trying to get over the front, the small planes became separated from the group and got lost. Peck had rounded them up and they had flown in with him, scissoring on his tail to hold down their speed. We turned "Frisco Gal" into our parking revetment, locked the brakes, and killed the engines. Over against the trees was the battered wreckage of another Black Cat, suggesting the image of a nighttime attempt at a landing with a similarly hairy crosswind. Overhead, Peck's three aircraft were now fighting the wind and making their way in, and in the distance the other formations were just becoming visible.

We watched as one by one they landed, each struggling with that fierce crosswind, each settling unsteadily on that high landing gear and rolling to a stop. We counted as they came in and breathed easy as they were all accounted for, including one covered in oil from cowl to rudder. Peck must have been living right — as he rolled to a stop, his port engine started popping and cutting out. He added a little throttle and it quit completely and would not restart, a most reflective situation considering the landing he had just made. Ray and I had gone through training at Corpus Christi together and he had certainly become a savvy pilot. Judging from his thinning hairline, you might peg him as a worrisome type, but he was another of these California boys that had a way of just letting things roll off their backs.

Quarters were at the transient camp, screened in frame buildings with sixteen cots apiece. Fresh linens were the whitest I had ever seen overseas, and as the shower opened up, we cleaned up a little until the water bag gave out. Then it was on to mess for a well deserved dehydrated dinner.

I noticed quite a number of natives performing odd jobs about the camp. A few of them were working in the galley, some loading trucks, others building huts. They were a handsome lot, cinnamon-skinned with clean-shaven complexions and good builds. Each had a peculiar swagger when walking about, barefoot with head held high, like each was a chieftain in his own right. Most were dressed in a piece of khaki cloth wrapped about the waist to just below the knee, a few in brightly flowered costumes, sometimes including a ring in the left ear. While they always flashed a ready smile in passing, they seemed hesitant about speaking with us. I was interested to learn that they were signed up in labor battalions for a year at a time and paid $7.00 a month by the government. Many of them had not seen their families in three years, although they lived just across the lagoon.

We went to a movie about dusk at one of the island's two open air theaters, about a ten minute walk. Most evenings on these bases, it was possible to find a movie somewhere. They were very popular, so much so in fact that no quirk of the elements, sudden or prolonged, would prevent or interrupt a scheduled show. The theaters were generally cleared spaces on the side of a hill with a projection booth protected under cover. Various films became available and were treated almost like currency between bases, with more sought after pictures being traded for others as part of carefully crafted deals. It was exceedingly amusing to me the importance all these men, myself included, placed on those two hours of entertainment. Wouldn't it seem even more astounding some day when I'd again be driving to Loew's Palace on Meridian with my date beside me, instead of bumping down these dusty roads on a truck with forty other guys that managed to climb on before me. Just imagine, reclining snug in plush seats with dry peanut shells on the floor, instead of huddling under ponchos in ankle deep mud with water actually flowing past our feet, yet somehow scarcely noticing anything but Rita Hayworth.

> No, we couldn't make do without the movies.

The men usually made good audiences, although there was generally criticism of the servicemen lucky enough to be back home (the U.S.O. Gang — of course, any of us would have gladly traded places with them), or the tendency by movie makers for inauthentic characterizations of aircraft and blatant propaganda. We wanted the stuff that reminded us that America was still America, and that meant Cary Grant and Ginger Rogers or "Star Spangled Rhythm," but with about ninety percent less flag waving. Of course, there was the ongoing, but good natured, rivalry between the services that required heckling whenever the Army appeared on the screen. No, we couldn't make do without the movies.

So while tonight's selection was kind of an uninspiring choice between "A Trip to Paris" or "Klondike Annie," we were still grateful for the diversion. The sun had just set across the lagoon, and there were still beautiful reflections from the clouds and the lights on the strips. A seaplane was just coming in throwing up pink spray behind it. Silhouetted against the sky were the ruins of an old stone mission, which had been camouflaged but hadn't fooled the Japanese bombardiers. The walls were pitted by flak, and the roof and windows had completely disappeared.

After the show, we spent some time trying to get Peck's engine going. It was raining again, but the men worked attentively while the skipper and Major Moran watched. The major summoned over one of his crack mechanics, and eventually, they determined the distributor was at fault and parts that were not available out here would be required. They sent a dispatch for another plane to catch up with us as soon as possible. Peck was broken hearted about having to stay, but we knew he would run us down in a day or two.

Once again it was up before dawn. Breakfast was scarcely worth describing. It seems that ships just didn't stop any more and supplies were scarce. So it was off to the runway and shortly we were taxiing down the strip into a brightening sky. As we rose off the mat, hastening the dawn, we could see a severe buildup and shower activity in our path. Climbing to 10,000 feet, about the edge of our comfort zone, only gave us a better view of the towering clouds still above us. We headed toward a hole to port and could barely glimpse a patch of blue sky in its center. As we made for it, it quickly closed and the plane was veiled in white, so we went on instruments for several minutes. Then all at once, as if the blindfold had been snatched from our eyes and we found ourselves walking over a 10,000 foot cliff, the clouds fell away straight down to the ocean below. Before us lay the most colorful panorama of endless dark blue water. Puffs of cumulus clouds, distant "cumulons," and the stunning color effects from the rising sun behind the clouds we'd just come through were dazzling. We swung back to our proper course, set up on the automatic pilot, and relaxed to enjoy the sight.

The information on these tiny islands was kind of sketchy, so we came prepared with a beautiful new K-2 camera to photograph the groupings and details. One below us was still in darkness but a crewman tried a shot anyway, and soon we passed over a larger one before hitting open water the rest of the way. We were making better time than I had expected at 10,000 feet and were surprised to spot our next check point over the starboard bow. There was a radio report that the last of the planes was a little late taking off, and we were a little early, so we decided to swing over the next in the chain of islands and photograph them from several angles. I zigzagged between them as the guys in the blisters did the camera work, and I would identify the island on the map and spell it out to the men, so we could coordinate it with the film. Then I decided to pull out my trusty little Argus for a few more shots, hoping the long stint in the tropics hadn't caused the film canisters in the case to get moldy.

Bob informed me that the equator was just ahead, and looking at the chart, I discovered a little island only a few miles from the zero parallel. We took the range on the island and once at a defined distance, set a proper heading and circled twice, giving us a whopping five crossings in just those few minutes.

We shot a few more reefs, and a crew member advised me that the film counter indicated a film change. After a few moments, his voice over the inter-phones was noticeably faint, "Sir, there doesn't seem to be any film in the camera ..." Up in the cockpit, Bob and I couldn't stop laughing. I mean, it seemed a shame, all the pains we had taken to catalogue them, the maneuvering and all, but hell, it was funny.

Some of the men seemed pretty disappointed, but unhappily, those "aero" cameras didn't have any way of telling about the film without opening them in a dark room, and they handed it to us "ready to shoot." So we stuck in another roll, took a few more pictures and headed for our destination, Tarawa, on the horizon.

By the time we arrived, several of the planes had already landed and others were circling. Below us was an airstrip located on a tiny island that showed signs of a terrific bombardment, honeycombed with submerged shells and craters. I tried to imagine what it must have been like. The other field was over on an untouched part of the reef, above a few sunken ships, barges, and some plane wreckage and in stark contrast to a peaceful native village with beautiful gardens. That's where we headed.

Our turn to set down came just behind one of the transports. The strip was framed in green with palm trees, and we climbed down onto the mat and into the intense heat and glare of the equator. I ordered a man to sleep with the plane, then signed in with the duty officer. He told me, "We don't have much of anything around here, but you're sure welcome to what we do have. Let us know."

It was a short drive through the sights and to quarters; it seemed a rather lovely place. After learning that chow could still be had, we hustled over to the mess hall for lunch and were astonished to see ahead of us a long table covered in white, adorned with bread, butter, lemonade, celery, and radishes. Stewards served a fine meal of roast beef, mashed potatoes, frozen peas and, finally, ice cream!

> Within a mile or so, there was the "Seabee" camp, and again, you had to marvel at the ingenuity.

Back at camp, we refreshed with cooling showers, courtesy again of those clever Seabees. They had rigged up wooden pedals to operate the spray nozzles while conserving water, and nearby, there were shaving bowls made out of regulation steel helmets painted white on the inside and set into holes on a long wooden platform.

Reinvigorated but restless, some of us went for a hike along the beach. Within a mile or so, there was the "Seabee" camp, and again, you had to marvel at the ingenuity. Every hut had a small windmill facing into the prevailing wind, ranging from makeshift two bladed soapbox affairs to elaborate sixteen-bladed all metal versions. We discovered they drove a shaft and gears in the huts working a plunger up and down in a drum of soapy water, an inventive washing machine. Rumor had it that it also performed admirably as an ice cream maker.

The "club" was open, so we secured the necessary chits and each bought a beer. Out on the lanai, you couldn't but be impressed with how much cooler it was under the thatch of these simple structures. The drinks and the ocean breeze were refreshing; what a pleasure to kick back and discuss the trip and enjoy the impressive cloud formations. In the background, it became apparent a couple of the flight crews included a musician or two, some covertly bringing along harmonicas, even brass instruments, and the air had a pleasant melodic feel. I often wished I had learned to play an instrument, and at times like this, it would have been wonderful to be talented enough to join in.

As a child, I had labored through a few piano lessons when we could afford them and, in college, had "banged the skins" for a few weeks on a friend's drums while he was gone over Christmas break. The music now reminded me of that same first year in college. I had not been pledged to a fraternity and was automatically accepted into the large "Garfield Club." During Winter Carnival, the various fraternities and organizations were all in search of musical talent, and our club sent scouts clear to New York to try to sign a band for the occasion. Our group returned with the disheartening news that none of the name bands were available for a small college event like ours. Regrettably, there were only two "unknowns" around that would be available at all: someone named Harry James and another called the Glenn Miller Band. So it all came down to which of these had a female vocalist as part of their group, and since Mr. James did, his group was selected to perform. That Saturday evening, with some ten other bands on campus, nearly everyone ended up at the Garfield Club as Mr. James blew his unknown heart out while the lovely Connie Haines sang.

I was sitting and enjoying the whole thing and thinking it was too bad that Peck wasn't here to join in. He was a solid trombone player and a talented, mellow voiced singer. Suddenly, it dawned on me that the skipper, having landed in the bay over at the other island, would probably be needing to get over here to "pow wow" with the brass about tomorrow's flight. Phones were not operational on the island, and it would be a two hour trip by boat, so it seemed natural enough to fly over and pick him up.

We took only a skeleton crew, but a lieutenant wanted to come along and soon four bystanders asked to join us as well. A heavy squall was closing in, so we hurriedly taxied out, checking the engines along the way, and just beat the worst of it as the plane got airborne. The lieutenant came forward and, coincidently, was heading over to the bay to look up the skipper, so I contacted the tower to request landing clearance and to ask that they locate him for us. "Sorry, boys, the commander just took off in a cub for the other field," the tower responded. Now feeling useless, Bob "Rogered" back and told them we would just head on in, and if the weather worsened, might return again. On our approach, it was obvious conditions back at the field looked fairly rugged, but it seemed like we could get in under it all by going in immediately and very low. We made a straight in, power approach, dragging over the mudflats and crabbing into the wind. A sudden downdraft surprised me, pushing the plane below the end of the strip and before I could correct, the plane struck the sloping embankment about fifty feet short. It was a powerful deflecting jolt, which knocked the passengers all about the cabin. The parachute pack hanging over the lieutenant seated at the navigator's table broke loose and fell into his lap (he later said he thought it was his head). The plane now sailed back into the air and from instinct, I added throttle and regained safe airspeed. The "feel" of the bounce suggested to me that the landing gear had not given way, so I eased it very gently back on the mat, ready to pour on the coal and come up again if anything felt wrong. It stuck and held, and I slowly lowered the nose in case a tire was blown. Everything seemed OK, and looking back, I noticed too many men aft; it was fortunate we hadn't caught our keel. Slowly, I tiptoed along the mat in silent hopes that no one had really noticed, only to swing around and see every fire truck and emergency vehicle on the strip was already speeding our way.

For the next couple of days I felt sick about that landing. You blame yourself for something like that even when logic tells you that there were particular factors beyond your control. It taught me a few things, and I finally persuaded myself that any landing you walk away from is still a good landing. The lieutenant chimed in, "Oh, it wasn't that bad. We bounce our R4Ds all the time."

While I didn't answer, I was thinking, "Well, we don't 'bounce' our PBYs." I vowed to never let it happen again.

The next morning at 5:00 a.m. sharp word came that we were not moving because the airstrip at the next checkpoint was not completed. The small planes were to remain here indefinitely and our Dumbos were to return to base. This was a dispiriting. By now, all of us had become acquainted and felt somewhat attached to the planes and their crews.

So we went to breakfast kind of low. The lavish assortment of eggs, pancakes, and even orange juice couldn't shake us out of it. After eating, the guys and I took a few moments to talk it over, but our attention shifted to a group of natives and an enlisted Navy man apparently in charge. One of the group was dressed in khaki with sergeant stripes, obviously quite proud of his status. He would bark orders in his native tongue to his men and they would quickly and skillfully perform the required task. It was fascinating to watch as several of them scampered up the trunks of the towering coconut palms with the agility of a jungle creature, pulling down dead fronds and coconuts to the delight of a growing group of onlookers. They would drop the fruits, carefully spinning them to land only on their points and unbroken, then hop down and hack them open with one swipe, a drinking hole in each, so we might enjoy the milk. For all this, each was rewarded with a couple of packs of chewing gum.

Around noon, we heard the sound of planes approaching and realized the second echelon was arriving. I counted four PBYs and guessed that Peckham must have gotten his replacement plane and was among them. Three of them landed and we were soon reunited with Harry, John, and Peck. Ralph in his Seacat made for the lagoon and would join us later. Again, all the planes were safe and accounted for. The island was gaining in population fast, so we decided to get a head start toward the club, which was opening at 1300 hours. It was a reunion of sorts and called for a beer.

That night after the movie, we sat on the lanai watching the lights of the crab fishermen moving over the reefs. One of my crew came running up to us with news, "Everything is on again! We move in the morning!"

"Better hit the sheets," Peck commented as he stood and stretched. "Man oughta get some sleep if he's gonna fight the war tomorrow."

In the morning we gathered our gear, still savoring the last of yet another banner breakfast. After a quick briefing — weather dope and recognition signals were handed out — Peck told us he'd like to make the early takeoff. He raced down the runway and I watched as our plane was loaded. I then passed the word that we had decided to cut our takeoff intervals from an hour to thirty minutes.

Our course led us between two Japanese-held islands and I dreaded to think of having to make a rescue near one of them. It was now common knowledge that all the islands along the route were unfriendly, allegedly because the Japs had been talking up head hunting with the natives. If you went down in sight of land, the natives would paddle out and get you. It brought to mind those pictures of hapless adventurers sitting up to the neck in great cauldrons over ceremonial fires. I had Roger plot a course to a point midway between the islands and then figure a new heading from the other side. I wasn't ready to be soup.

As it turned out, the flight was uneventful. Even the weather was cooperative, some occasional weaving around buildups and some thicker cloud cover, especially around the islands (we were happy about that), and things improved as destination three came into view. The other planes had already arrived and, as we circled, our tally again looked good. The skipper was letting down into the seaplane area and I hung in formation with Peck while waiting a turn at the traffic circle. This strip was much like the last, showing signs of scarring and damage, disfiguring a once beautiful South Sea isle. Other than the scores of planes on and around the landing site, it seemed that endless rows of barracks covered most of the rest of the island. Finally, Peck gave the "kiss off" and dove into the 1,000 foot circle, lowering his wheels as he went in. We followed.

Things were bustling. A strike was about to begin with some dozen or more B-24s loaded and taxiing into position. I asked one of the army guys on a fuel truck about it, and he said they were headed out to bomb the islands we had just passed. I wondered aloud if they knew about the weather out there around most of those islands. "We lose a seaplane now and then," he went on, his voice nearly screaming over the aircraft clamor.

"Japs still have some ack-ack. They hit two P-38s yesterday, got 'em with .50 caliber stuff, too. They were going in low for photographs, one was shot down, the other came in on one engine."

A truck gathered us up as I asked the plane captain to look at our starboard engine. One of the crew had noticed a light oil leak. The shuttle scurried up a slight hill to the GroPac (Navy base) duty office and the crew unloaded, signed in, and hurried off to chow.

We didn't like Kwajalein, or "Point D," from the first. It was torrid and dirty, and so closely packed that it felt like the industrial section of a large city. There wasn't a tree in sight; the island was another victim of fierce fighting six months earlier.

The chow had returned to normal, dehydrated potatoes and beans. Afterward, they sent our group off to some abandoned barracks with an assortment of folded cots, six of us sharing the very crowded lower deck while the others went upstairs. It was hot and sticky, and the movement by the men upstairs created a dust cloud that persuaded the rest of us to head back and check on the plane.

It appeared the army mechanics there had never worked on a PBY before and weren't fond of the idea. An hour or so of seeming to make things worse persuaded us to ask that they just let it go. The barracks were no more inviting than before, so we headed in search of an 'O' club. Of course, there would be no club, but we were grateful to be allowed one bottle of beer each after chow that night.

The barracks had now been invaded by another fifty or so Marines and was crowded to overflowing, so the best option seemed to be staying outside to keep cool and count the minutes until dinner. After chow, all fingers were crossed on the way to the movie venue. About this time, we thought there was nothing about this place to like, but were pleasantly surprised to find Point D had what might be the greatest concentration of movie titles short of Times Square, multiple movie sites, and a bulletin board with fifteen or twenty choices — the ones within walking distance highlighted in red. Red Skelton filled the screen as the rain started to come down; it felt great and I wasn't even sure I wanted to use my poncho. It was just what everyone needed.

After the movie, we walked a short distance before stumbling across an old abandoned Negro mess hall. Rather than dealing with the mob back at the barracks, the hall appeared to be a better option, and we hastily shifted our cots into our new digs. Most of us were still fairly wet, but slept in our clothes anyway. Some time before dawn I was startled by the bugler from the Negro camp blowing reveille. He wasn't satisfied until he'd blown it at least a dozen times, as he marched closer and closer until I expected him to stick his bugle in the window. Breakfast was prunes or something, and we soon had our gear loaded and were headed to operations. The crew was only too glad to make the early takeoff and I wondered if GroPac would ever find those six missing cots.

> As the image became more distinct, we were startled to see the silhouettes break up into hundreds of independent pieces.

This time we headed along the reef to depart from the northern tip and over the seaplane base of Ebeye Island, but it was impossible to determine whether the skipper's plane was still among those on the water. At the farthest tip of the atoll, there was another airstrip called Roi, and there I swung around to the west and took up a heading for Eniwetok.

For some reason, the progress on this leg seemed rapid, the weather hazy but good, with ample tail wind. There were several checkpoints along the first part of this route and, as we left the last of them, there were already visual indications of our next stop on the horizon ahead. As the image became more distinct, we were startled to see the silhouettes break up into hundreds of independent pieces. I now figured this must be a pool base for the small landing craft that were being used for all the beach approaches. Another few miles and the "landing craft" grew in size, becoming battleships, carriers, and an entire fleet of warships anchored within the atoll's barriers! It was a breathtaking and most astounding sight! Here was a battle fleet so huge it must certainly be invincible, something I had never seen before or expected to see again.

The Eniwetok landing strip was on the far left, with many of our transports circling overhead and formations of fighters taking off and landing, acting as the CAP (Combat Air Patrol) for the fleet. I explained to the tower that since we were in ahead of the Marine boys it was important to hang around up here a while until they arrived, and then headed off to get a closer look at the flotilla.

Heading down the coastline to review the fleet, it became even more apparent how huge and forbidding it was. There were seven large carriers and as many CVE's (escort carriers), six battleships, twenty light cruisers, scores of DD's and DE's (destroyers and escorts), along with tenders, tankers, and supply and troop ships. There were over 400, not counting the tinier craft buzzing around between them. A couple of OS2Us from one of the cruisers quickly popped into formation with us to look us over, much as a vigilant watch dog would sniff at a passing neighbor before losing interest and moving on.

The huge circle of the fleet brought us nearly back to Stickell Field where our sections were now arriving. Peckham pulled into the landing circle ahead of us and the other members of the "Skytrain", while the transports were landing. John was bringing up the rear. Peck was waved off for some reason, so I went in next. The strip was lined on each side with Liberators, transports, and fighters, mostly P-38s and F-6s, so much so that there was no parking. Eventually there was a place big enough to shoehorn ourselves in along one of the back taxiways and, finally, it was time to step out into the heat, dust, and chaos.

A messenger intercepted us with word that the majors had discovered we shouldn't even be here and, in fact, there was a dispatch ordering us to return to Kwajalein immediately, or in other words, Point D. There was no room for us up the line and, tired and hungry as we were, the whole thing would need to be repeated again in due course returning us to that gem of the Pacific and its cozy mess hall. So we hung around about an hour to get a confirmation, ranting all the while, until one of the majors approached in person and said, to our considerable relief, that they had gotten it worked out. Engebi Atoll, a little further up the chain, would now be our home for the evening.

The gang of us scrambled our planes before anyone could change their minds, and followed the R4Ds down the strip. By the time the ships again passed below us it was obvious that, even using excessive power, there was no staying with these guys and, slowly, the Skytrain passed us by.

After we braked to a stop on Engebi's short runway, our escort jeep signaled for us to follow them down the taxiway. I was intent on staying with the jeep and barely noticed some telephone lines stretching across in front of them. Just as we passed under the lines, it hit me that the props might be high enough above the wing to nick them. Needless to say, I cut the throttle a moment too late and clipped them cleanly. Fortunately, the wires hadn't fouled us and, after giving a shrug, the escort motioned us on ahead. I judged we were the first PBY they had ever had on that strip — at least now, the way was cleared for the others.

This was a rather pleasant place with Seabee written all over it. The tents were situated right on the beach, looking out onto the deep blue of the water and the white, clean coral. It was peaceful, save an occasional plane passing overhead, and the water was inviting. We lost no time getting out of needless clothes, lighting up a couple of cigars, snacking on peanuts, and with Point D still a vivid memory, counting our blessings. After an afternoon and evening of relative luxury, it was quite agreeable to spend a little time at their rather sophisticated club before retiring for the night. The last thing I remembered before drifting off was the sound of the CB's holding a "smoker" nearby, and the applause after someone had recited what seemed to be a pointless joke.

Ray had "first" this day, as we prepared to make our way to the Marianas. The forecast was promising and everyone seemed eager to be on the last leg of the trip, especially the boys in the transports who had to sit, parachutes strapped to their backs, for these five- and six-hour stretches. Even on this short runway "Frisco Gal" made it off in two-thirds the distance and circled around over the still waiting fighters before striking out to the northwest. Within minutes, I could see the dim line of the reefs withdraw into the haze on our port beam.

All was going well. Behind us, the others were gaining and beginning to join up while we broke out and test fired the guns and all maintained careful watch. Just south of us lay the mainspring of the Japanese installations in the Carolines. They were operating patrols out of Truk, a large base, and several "Bettys" (Japanese bombers) had been spotted in the area. Our orders were to take no chances, so we hung near the broken layer of clouds and tried to remain inconspicuous.

As the last of the formation caught us and again disappeared into the distance, it seemed our job was done — in all likelihood it would be solo flying from here. Then we began picking up fragments of a conversation that sounded as if someone might be in a little trouble. It became clear it was the skipper, and he was giving his position to someone, probably Peck. Apparently by now, they had made visual contact and were limping home O.K. and, a couple of hours later, the outline of the first island of the Mariana group, Guam, was visible up ahead. The sheer, rising cliffs profiling the shoreline were a sharp contrast to the low-lying atolls with which we had become accustomed, and the spit of land at the southern tip was peculiar to Guam. The strip came into view from behind a shower. Numerous ships were anchored nearby with several destroyers plowing back and forth, covering them from hostile subs.

It was clear the shoreline had undergone a ferocious bombardment in recent days. The wreckage of landing craft, trucks, and tanks was strewn everywhere. In one or two locations, there was evidence of what might once have been small towns, now crumbled foundations and twisted, corrugated metal roofing.

The peninsula itself was some hundred feet above the water, with abrupt cliffs forming its edge. Caves dotted the volcanic rock and, flying above the surface, you could see it was pitted with bomb and shell craters. The airstrip ran down the center and, instead of the white of the coral strips, this was the reddish color of the soil in the area, almost symbolic of the recent bloody strife here. Each side of the strip was lined with planes and, as yet, there was no dispersal area. Curiously, the runway had a slight bend in it about halfway down. It had me wondering if I was seeing things.

Peck was still circling as he waited for some homecoming fighter sections to pancake. We made one pass at the field and got a red light and zoomed out low over the cliffs to re-enter the circle. The tower finally saw fit to bring us in, and I made a careful approach. The strip was quite narrow, so much so that it seemed that our wing tip would surely come in contact with the parked planes. The surface was anything but smooth. Puddles of water stood here and there, and soft spots indicated recently filled bomb craters. The tower was part of an old reclaimed Japanese building, and we taxied alongside and parked across from the wreckage of some Jap planes.

When the skipper arrived a little later, he explained that his port engine had begun vibrating so badly that he had to feather it and throw much of the gear overboard, including his guns, to stay airborne. He came nearly 200 miles that way on one engine and landed in the harbor at a seaplane tender where the crew was to spend the night. This sounded good to us, as we had expected to sleep under the planes.

A jeep came by to shuttle us over to the tender. The driver indicated that while the Japanese had been driven back into the hills, a half hour ago one of them had blown up a Corsair right on the field. According to the report, an enemy infantryman climbed into the baggage compartment with his confidential papers and a helmet full of hand grenades, intending to blow up the plane in the air. The pilot was later sitting in the cockpit writing a letter to his wife when he heard a disturbance and spotted the soldier in the back of the plane. He scrambled out as the intruder pulled a grenade, killing himself and blowing a hole in the Corsair. I decided to post a double armed guard by the "Frisco Gal" that night.

On board the tender we were treated to a great meal of sardines, cheese, and spaghetti, all served on white linens with real silverware. Later, over cigars, the crew gave us the detailed account of the ongoing campaign. They spoke of the three-week long bloody battle with over 7,000 American casualties. Some of the Marines encountered heavy surf around the reefs and weren't able to navigate transports any closer. They had to nearly swim the remaining distance, scrambling through heavy fire, before reaching whatever cover they could on the beach. Like most of the island conflicts, the Japanese never seemed willing to surrender, preferring to continue fighting in the jungles to the last man. A Navy radioman hiding out on Guam throughout the war had been pulled out only a couple of days ago. It was humbling.

The following day, we found the mechanics had scratched up enough parts to get the skipper's plane airworthy. Our time as escorts for the Marine boys was over, and we would continue on to Saipan in the morning without them. A few of us decided to nose around a little. The road was soupy after the morning downpour, and we gingerly walked along, testing every few steps so as not to sink entirely. There were signs of a normal civilization here. It was the first real "on foot" contact I'd had with a Pacific battleground. Up on the hill, there was the grim wreckage of the old Marine barracks and the Pan American Hotel, once famous landmarks. The barracks were already being repaired to house advancing American forces. Walking along through some fields, past junk piles of Japanese aircraft already searched and stripped by souvenir hunters or intelligence, we weaved around numerous craters, some used as machine gun nests and still containing ammunition or wrecked guns. Everywhere were heavy fragments of bombs and shells, torn rusty hunks of twisted steel. I shuddered to think of those things flying around down here.

The skipper happened along and indicated our flight in the morning had been postponed. Our small collection of artifacts piqued his interest, and we all set out, still armed to the teeth in anticipation of a chance run-in with a Jap sniper. Ahead were several gun emplacements that bore the signs of a frantic last stand. Empty shell casings were strewn about, as well as grenades and machine gun belts, used and unused. An assortment of battered tanks and trucks and several dugouts, some with dead enemy soldiers lying in them, covered the entire area. In an old shack, perhaps some sort of headquarters, I picked up some interesting pamphlets and documents. I also decided on a rifle with bayonet and a helmet, while the others looked around for whatever articles they found intriguing.

On the way back we stopped at operations to file a new flight plan. They immediately jumped down our throats because they thought we had already taken off and had not arrived at Saipan. Worse yet, they had us so far overdue that they had already initiated a search with a couple of planes and a destroyer. I quickly held up my hands, exclaiming that not only had we sent word to them that our flight was postponed, canceling the morning flight plan, but, "Hell, do you know what a PBY looks like?" Our two planes were still sitting down there, big as life, and the only two aircraft on the field painted a dark shade of black.

Before long, the skipper's plane passed overhead and we too hurried to get airborne. Heading up the coast of Guam, I swung clear of the enemy-held island of Rota, then made a beeline for Saipan and Isley Field. This was a brief stop before traveling the final twenty minutes to Tinian, our eventual turn-around point. While fighting was still in progress on Tinian, two airstrips were being put into shape and one was now serviceable. I found myself considering the long climb back down the rungs of the ladder toward Santos base again. Upon our return, the jaunt would have lasted two weeks, and while it had been an adventure, we felt pleased with the outcome. I could sense the growing confidence driving the war effort. Our Dumbos would now regain focus on making sure that we gave our downed pilots every chance of finding their way home.

PBY on island runway

Island Navy base

Howard's flight notebook - one of a dozen
Recognition page sketches showing profiles of friendly and enemy ships as seen from the air.

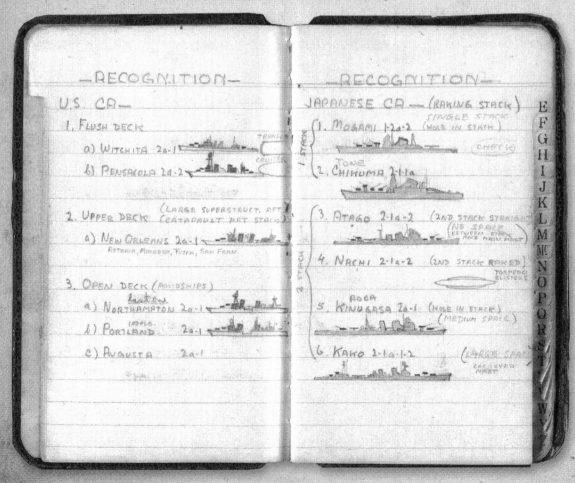

SECOND MARINE AIRCRAFT WING
FLEET MARINE FORCE
IN THE FIELD.

7 August 1944.

SECRET

SPECIAL OPERATIONS ORDER)
NUMBER   1-44)

Task Organization.

   (a) VMTB-131   (22 Avengers)   Major G. E. Dooley, USMC.
   (b) VMTB-242   (22 Avengers)   Major W. W. Deane, USMC.
   (c) VMR-253   (17 Skytrains) Major J. F. Moran, USMCR.
   (d) VP-54   (2 Seacats)   As assigned by ComFairWing-1.
                  (4 Landcats)

1. ComTaskFor 57 has directed the movement of garrison Avenger squadrons from the South Pacific Area to the Marianas via own aircraft accompanied by escort and Dumbo aircraft. This order is promulgated for the purpose of coordinating the transfer flight of the subject squadrons. Upon arrival at destination this order will be cancelled and destroyed.

2. Squadrons will proceed from Espiritu Santo to airfields in the Marianas Islands group along the following approved route: Santo, Funa Futi, Tarawa, Kwajalein, Eniwetok, Marianas.

3. (a) MarTorpBomron 131 will proceed on or about 9 August in flights of six or less Avenger aircraft, each flight to be accompanied by one Skytrain.

    (b) MarTorpBomron 242 will proceed on or about 10 August in flights of six or less Avenger aircraft, each flight to be accompanied by one Skytrain.

    (c) MarTransron 253 will provide Skytrains to accompany flights of Avenger aircraft. At least one Skytrain will precede each Avenger squadron by two hours to observe weather conditions along the route to be followed. Remaining Skytrains will be made available to trail the squadrons and to be utilized as advance weather planes in event the squadrons become separated by delays enroute.

    (d) Patron 54 will provide Seacats and Landcats for Dumbo rescue along the entire route. There will be three Dumbo aircraft assigned to cover each squadron and accompanying Skytrains. One Dumbo will depart in advance of the squadron at such time so as to provide rescue coverage for the last one third of each leg of the trip at the time the main body of the squadron passes through that area. A second Dumbo will depart in advance of the squadron in order to provide rescue coverage for the center third, and a third Dumbo will do the same for the first third. Upon arrival of the squadrons at their destination the planes of Patron 54 will be relieved of this temporary additional duty and return to their organization, or to such other place as may be designated by higher authority.

    (x) (1) The Commanding Officer MarTransron 253 is the officer in charge of the entire flight. He will coordinate Skytrains and Dumbo departure to provide for coverage of strayed or delayed aircraft.

- 1 -

"Taking a Break"

Howard and crew members awaiting instructions?

Ray Peckham

Japanese dive bomber wreckage

Crew of the "Frisco Gal"

Leap Frog

The battle of Peleliu was underway. The Marines had driven the enemy into their network of caves and tunnels, and finally gained control of the airstrip after a brutal and costly battle. This effort was all the more extraordinary due to the 110-degree heat and a near complete lack of water. The rumor was that the Japanese had poisoned the wells so that what water there was came from Guam.

The theory of sending out small task forces of PBYs on combat missions continued, and with it our nomadic lifestyle. A number of our Black Cat crews were sent over to Palau[*] to assist in what we were told was a mopping up operation, although Del and two other crews arrived first and were instructed to come in at thirty feet because of the shelling that was still going on above them. At night, landings were accomplished using a makeshift airstrip lit up with jeep headlights and, in fact, VPB-54's planes were the first to touch down on the island since the invasion began.

Peleliu was an awful mess — there was little left of it but broken palm trees. Things had improved somewhat by the time our crew arrived, but Marines continued to work an upland area called Bloody Nose Ridge above and just north of the airstrip. It was an active and threatening place with sniper fire still killing

---

[*] Palau is the largest of this Island group, although the most intense fighting took place on Peleliu, a roundish, smaller island about forty miles southwest of Palau near the end of the group.

men down here. Much of this island's surface was coral, but the northern portion included high hills, cliffs, and steep terrain and was very different geologically. Many of the caves were early mineral and mining tunnels dug out of the clay and lava, and now the enemy had connected them and added hundreds more creating an underground complex to move around personnel and conceal artillery.

The Seabees arrived about the same time as the first of our PBYs and had gone immediately to work rebuilding the runways, even as the Marines continued firing mortar rounds over their heads into the northwest hills. Some of those barrages made our takeoffs a little dicey, as well. There was at least one skirmish between Japanese soldiers and the Seabees who, using everything they had including shovels and bulldozers, quickly sent the intruders scurrying out of a pit and back into their caves.

Bob and I found the Operations Tent and checked in. I saw my name on the schedule board for the next morning with the comment "Napalm Strike." After searching through several charts, I was unable to find a place around there called "Napalm," so I asked a lieutenant about it. It was then explained that napalm was an inflammable liquid to be carried in droppable wing tanks! Each tank held about 250 pounds of the stuff.

The idea was to hit the mouth of the caves and effectively burn the occupants out. The targets were so close that we practically stayed in our traffic pattern, simply taking off, circling over the ridge for the drop, and then back in again for a reload. We scarcely reached 400 feet in altitude and were putting the landing gear down again in five minutes.

This went on for a serious part of the day and made you wonder how anyone could survive in those hills for any length of time.

After a day off, we were again readying "Frisco Gal" to Dumbo for an airstrike, this time on Yap, another small island about 300 miles north and east of Pelelieu. I put my earphones on as I stared out the windshield at the 200 foot ridge that a short time ago was smooth, green, and tree laden all along the western edge of the island. A magnificent sunset was developing, painting in crimson these now jagged war-torn cliffs some three quarters of a mile away.

"Standing by, cockpit ..."

The tower responded, "Ready, starboard engine?"

"Standing by, starboard," I replied. The rising hum of the energizer filled the cabin as I continued to gaze at this changed landscape.

"Contact, starboard."

"Contact, starboard." The prop slowly moved, hesitated, turned a few more times, and then finally caught as the engine sputtered once then streamed exhaust.

The grotesque skeletons of once towering trees gave way to a chalky white area of landslides and crumbling cliffs where not so much as a stump remained of the original forest. Nature, herself, in one of her wildest tantrums could not have created any greater havoc. The port engine was now ready and I reached for the ignition.

"Contact, port."

"Contact," I replied. The engine flashed flame as it roared to life. "Oil pressure up."

I glanced at the instruments, setting altimeters on twenty feet and making adjustments, then settled back to wait as the engines warmed up and traces of the soft bluish haze from the exhaust drifted gently through the cabin.

A dark cavern beneath an overhanging rocky crown crumbled away as black smoke billowed from it. I counted the seconds. On the fourth count, an explosion with a concussion that jarred the plane was followed by several more, the red flashes lighting up the sky and some sending showers of white in all directions —

phosphorous shells. A tracer streaked from atop the pinnacle and across the runway into a group of parked planes.

I picked up the binoculars and now could clearly see what was unfolding. The small canyon's shattered walls stretched far back into the hills and the stream that had formed it was slowly being backed up by the crumbling rock. Above it, the smoking cavern was actually a cave entrance, one of many connected by a network of tunnels. Marine marksmen were now hitting the cave, pumping round after round cleanly into the slit, with an occasional tracer lodging in the opening and glowing brightly in the shadows. For a few moments, a volley of return fire sprayed wildly back out of the slit. A glancing tracer raced by us, causing me to instinctively duck, and then the cave went quiet.

There was more going on. While I had been studying the spectacle through my glasses, some eighteen planes had been taking off on the runway between the hills and my vantage point. There was a roar as each would come into view overhead, the colored wing lights suggesting a profile. I could see the pilot peering out over the long F4U engine cowling as he worked the controls to hold the plane in line with the runway. The planes all carried a belly tank and had formed up into three six-plane sections. I noticed all the tracers and artillery firing that had been pummeling the cliff openings had ceased. The lead Corsair abruptly broke away from a section into a long run, the others peeling off systematically behind him. He then let go of his belly tank, and I realized this must be a different kind of napalm run. The tank burst open and sprayed its contents all around a cave entrance before tumbling down the rock face. This material was like the fuel in flame throwers mixed with two parts wax that created a rampaging fire when ignited. I had heard the resulting inferno sucked the air out of the tunnels while providing cover for our advancing troops. One by one, the planes honed in on the rocky ledge and discharged their tanks.

A voice over the headphones pulled me back. "Engines ready for test, sir."

I revved the starboard engine to 1,800, adjusted the prop pitch and watched the tachometer drop off to 1,050, then rise again to "high." The plugs were cleared with the engine at 2,200 for a few seconds, both mags checked out OK, and the idling RPM fell off properly to 575. I eased back on the throttle, as a blinding glow drew my attention again to the hills across the runway.

The planes had finished their runs now, and nearby some dug-in Marines lobbed mortar shells igniting the area and creating a seething red flame that spilled down the hillside and over the caves. I still couldn't imagine how anyone, even with the protection of caves, could hold on in this hellish environment. It had come to this. A cunning and stubborn adversary hiding deep inside the cliffs had effectively sealed their own fate, forcing a new type of warfare. This steep rock was nearly impossible to scale, and that combined with the honeycomb of tunnels, made it the most rugged and costly kind of conflict. Eventually, when the methods our guys knew came up short, they would invent new ones.

"All instruments check out OK in the tower, sir," came the voice.

"Very well, are all stations ready to taxi?" The stations were secure and ready. I released the brakes and the big plane swung into the taxiway. It was dark now, and in front of us the runway lights stretched almost to the horizon.

I spoke over the radio. "Hello, Jungle Tower, this is five-two-Baker, how do you hear?"

"52-B from Jungle Tower, you are cleared for takeoff, course zero-five-zero, over."

We taxied down the coral mat toward the sea, then turned about. The runway lights formed a pointer toward the foot of the hills where a glowing star shell burst and drifted slowly downward bringing the brightness of day to the battlefield. I could make out the ghosts of other regularly spaced flares that had gone up and burned out. Another sailed aloft and soon there were four at once. "Frisco Gal" was ready to go. She shuddered momentarily, then slowly advanced toward the light. As we gained speed another assault began, a battery of shells exploding over the canyon into white phosphorous sprays and fiery red flower-like petals. Long strings of speeding tracers careened in as the explosions grew more intense. The detonations that we couldn't hear above the engines were clearly felt throughout the PBY, and flash after flash and thick smoke enveloped the hillside as our wheels left the ground. We slowly climbed above the fray, peering down at this once peaceful South Pacific island. The power of this offensive was breathtaking, and there was a sense of pride among us that we were doing what it took to drive the enemy out of here, but I couldn't help wondering, "How would it ever recover?"

The smoke covering the hillside dimmed the flashes as our altitude increased. Ahead, a last bursting shell fanned out in the clear smokeless sky like a brilliant American star to light our way.

Del's crew,
Plane Captain Harold Koenig

That night, after the plane was parked and we had eaten, I was watching as an F4U* stalled on the runway while taxiing. He was headed out as part of another airstrike and suddenly he was in a fix, parked right in the middle of the semi-dark airstrip. The pilot in a near panic rushed out of the plane to summon help. The tower immediately fired red flares and tried blinkers, but it wasn't in time to prevent a two-plane section from attempting a takeoff unaware of the obstruction, and one of them collided with the stalled plane. There was an explosion, but somehow the pilot escaped. The second plane knocked off a wheel, managed to get airborne, but shortly realized his predicament and bailed out over the water. Two more planes collided while taxiing in the confusion. The firefighters, thinking the pilot was still in the stalled plane, moved in on the fire unhesitatingly, with the ammo, fuel, and eventually bombs blowing up more or less in their faces. I was about 200 yards away lying in a ditch, and even from there, the fallout and shrapnel were flying by and raining down all over. I lay there in awe of the bravery of those rescue men. They were amazing.

There was no doubt that confusion was a big part of things out here. Several of us were flying escort for another airstrike on Yap when word came in that an F4U had crash landed on the return leg. Del's plane captain, Harold Koenig, told us that

---

*The F4U Corsair had a distinctive bent wing profile intended for aircraft carriers. Early difficulties with engineering of the plane were resolved and it went on to become one of the premier fighters of WWII.

when they arrived at the crash site, they could see one of the marine aircraft had been trailing gas and the pilot was on the wing with his Mae West[*] strapped on. They landed and taxied toward the location, but the pilot had by then vanished! Two Marine fighters made runs at the water, presumably above where the airman had last been seen and Del moved the PBY toward the spot. The pilot surfaced, swimming furiously, then disappeared again. It turns out, his chute had deployed, and in spite of his life jacket, the parachute began acting like a parachute, only under water, dragging the poor flier with it. Finally, Del's ordnanceman, Andy Decker, jumped in and was able to cut him loose, and with the crew's help, succeeded in getting him on board.

Just a few nights later, another crew was returning from a mission to the somewhat still unfamiliar base and landing area. The runway lights suddenly appeared and the pilot turned to make his approach. At the last moment, he realized something didn't feel right, and pouring on the power, narrowly escaped a trap set on an enemy held airstrip.

Tiny Peleliu was definitely an active place. In spite of all this, we still were foolish enough to explore a few of the abandoned caves during some down time, again on the lookout for a few souvenirs, sabers, and such and were lucky enough not to have picked up a booby trap instead.

Our Dumbos were on the move again, as they had been almost daily since this latest excursion began. I spent several extremely rainy days in a tent at Emirau Island. The base was on a bend in the river and the mess hall commanded an excellent view of the water downstream. It became our custom when returning from our frequent sorties to form up in three-plane formations and come down the river to zoom the mess hall. PBYs were not fast but they were majestic just the same, and a low flying formation was awfully impressive. A couple of us were standing beside the airstrip when the base commander drove up in his jeep. He was kind of hot under the collar, announcing, "You guys have got to stop these buzz jobs! I laid down the law to my own fighter jocks already, and I won't tolerate it from you guys either!" We could see in the distance behind him, Gewin leading a trio of Black

---

[*] "Mae West" was a nickname for an airmen's life jacket.

Cats in from the two-week task force operation at Palau. He was sneaking up the river in a gorgeous three-plane alignment to celebrate. They barely cleared the palm trees, rattling the very bones of our bodies and stunning the commander speechless before sending him off, wheels spinning, in his jeep.

On that day, we all had our sights set on a wonderful swimming hole about a mile from where our camp was perched high up on a cliff overlooking the sea. We hopped a jeep down the winding roadway cut out of the very face of the cliff and continuing through the green woods to the road's end at the beach. Here the Seabees had blasted a hole out of the reef about the size of a large swimming pool and built concrete walks across the coral from the beach out to it. A few yards beyond, a channel allowed water to enter at low tide and at high tide the waves would crash into the pool over the coral on all sides. At either end, they had installed concrete platforms with ladders into the pool and what looked like the remains of a diving board that had been swept out to sea by a storm. Tides changed quickly here, affecting both the dynamic of the pool and the beach almost before your eyes. Stray sea life was abundant, even octopus.

Nearer to camp and sitting high on stilts over the breakers was the outhouse. It was a ten holer that would spray up at you from below, a peculiar sensation, to say the least.

Our quarters were framed mahogany huts, screened in with a standard tent style roof that, given the nature of rain around here, was leaky but did a fair job. Many of the crewmen had used discarded flare parachutes to double up the tops. Sometimes at night "Old Charlie" would drone overhead and we would dive for the dugouts, not so much from our fear of "Charlie" as the danger from falling shrapnel from our own planes and anti-craft guns. His flights overhead were still part of the strategy of harassment to keep us from sleeping, a favor our PBYs were more than happy to return. With Charlie, if the searchlights were quick enough, they would catch him like a moth at a lamppost. Suddenly, a spray of tracer fire from a Marine night fighter would spit at him and in a little puff of orange flame, he was gone! Some of those night fighters, PV-1s and F7Fs were racking up records of eight kills a watch.

Jack and I finally returned to Espiritu Santo from this marathon 6,000 mile round trip and were feeling awfully glad to be back, and had, ourselves, zoomed the camp in celebration. It seems habits died hard out here. Our path had taken us to the Russells and Bougainville, and then Emirau, Owi, and of course Jungle Tower at Peleliu. We Dumbo-ed * for a strike at Kossel reef and tendered for a night at the USS Pokomok and later at the USS Hamlin (but more typically found ourselves in huts or tents, sometimes with cots and mattresses, sometimes not, and sometimes in cots under the wings of our plane). There was more Dumbo coverage for the Yap strike, then on to Ulithi Reef, Peleliu, and Kossel again. There was a day-long sub search with one of our DDs (destroyer) southeast of Palau. We returned to Palau to evacuate five wounded on a nine-hour leg to Momote and Setter Tower. In the morning, we headed back to Emirau in time to see Gewin's buzz job and a few days later, hopscotched the rest of the way through Green Island (Ocean Tower), Russell Island, and Guadalcanal, finally skimming the mess hall of camp and rattling some glasses of our own. We figured we had it coming.

Now back at Espiritu Santo, the crew tried to unwind. I wrote some more stories and tried to sketch some of what I was seeing, and of course, there were still basketball games, horseshoes, and some general craziness mixed in. However, we were facing a new crisis: our shipment of booze had never arrived. Rumor had it that it had been sent up to Tarawa, perhaps from some confusion about our whereabouts during the Task Force trip. Eventually, as desperation set in, we sent a plane down to Nouméa, New Caledonia, to bring back whatever was available from the French down there — mostly brandy and (ugh) crème de menthe. Anyhow, at least there was something under our bunks for snake bites. In a few days, quite unexpectedly, our original shipment arrived relatively intact from Tarawa. Now our new burden became where to put all of this good stuff along with the French junk. Interestingly, during our time away, the camp had added another new and unique feature, a latrine room. Here, an entire wall was constructed as a monstrous, backlit urinal fashioned from beer bottles set in mortar. There, emblazoned in large red letters was the word "Tojo," for all to pee upon.

As might be expected, the work could be as preposterous as the play. Al Wilson, Pete, and Peckham drew the assignment, an army request, of bombing a small isle nearby to clear the land of foliage. They presumed it had something to do with security. They set about dropping 500 pound bombs, but with poor results, so they

---

*"Dumbo" is a term applied when the PBYs served as escorts for other attack aircraft providing some rescue capability for them.

rigged up homemade daisy cutter fuses on 1,000 pounders and let them go. This did the trick. Turns out the army wanted the cleared circles for target practice.

When Willie Sneed arrived back at camp from Palau and Yap, he told us he had gotten himself into some hot water. Up at Yap, the enemy still used the runways and the place functioned as a refueling and resupply point for their aircraft. According to Willie, the Army had planned to take fifty or more B-17s and B-24s to completely annihilate the airstrips, but intelligence and coast watcher reports showed the island to be well fortified with men and anti-aircraft. So they went in expecting the worst. Willie's crew along with John Love and Gewin McCracken were spread out over about 200 hundred miles to Dumbo for them in case anyone needed to be fished out of the water and were orbiting at low altitude to avoid detection. They reckoned that between them they could respond in thirty minutes to any situation, and they anxiously awaited the arrival of the bombers, expecting to see enough raw power unleashed in the attack to turn the entire island to shambles. Then suddenly through the cockpit bulkhead, Willie's radarman begins punching him in the leg and yells, "I've never seen so many blips in my life! Thank God they are friendly!" The rest of the crew now searched the skies, until one of the boys in the blisters spotted the entourage and Willie swung the PBY about to watch. At 20,000 feet or more and in perfect formation was a most magnificent war time sight: more U.S. bombers than any of them had seen in the air at one time! Suddenly, it was "Bombs away!" as the lead bombardier began the attack. Down rained the bombs from the dozens

Willlie Sneed

of bellies of those gallant fighting aircrafts. The crew watched. And as they followed with their eyes this awe inspiring free fall of bombs of every size and shape, what happened next was best expressed by Waist Gunner Grover Smelley:

"Aw, Shit!"

If this perfect pattern had been just 1,000 feet east of where it had exploded, that island certainly *would* have been in a shambles. Not a bomb touched anything.

Over the plane's intercom, Smelley spoke first. "Hell, I can do better than that with these thirty calibers!" Within seconds the airwaves were jammed with everyone in the crew wanting a piece of this. Willie made the call and decided to try a strafing run on the airfield, the assumption being that the enemy must all be underground, hiding from the bombers, and would never be expecting a lonely PBY. They dove in at 180 knots with guns blazing and left four planes and a number of fuel tanks afire without so much as a single return shot from below. As they slowly made their assessment from the safety of a cloud, they concluded, "Why not have another go?" In they came again, blasting away from the blisters and now someone had joined in with the twin thirty calibers in the rear hatch. It then became painfully obvious that the enemy wasn't hiding underground anymore and as the PBY gained speed, "All Hell broke loose!"

They finished their daylight run and "skedaddled," with several of the crewmen arguing with Smelley over who had gotten the hit on the ammo building that was popping and smoking behind them. The bombers had long since left the area with no apparent casualties to be picked up, so Willie joined in with John and Mac and headed back to Peleliu.

Once on the ground, they looked over the plane and saw it had sustained some damage to the fuselage and had several more holes in the wings. Regardless, there was a great sense of satisfaction that the crew had been up to the task and performed well together and they headed back to camp to unwind.

It was at this point that Willie, now out of his flight suit and lounging in his tent, was summoned to the skipper's office. There before him stood a row of Navy officials and "five sour-pussed" army officers, including a one-star general. They had informed the skipper that a PBY on duty at Yap had interfered with their Primary Bomb Run and that, as Willie put it, "... they wanted the responsible individual to be sent off to Leavenworth to cover up their mistake of missing the whole damn island! Yes, at rigid attention, on a coral island 8,000 miles from home after flying over ten hours that day, dressed in shorts, t-shirt, and sandals, no officer insignia, we took the ass-eating of our lives!"

But there was a happy ending to his story. A short time later, Willie and his copilot were again called into the skipper's office and arrived thinking, "What now!" The Army brass were gone, but the skipper still looked stern and military. "Tell me what happened."

Willie, still at rigid attention, told the story as truthfully as he could. "At ease." At this point, the skipper broke into a wistful smile and pulled a bottle of whiskey out of a drawer and set it up on his field desk. "Let's all have a drink and relax. And dammit, Willie, I wish I had been there with you. We might have made a third run over Yap."

Election day arrived and so had my absentee ballot. I had returned it promptly and wondered if it arrived before the election took place. The sentiment around here seemed almost evenly split, and although the president won handily, it had to be a rough time to be the leader of this country.

As November wore on, we continued to move things and people (sometimes wounded, sometimes brass) around, do sub searches, drop supplies, and provide coverage for planes or ships when needed. Then there was always some practicing of water landings and check out time in other planes to keep us sharp and occupied. They even called test alerts for our Dumbos, more like a contest, really, to see who could get airborne first from a cold engine start. When a crew was on "standby" they normally hung around the operations tent and would then jump into action when an "alert" was sounded. The idea of the "test" was to determine readiness of each crew. This particular day one of my crewmen happened to overhear a conversation that a test alert was being called for our crew and mistakenly thought it had already been called. Eight of us raced out onto the strip, scrambled aboard, fired up the engines, and started taxiing while I contacted the tower for clearance to takeoff.

Bob Pinckney (lower left) and Elliot Schreider (3rd from left, front) - Skip Marsh's crew

Before I could speak, the voice on the radio said, "Be advised, a Dumbo alert has just been called." The plane was already moving toward the runway and we looked at each other in disbelief, hit full throttle, and were airborne in ten-seconds flat! The crew of the "Frisco Gal" stands proudly behind what we are quite sure is a record that will live forever.

The crews had banked some serious hours over the last several months and were in need of a break. Fatigue is a sneaky thing, mistakes were becoming more common and tempers shorter. After taxiing for twelve hours and eighty miles following an emergency landing due to an engine problem, Bob Pinckney found an unfamiliar harbor and a traffic jam of vessels to maneuver through as he tried to get to a tie-up point. He was beat. He and his radioman were each standing on their seats and out of the overhead hatches signaling back and forth with a lantern, while peering around and at each other in the darkness. Bob, intending to wave him off, quickly thrust his hand out ... and into the idling prop's blades. It gave him quite a whack and he very nearly lost two of his fingers.

Pete and Willie were the best of friends and nearly came to blows over some silly thing. Pete was a big guy. Willie, was an oil derrick worker, only about 5 feet, 10 inches, but an impressive, solid, and very muscular fellow. It ended when Willie grabbed Pete and simply picked him up and held him there.

The break came in Suva on the island of Fiji, two days of R&R in an island paradise. Suva was a small town, not quite the size of Crawfordsville, Ind., and had more of what you might describe as a "civilized" feel, at least from a typical American perspective. Most of us were surprised to find the town had a rather modern hotel called the Grand Pacific, and it was there we put up for the night. It was in stark contrast to the thatch roof huts so common along the beaches. It also was far different from our experience at Nadi, then staying nearer the airstrip over on the opposite side of the island on our initial voyage to Guadalcanal almost two years ago. For a pound a day, about $3.75, you relaxed in a comfortable room and enjoyed three marvelous meals.

The natives here were of fairly harsh appearance, more like Melanesians than Polynesians. They had their hair stiffened and swept up Afro fashion and, again, it was whitened with some type of wash. On their faces, they used generous amounts of a red dye, and they all chewed betel-nut, a habit a little like chewing tobacco, which ostensibly gave the chewer some kind of a "high." They collected the seeds from the Areca palms grown on the island. One of the young men took a liking to me and wanted to return to the United States with us to be my "personal servant."

Outside the hotel, Jack met us at the door. "Have you seen this? There is enough food to feed a carrier!" Each menu showed a whole host of delicacies, course after course and seven, eight, who knows how many options. It was an endless feast. They had us feeling like wealthy American tourists instead of military folks.

In the morning, Jack and I rented bicycles and pedaled all over town and out to Lauthala Bay airdrome where we landed.

"Jack, let's take the shore road back to the hotel. There is supposed to be a botanical garden along the way."

By afternoon, we had hooked up with an old Indian guide and ventured into the hills and a Fiji native village. We spent several enjoyable hours sitting on the floors of village huts and conversing with the families and getting to know them. The Indians were originally from various parts of mainland India and were first brought to Fiji as laborers for sugar and other agricultural industries here. They were also known for their gorgeous silver work and jewelry. The Fiji islanders were truly natives, born and raised in villages and a proud people. Their native handiwork and crafts included beautiful baskets and weavings. Naturally, there was a little trading. I decided to paint a scene from the village depicting the Islanders near the beach, the surf breaking in the distance, with indigenous pandanus trees standing like Spanish bayonets in the foreground. It would be a perfect birthday gift for my sister, Marian.

Even after nearly two tours of Pacific flying, this island's waters were an astonishing emerald blue, seemingly exceeding the delightful hues of other coastal bays and lagoons throughout the myriads of south sea islands. This place was just what we needed.

Two days later, "Frisco Gal" was winging her way toward Espiritu and Buttons Base once more, and her crew would spend the remainder of November bouncing between there and Guadalcanal.

I heard my brother Mac's unit mentioned on the radio and I now knew where he was. According to the weather reports, Mac and the boys up on Leyte were enduring torrential rains, suffering from monsoon storms and wind (typhoons happen here) and I was thinking how he'd appreciate some dry clothes about now. Tents won't stay put in those conditions, the ground softening so much the tent stakes pull loose and the wind does the rest. You can try acting as a human stake the rest of the night, which didn't always work, and soon your stuff on the inside was outside getting wet anyway. It was all too familiar and I felt for him up there.

As Christmas approached, VPB-54 itself loaded up and flew lock, stock, and barrel up to Leyte. The airstrip had recently been secured, but it was crowded with planes parked wing-tip to wing-tip, so we landed in the bay and tied up to numerous buoys anchored around a small seaplane tender, the USS Orca.

Certainly a big part of being a Navy pilot involves working with the fleet, but none of us had been based aboard a ship before. Being assigned to flying boats, we would know no carrier duty and felt a bit shortchanged, and all our efforts at transfer to attack aircraft had not panned out. So at long last, we had a ship and felt a lot saltier. Oddly enough, our flight crews had become the envy of the shipboard brass, simply because our gold wings and collar bars had picked up plenty of bluish corrosion out there in the jungle and it made us look as if we'd been at sea for a good while. Being based at sea even gave us the chance to acquire some Navy skills that we hadn't been exposed to yet. In my case, I had an opportunity to spend some time with the signal men who operated the semaphore flags and lamps, chatting about their craft.

```
POOR RECKLESS YANKEE DOODLE

DO YOU KNOW ABOUT THE NAVAL BATTLE DONE BY THE
AMERICAN 58TH FLEET AT THE SEA NEAR
TAWAIAN (FORMOSA) AND PHILIPPINE.

JAPANESE POWERFUL AIR FORCE AND SANK THEIR
19 AEROPLANE CARRIERS 4 BATTLESHIPS 10 SEVERAL
CRUISERS AND DESTROYERS ALONG WITH SENDING
1261 SHIP AEROPLANES INTO THE SEA.

FROM THIS RESULT WE THINK THAT YOU CAN
IMAGINE WHAT SHALL HAPPEN NEXT AROUND PALAU
UPON YOU.

THE FRAUD ROOSEVELT, HANGING THE PRESIDENT
ELECTION UNDER HIS NOSE AND FROM HIS POLICY
AMBITION. WORKED NOT ONLY POOR NIMITI BUT
ALSO MACCASIR LIKE A ROBOT. LIKE THIS
WHAT IS PITY. MUST BE SACRIFICE YOU PAY.

THANKS FOR YOUR ADVICE NOTES OF SURRENDER.
BUT WE HAVEN'T ANY REASON TO SURRENDER TO THOSE
WHO ARE FATED TO BE TOTALLY DESTROYED IN A FEW
DAYS LATER.

ADD TO YOU, AGAINST THE MANNER OF YOUR ATTACK
PAYING NO HEED TO HUMANITY, YOUR GOD SHALL MAKE
JAPANESE FORCE TO ADD RETALIATIVE ATTACK UPON YOU.

SAYING AGAIN, AGAINST THE ATTACK PAYING NO
HEED TO HUMANITY CONTRARY TO THE MUTUAL
MILITARY SPIRITS. YOU SHALL GET AN VERY STERN
ATTACK. WE MEAN AN CRUEL ATTACK!!!

                                    JAPAN MILITARY
```

Leaflet dropped on camp

Pelileu aftermath

Ray Peckham surveys wreckage of "Japanese Betty" on Peleliu

Black Cat with flak punctured tire caused an accident, sliding off runway and scraping through fuselage and into the boot of a crewman, not breaking the skin, but ruining the shoe

Formation of Black Cats returning from mission

Seaplane tender, probably "Orca"

Shelling of hills near Peleliu Airstrip from behind the "Frisco Gal".

How's the fishing?

Every day or so I would be assigned a rescue mission somewhere in the midst of all these islands. It was exciting work. Signals were arranged in advance with friendly coast watchers, we would arrive at a specific location, appraise the situation to determine how to best handle a water pickup, and hopefully accomplish the rescue. Not an exact science. If a landing was attempted when the swells were too rough, there would be no subsequent takeoff, one way or the other. Bad conditions could put nine or ten, perhaps more men in harm's way, so it could not be an emotional decision. You had to read the sea. The frequency and size of the whitecaps told the direction and intensity of the wind accurately enough. Up to a point, the stronger the wind, the easier the landing. The swell could be treacherous, ten to twenty feet high and like a brick wall in your path. So we would try to land along the top of it. But there were other issues. This might be a crosswind! Don't drag a wing tip float and break it off! Is there a secondary swell from a different direction to contend with? It was touchy business.

One morning, a B-25 crew was making a run to Los Negros when their plane caught fire down in the bomb bay. The crew bravely fought back against the fire, knowing that any of the bombs on the heavily armed bomber could go off, and it would only take one. The navigator, unable to control it with a fire extinguisher, was backed into a corner and lingered there facing away as his backside became seriously burned. At this point, the pilot had no choice but to ditch, and when we found the crew floating in their life jackets, the skin on their fingers was hanging and they were in shock. Our pharmacist did an amazing job of first aid on them in flight, although he decided against working extensively on their faces, leaving that to the doctors back at base. The pilots didn't suffer from burns and, although banged up, came through it in good shape. We were later happy to learn that the entire crew had made a decent recovery.

Since most of our work was in enemy territory, we skulked along following the irregular shore lines. Radar was still in its infancy, but our plane, like many PBYs, had a movable antenna on each side. With one set abeam, we could maintain a three mile interval off shore. One crew member secured — probably through "midnight requisition" — a second set of antenna and he mounted them facing aft. During a night mission, he was playing with this new toy and advised me that an aircraft was following us.

"I think it's squawking a friendly signal, but I can't make it out, sir."

I asked him to check it out on our own IFF (identification, friend or foe signal). He did so and reported our transmitter had been off and that we had apparently tripped a circuit breaker. We quickly reset the breaker, regaining our signal indicating we were a U.S. aircraft, and the unknown plane, after several long minutes, broke away. We could have easily been shot down by our own plane that night had it not been for our rudimentary radar.

The Catalina was a slow and methodical but very durable airplane. When we flew without escorts, we would take them up in almost any weather and cancellations were rare. The joke was, "Aerology predicts practically impossible weather, all aircraft are grounded, but that will not affect you guys. You are flying PBYs." Or sometimes, "Roger Tower, our weather en route: headwinds at all altitudes forty to sixty-five knots, frequent heavy thunder and lightning squalls, severe freezing conditions, ceiling zero, flying conditions average ..." This might translate into a very exciting ride depending on the squalls and whether they were avoidable — a severe downdraft could drop us hundreds of feet faster than a PBY could fly, leaving crewmen scattered about the fuselage or even temporarily pinned against the plane's upper cabin frame. There were times that you wondered how the old Dumbos held together. Sometimes, it was the takeoffs or landings that tested the mettle of the metal. Large swells or waves could stretch the planes' skin to its limit, popping rivets and letting in the sea. Golf tees and pencils were standard issue onboard, making a fine patch for rivet or small bullet holes.

Frequently, PBYs would have fighter cover, generally a formation of F-51s (Mustangs) or F6Fs (Hellcats) zigzagging around high above them so as not to outrun our lumbering Catalinas. Our range was much longer, so oftentimes before we could even complete a rescue they would need to bid us good luck and good hunting and head for home. With only light armaments, our big planes were generally sitting ducks the rest of the way.

I had spent another New Year's Day in the tropics, more specifically, the islands near the Philippines. By Jan. 4, we were about sixty miles east of Manila, searching for a downed B-25 crew reported somewhere in the area. The skies were cloudless and clear, and we made our way up the west coast toward the islands of Biliran and Maripipi. Our fighter cover, "Beware Red," consisted of two P-38s (Lightnings),* and they maintained a watchful eye as all of us made our way north between a pair of Japanese held islands guarding the San Bernardino Strait. I now swung to port around Rapu Rapu and into the Lagonoy Gulf and could see ahead the 8,000-foot cone of a volcano just south of San Miguel Bay. It reminded me of Fujiyama and, at the time, seemed quite as much a part of Japan. Just south of the Polillo Island group, our first relief fighters, "BewareWhite," took over for "Beware Red."

Jomalig, the outermost of the group, was held by the enemy and it seemed unlikely any survivors would be there. Polillo, the largest island, had a number of Jap positions and it seemed equally likely that any survivors in the hands of the natives there would have been escorted elsewhere by now. The most logical island was Patnanungan in between the other two. A squall had nearly covered this piece of land, and since fighters are notably skittish of reduced visibility, we concentrated on the small islands, rocks and reefs, and even native canoes first. Two B-25s arrived into our airspace to assist but, unfortunately, only managed to send us off on several

---
*This unique looking aircraft from Lockheed had twin engines and two tails. It was heavily armed and could reach a speed of 400 mph, the fastest fighter in the world at the time. The Japanese knew it as "two planes, one pilot."

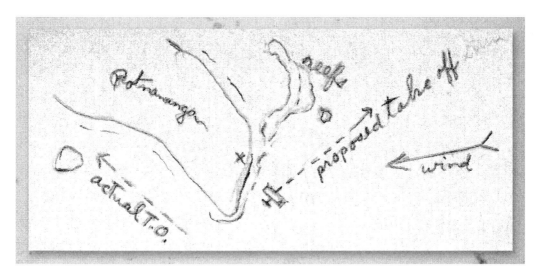

wild goose chases investigating native people whose excitement had induced them to frantically wave whatever they could get their hands on, usually a white flag.

After an hour or more, the squall drifted west and we started following the southern profile of the island. A group of natives caught our interest ahead about the same time as a brilliant red flash from a long arching trail of smoke popped right in our faces. There was something yellow, perhaps a raft, in front of them and as we drew closer, someone was distinctly waving what appeared to be a life jacket. I made another low pass thinking surely this must be our crew, but it was impossible to clearly distinguish any American airmen anywhere among the group. We decided to go for it.

Naturally, the natives couldn't be expected to select a pickup spot out in the deep water off the point, and instead had taken the crew to a beach location surrounded by shallow water and reefs. After one low pass to size it up, we headed in, landing in a power stall and taking a few good smacks before settling. It was a long way to taxi, down and around the point, and catching sight of the breakers across the coral well ahead, we stopped, dropped our sea anchors, and circled. The B-25s and fighters cavorted overhead like interested parents and made occasional passes at the group on the beach.

In the distance was what seemed to be a tiny yellow raft bobbing violently up and down in the breakers, slowly making its way toward us. We chose not to cut our engines and continued to circle as waves dashed over the bow, also standing ready at the guns until we had some kind of confirmation. Looking through the binoculars, there still wasn't any sign of an airman in the raft. It was now quite close and at that moment, one of the group leapt up and waved. He was wearing the unmistakable tapering hat of a Japanese soldier! We hit full throttle, sending spray and having every intention of getting into the air, anchors and all, but as I swung her away from the raft, several of our crew caught sight of another man, distinctly American, with a very puzzled look on his face.

Slightly embarrassed, we quickly headed back, confident that, although we weren't particularly well armed, there should be enough firepower to overwhelm a rubber raft.

The gap between us grew smaller and as they pulled alongside the blister, a crewman threw out a line and pulled them in, including the bedraggled B-25 copilot, Army Lt. Charles Yackiw.

The challenge now was to get us all back into the air, and in these swells, it would be a bouncy, rivet straining try. I decided to taxi around the point to the more sheltered side, which in itself was about two miles and a little tricky heading downwind. It was a good call, and after cooling down a short while, we took off easily and acknowledged the "Nice work" message from the fighters and bombers on radio as they headed for home. Unfortunately, our radio reply also informed them that we had only one of the crew, and that the others had been in another raft and had become separated. It was too late to look any more this time, fuel was getting low and Roger would already need to find a shorter way back. The objective was to beat nightfall and avoid a landing on the water and in the dark.

Roger gave us a heading straight for the narrow neck of Luzon Bay, swinging clear of several Jap towns along the way. Before long "Beware Red," freshly refueled, came into view and completed our entourage for the balance of the trip.

The sun had set as "Frisco Gal" touched the water beside her tender. It had been a long day and a cold beer would taste good. Two bombers flew above us as we tied up. I thought to myself, if one of you should happen to stay overnight up there somewhere, we'll be up in a few days to bring you back.

Two days after picking up Lt. Yackiw, headquarters received a call from the Guerrilla Army about a pilot at the Port of Borangan on the east coast of Samar. Our crew was to arrive there at 10:00 a.m. and look for two signal fires on the beach. Roger again went to work, plotting a course directly across the island, crossing its mountains and then winding down a valley where we leveled off at 800 feet. Up ahead was a bay with two islands protecting the entrance and inside would be a small peninsula splitting the back-end in two sections. We expected the fires to be on that peninsula.

I took her into a sweeping arc, crossing the bay just above the groups of coconut plantations, rice paddies, and huts, several with tin roofs. Some natives were plowing with water buffalo, others were fishing with great heart-shaped traps built out from the shore. Shortly, the peninsula was in sight and there were, indeed, the two fires being tended by locals, but we had not, as yet, seen any sign of our pilot. Another pass revealed nothing new. Then as we crossed a pier, there it was, a tiny launch tied up next to a small group of people. Walking down the pier with a bundle in one arm and waving his other was a figure that seemed likely. I could see his wide brimmed straw hat, and he seemed to be making signs with his arms rather than just waving.

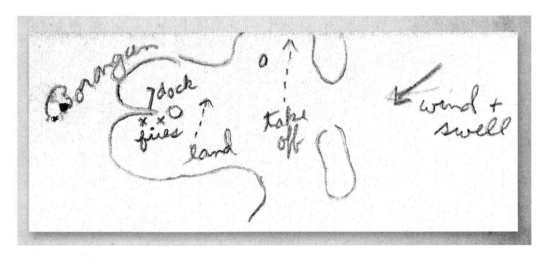

The landing would be easy enough, now we just needed to find the best way back out, noting the fairly heavy swells despite the protection of the islands. A takeoff along the shelter of the island with, hopefully, enough space to get off before the reefs came into play, seemed to be the best choice.

We power stalled in and taxied on the swells toward the pier. The launch was already heading our way, trailing a heavy stream of black smoke from her stubby stack and enjoying a large escort of native canoes. They pulled alongside with a number of armed guerrillas and an American, who looked every bit the Texan fresh off the plains, with his broad brimmed hat and his gun belt. The launch had a high pole with, unbelievably, an American flag in plain sight on it, but even after dropping the pole, the risk of a swell against the fuselage dashing the launch seemed too great. He finally hopped in a canoe and shuttled in close enough to get him aboard in one piece.

The pilot, Lt. Ellensberger, was a red haired P-47 man and quite a character. He even came bearing gifts! First he passed around some fresh bananas, then proudly unwrapped the yellow cellophane around a small package and displayed what appeared to be grayish dough. "Guerrilla Goo," he explained. It tasted a lot like Ralston.

The lieutenant went down on Dec. 26 after being sent out to strafe what he thought was a battleship in a Jap task force coming down to bombard Mindoro. He had only had an hour of night flying in a Thunderbolt, and the idea of strafing this ship hardly appealed to his largely pacifistic nature. He went ahead and made a couple of passes through the wall of tracer fire, then headed for Leyte. The strip at Mindoro was now under siege. During all the intense activity, his chart blew away and he had to guess at the heading. He came surprisingly close, but became lost enough to miss Leyte and run out of fuel over the mountains of Samar. He hit the silk in total darkness and came down in the top of a big tree. Peering down, he thought he was close to some tallish bushes, but being fairly tangled up, decided to hang there all night and cut himself loose in the morning. After sun up, he looked down at what he had thought was the ground and realized it was really the tops of smaller trees.

"So I managed to climb down a vine and through the underbrush, finally reaching a stream. Damn likely it would head to the beach sooner or later, so I followed it for six days. Nothing to eat besides a li'l bird that I shot and ate it raw. Well, it may have started as a stream," he said, " but by God, it ended up a full blown river. Big 'un, too. Finally found a small empty hut and bedded down for the night. Spent the whole next morning dryin' clothes. A young native kid walked up and wanted to get acquainted, said he would take me to his village. When we found it, they all thought I was a Jap and lit out of there. Finally, I guess they got curious and came back." He paused long enough to savor a bit of the Guerrilla Goo, "Anyways, I figgered one of you boys would be out this way before too long to see how the fishin' was."

Our takeoff was a bit more exciting than I'd hoped. I had taxied well out into the bay and rougher water, needing to put some distance between ourselves and the reefs upwind. As we neared the reefs, there would be a point where a decision had to be made to stop or go. We charged into the swell, climbing onto it and pushing through the bounces, finally gaining the shelter of the island again and calmer water. Our speed was now increasing rapidly, but I eased off the throttle slightly to leave a little in reserve for when she bounced. She bounced one more time and was over the reefs in good shape. We climbed up the foothills and headed for home. Bob asked Lt. Ellenberger, "What in the hell were they burning in that motor launch to create so much black smoke?" He replied, "Coconut oil."

Our crew had moved back to the "Tangiers" at Leyte after a couple of nights on the "Half Moon" and "San Pablo" in Mindoro. The Tangiers, a much larger vessel than Orca, included an on-deck hangar where cranes would hoist our planes for servicing. December had been a busy month and much of our time was spent bounding around between a variety of islands like Palau, Owi, or Biak. Now, sometimes we would work right in the bay.

Many of the flight crews stayed aboard the Tangiers. Art Bonnet and his copilot, Alex Catlow, had just returned from a short hop and told me it included a side trip to a party with, of all people, the governor of Leyte. Now that the Japanese had left the area, the locals were very appreciative and were in a celebrating mood. Many of them were guerrilla fighters and they had developed a fearsome shotgun-like weapon made out of a larger and smaller pipe, some sulfur (derived from matchheads) or gunpowder, a nail, and everything from rusty metal fragments to urine and feces stuffed into the barrel. The Japs hated it, and Alex guessed they were more than happy to give back the property.

Pete and I never met the governor, but we both had brief but entertaining episodes with admiralty while flying in the Philippines. One morning poor Pete found himself saddled with the awesome responsibility of transporting Admiral Sir Bruce Fraser, the British Fleet Commander, on a longish jaunt from Lingayen, north of Manila, down here to Leyte. No matter how he tried, he just couldn't relax during the first hours of the flight. He was sure Japanese fighters would hit them and he would go down in history for all the wrong reasons. The admiral's friendly, calming demeanor must have finally won him over, and as it turned out, the flight was relatively routine. Pete said he was quite impressed with Fraser, especially after the admiral promised to look him up after the war, or if Pete ever found himself in London, he shouldn't hesitate to do the same.

A brief time later, I was up at Kossel Passage on Palau Island to pick up two-star Admiral Oglesby along with a captain. It was a bouncy, rough day and we nearly dropped the admiral into the sea just getting him from his barge into the blister. He was dressed sharp and immediately stuck his head into the cockpit and introduced himself to me. As expected, the takeoff was a bouncy, turbulent affair, with swells breaking over the whole

Navigator Salley, Art Bonnett, and Alex Catlow

plane and leaking into the compartment and onto them both, thoroughly soaking each. He was very good natured about it, and later came up and spent the rest of the flight in the copilot seat. As we were chatting, a voice came over the intercom asking if I'd checked out the "old man" yet. Much embarrassed, thinking it was a careless member of my crew, I asked, "Uh, would you repeat that statement? WE couldn't make it out?"

"I said, have you checked out the 'old man' yet?" the voice repeated.

I asked him, "Who is this speaking?"

"Captain (so and so)." I was very relieved that it was his own captain and wasn't part of our crew. And the admiral was having a good laugh about it. As we approached Peleliu strip for a mat landing, I lowered the wheels from their rest position alongside the fuselage and started a glide in toward the runway. I couldn't help seeing the admiral squirming and looking increasingly uncomfortable in the copilot's seat, so as we started in I asked if he was O.K. He fired back, "Are you crazy? It's a runway!" I pointed to the wheels and chuckled carefully. He was still glowing red, but now it was more because he was somewhat mortified to admit he hadn't realized there were wheels on a PBY seaplane.

The natives here were an interesting group. Every morning they would paddle and sail for miles down the channels and out to the ships to trade and visit with us. There was a real need for clothing among them and a torn shirt or trousers was valuable enough to warrant anything from bananas to a monkey. The outriggers, some with large triangular sails, were frequently large enough to carry entire clans with men paddling, women under umbrellas, and half a dozen youngsters clinging to the structure. With a closer look you might see chickens roosting on the bamboo cross pieces, or a squealing pig somewhere on the deck, even monkeys dangling with arms wrapped around the mast. Eggs were plentiful. They were a congenial people, every one of them wishing us "Merry Christmas" on Christmas Day.

As the New Year began we maintained our hectic pace. For weeks, we had been in the air more days than not and welcomed a day off. It was a gray day today, a welcome break with the intense heat aboard ship. There was certainly an improvement in meals and living conditions while on board, but no shorts or shirtless flyboys were allowed. So while high temperatures hadn't changed much, clothing had. For the first time in several days, I slept well having snagged a vacated bunk just beneath a ceiling fan and was now on deck catching up on some letter writing as small boats purred by and planes circled overhead. I had been so involved that I felt that I had neglected my family and wanted to write to thank them again for making our Christmas out here so special. It was the fourth time in five years we had been apart on the holiday, and friends and family had spoiled me.

"Dear Family,

As I began my letter, I wished I could tell them more about where I was and what I was doing. Much about life in the tropics had improved, but the Navy censors, unlike the Army, were vigilant in their prohibition of any suggestion of location or assignments. Once the Army is established at any particular location, it is quickly common knowledge and the enemy is aware of what units they are encountering. The Navy ships seek to travel incognito and movements are cloaked in secrecy and that included us. It was still up to my alter-ego, John Caldow, to reveal clues to my situation. Today he was in San Francisco (Leyte), fondly recalling a day leading up to Christmas back in Indianapolis (Espiritu):

"OK, Miner, when are you going to open it?" Pete bellowed. "It's practically Christmas, let's see what's in there!"

A second package from home had arrived unscathed, and I had been debating whether or not to hold out until the actual day — my plan for package one. The guys were having no part of it. Christmas was barely a week away and our Quonset hut was decked out with two red paper bells and a twelve-inch imitation Christmas tree that Bonnie had lavished with candy and tinsel for decoration. Candy, we found, didn't hold up well in packages or anywhere around here. It too readily absorbed moisture. But it looked good on a tree.

The squadron had been swamped with packages in surprisingly good shape. Since we really weren't sure at this point where we would be spending Christmas, most of the gang had already torn into them. It now looked like my number was up.

"Fruitcake over here please, while Howard opens this up!" Bonnie and Del each had mouthfuls as I slid the wrapping away. "He got a tie!" Peckham blurted. "And look at that cocky little cap! You'll be the cutest one at dinner!"

There was more. We always enjoyed the small pleasures, a corkscrew and can opener, tape. Sardines made great hors d'oeuvres. Pete had gotten some cheeses and crabmeat, someone else the fruitcake.

By Christmas Day, we were aboard the Orca in Leyte. Del and I had saved two Christmas packages each and brought them along. Right after breakfast, we climbed up on his top bunk and opened our presents — we were kids again! Inside my first box were two layers of individually wrapped gifts. There was stationary, soap (monogrammed so it wouldn't get stolen), camera film, peanut butter, and photos from home. The other box from Georgia was stuffed full of more snacks, fruit cake, and playing cards — and finally, drawing pencils, colored chalks, a sketchpad, and erasers! We were set!

Our ship served a first class dinner that evening of olives, tomato juice, rolls and butter, sweet potatoes, potato salad, peas, walnut ice cream, fruit cake with flaming brandy, nuts, and cigars! Afterwards, several of us gathered on deck and sang carols.

"...So our Christmas was far from sad thanks to the efforts of the people back home. We all wish to thank them for their kind thoughts.

Hoping yours was joyful as ours and wishing you the Happiest of New Years. Perhaps we will be together again soon.

Love, Howie"

There was an abundance of time for reading and writing while based on these seaplane tenders, since we were a little short on land to move around on. Catching up on mail from home was a favorite pastime. Sometimes I would be surprised to find prints from camera film I continued to send home or newspaper clippings about activities in our area. Although it was January, it seemed strange to read about getting the car started in the cold weather, or Marian ice skating, or how good the Australian rugs I had sent home felt on those chilly, zero degree Indiana mornings. I found myself writing home every day or so, hinting that our stint over here might finally be winding down, but afraid to really say anything in writing to jinx it. Our mail service was great aboard ship, and we had a variety of periodicals to read and fill in the gaps about what else was happening that we couldn't see from our vantage point. One article caught my eye. Dave Crockett, a friend and another Wabash guy, lived not in Tennessee but nearby in Indianapolis and got his Navy wings about the time I entered training. He was apparently a German prisoner somewhere in France. Things were going badly for the Germans, too, and many of them were seeing their situation as increasingly hopeless. The commanding officer just walked up and surrendered to Dave, giving him his gun! Dave gladly obliged and marched them all off at gunpoint to the American lines.

Another letter was from our next door neighbor in Indianapolis (the one actually in Indiana), Mrs. Seet. She had written me inquiring about her son Bob off and on. She had recently heard from him that while at an Army receiving station near here, he had asked a rescued pilot if he knew who had brought him in. The flier replied, "A navy PBY, a Lt. Miner." Coincidently, a short time back, I happened to run across the island where his squadron was based. During a recent hop near his location, I made up an excuse to land and check around for him. The crew was over at the Red Cross getting a sandwich, and I did some inquiring, finally getting someone from his outfit on the phone. He was off on a hop of his own for a few days, so I headed back to rejoin the crew thinking we could continue on to our actual destination. When I tried to start the starboard engine — nothing.

After several more attempts, Townsley, our plane captain, said, "Sorry Skipper, she's not gonna catch. We need to open her up." We were now on a strange airstrip, no Navy for miles, and no place to stay. As we began tearing the engine apart, I sent a couple of guys off in search of an Army supply depot. A new booster coil was installed, and with fingers crossed we tried it again — still no luck! It was too late to get supper anywhere, but one of them did locate an Army casual camp that gave us a tent. First thing in the morning, we were up and at it again making every test we could think of until it began to look like we would be spending another night here. In went our last hope, a new magneto. After three tries, she caught and we were back in action. We wasted no time getting out of there, and in our haste, I never got another chance to call Bob.

I later learned he was killed while on a training mission.

Our carrier-based aircraft were pounding enemy installations all around the Manila area and an American invasion of Luzon Island was looming. Clark Air Base, taken from us back in '42, was being used as a hub for Japanese aircraft and was the scene of several fierce engagements. MacArthur's heavy bombers were paying daily visits to the area as well, in part, to deceive the enemy into believing our eventual invasion attempt would be coming from the South. We were called out to escort just such a strike.

The crew was ready and headed out early, our customary head start, but today "Frisco Gal" seemed sluggish and a bit unwilling. At any rate, we were only halfway to our target area when the bombers walked past us. There were several sections of A-20s and a large formation of B-24s and B-25s, and I watched their tails as they disappeared over the horizon. We were outrageously late for our rendezvous with our fighter escort, but they quickly joined us with a greeting, "Playmate Two, this is Attorney Blue. Do you read?"

We "Rogered" that and proceeded on to the strike location. By the time our PBY arrived, it was virtually over and most of the planes were already heading back. Particularly distressing was the possibility that some unfortunate one of them might have been in a predicament and waiting all this while for us, so Bob and I attentively listened for any calls for help. It seemed quiet and in the distance was Luzon, its shores the current home to our hated adversary. The enemy now feared American fliers so intensely that, once captured, none were spared on the bare chance they might escape and return to duty.

We checked once with our fighters before heading back. From high above, "Haven't heard a peep, I guess they're all O.K."

Just as we were about to acknowledge, a crackling very faint and garbled call interrupted. "Hello Playmate Two, this is _____." The rest was incomprehensible.

"Plane calling Playmate Two, say again?"

Even less distinct, a reply, "Hello_____ ___ this is_____ ___, ___ ___ reflection___west coast_____ 67." We called up to the fighters. "Attorney Blue, you get that?"

"We didn't, Playmate Two. Let us try them ..." And then, "Plane in distress calling Playmate Two, can you say again?"

"Playmate Two, this is_____ _____investigate_____west coast Snowball 67_____survivors on shore_____over."

"You hear that, Playmate Two? West coast of Snowball 67. Survivors."

"Roger, Attorney Blue, checking our index now, out." Snowball 67 was an area covering Subic Bay on the west coast of Luzon, just north of Manila Bay. That was one of the three big bays on the west coast of Luzon, certainly a hot spot and probably one of the targets of the morning raid. There would be some challenges getting in and out, and since the calling "plane" was unidentified, there was the additional risk of a bogus call to bait any planes they could back into the area to retaliate. We continued to try to reach the mystery plane, but to no avail.

> We continued to try to reach the mystery plane, but to no avail.

I had the crew strap on life jackets and all eyes were peeled as we cruised in at 1,000 feet, our fighter cover several thousand feet higher. "Bogey, three o'clock low!" The fighters were in hot pursuit of the plane about three miles starboard and quickly chased it into a cloud and out of view.

"Playmate Two, it was friendly." What is your position, we've lost you?"

There wasn't much to say here, we were a few miles south of Corregidor by now and heading toward Bataan. But, probably, so were they. A fine time to lose our fighters.

It was "pins and needles" now, but our misgivings aside, the rocky shore was in view and the mouth of Subic Bay was dead ahead. There was a towering column of smoke, perhaps the Jap Naval Base hit during the morning raid and maybe they would still have their hands full. I swung wide of it and around to the western cliffs of the bay.

We headed down to 300 feet and along the rugged wall of rock, then continued on past cultivated lowlands and eventually a beach. There appeared to be no gun emplacements, but no survivors either. Heading back toward the bay and billowing smoke, there was another island with some sort of fancy estate with white buildings and lawns. Nothing there, either.

"Playmate Two, we have you, over."

"Good to have you along, Attorney Blue, we're going in and drag the shore line, keep an eye out up there."

It occurred to me that perhaps the western shore in the message was actually the western shore of the western peninsula, and although it was rocky and precipitous along there, it might be worth a quick look before calling it off. We informed the fighters.

Around the point and north along the cliffs past an old lighthouse was a smaller bay with a couple of sandy spots, looking quite uninhabited. Then over a high promontory and another deeper bay, Nasaza, was a small spit of beach and a tiny native hut. Nasaza was exceedingly narrow, something like a Norwegian fjord, with walls too sheer and high to be able to navigate in and turn around in time to get back out. It was an unlikely place for anyone to be in hiding, and with the terrain and dangerous winds, it seemed to make sense to just give Subic another try and then head home. I banked around to the south, and just as the bay was passing from view: What was that! There was a bright flash from the beach area, and we quickly swung around again and returned on a heading toward that beach. Another flash! Then a whole series of them but no recognizable pattern, and it was blinding, more like a searchlight than an aviator's mirror.

This was a thorny little bay. While we could land in it, a scouting flight was impossible with mountainous cliffs at the end, too high and close to get up over and the whole canyon too narrow to circle back out. At 1,500 feet, we couldn't make out who the specks were, now gathered along the beach, so one of the P-51s, far more maneuverable, dove in to have a closer look. The arching trail of what must have been a signal star, probably a dud, wafted along behind him as he strained to climb out, just clearing the mountains. There now appeared to be some yellow cloth on the beach and we were becoming convinced these must be our boys. The plan was to land in the shelter of the bay, requiring a downwind takeoff away from the cliffs to get back out. I set her down into the crystal blue-green wavelets, and it was a short taxi over to within fifty yards of the beach where we dropped the hook and circled.

An outrigger was already heading for us, and as it drew closer, we could make out two bearded faces grinning ear to ear. A crewman called out from the blister, "How goes it?"

"Boy, are we glad to see you!" a brown faced flyer replied in very convincing Americanese.

Two airmen in ragged Navy flying suits, one with an American flag pinned on his sleeve, were sitting in the center of the canoe with a nearly naked Filipino rowing at either end. They clung to the rope and the boys all pulled as they swung along side.

The second flyer came on board, shaking his head and saying, "I just can't believe it." One of the two stuck his head into the cockpit, "Howdy, skipper, my name's Naylon and I'm mighty proud to be aboard. Can you hang on a little longer, we have three others on the beach ..."

Of course we would wait, but I wasn't sure about our fighters. "We're OK for a little while longer, but please hurry it up down there." I decided to kill the engines while we waited and followed the men back into the waist to watch for the others.

The brown faced flyer was with another crewman, a Minnesota boy named Clifford Schelitsche, also known as "Ski." He was a TBF (bomber) guy from the Wasp. Naylon went on to explain, "There are five of us that have gradually assembled here. We come from four different carriers and four different planes, all shot down during carrier strikes. I've been wandering around that rock since September. I'd just about given up ever getting off." He continued, "Roccaforte and Schelitsche here have been on an unpleasant task all day. They were up on that mountain. When they heard you land they nearly sprinted down the steep hill to the beach as I was climbing into that banka* there. You see, we got this big signal mirror rigged up on the beach. It's a big oval mirror we got from the Filipinos and it has one of those small survival mirrors with an aiming hole in it to sight through.

"Rocky's pretty good with it. We've contacted quite a few planes in recent weeks, but he wasn't down here today and, when you flew over, we couldn't get the damn thing to work. I was so excited, I was all thumbs. Thought I had missed you."

In the distance, I could see the native canoe now taking on more passengers as he continued, "Well, as I said, we'd made a number of contacts with other planes and they've buzzed us several times and dropped notes. Even had planes from my carrier, the Cabot. Thought we'd be out by Thanksgiving, then by Christmas. Then New Year's, then 1945!

"But I started to tell you about yesterday. We signaled an A-20, and he came in low to buzz us and drop a first aid kit, but when he pulled up to get over those mountains, he didn't have enough speed. He tried a fast turn but stalled, then he nosed over and caught himself, pulled up again and went right into the side of that mountain. Oh, it was horrible. We just sat down and cried. This place is a death trap. Another A-20 came in later and damn near did the same thing. He had just enough more speed I guess, and when he started to stall, he cut real sharp and got

---

* Banka - canoe

away with it. He could have looked right down his wing at the wreckage of that other A-20.

Schelitsche quickly added, "The ammunition in the wrecked plane was going off for three hours or more and we felt it wasn't safe to go up there. Finally, Rocky and I went up the mountain with some natives today to bury the guys. Just can't stop thinking about it."

The outrigger was close enough now that we could see the other three on board. As we started to pull them in, one with a fine black Abraham Lincoln beard stood up waving a long bolo knife and shouted, "You're the prettiest looking Cat I've ever seen!"

We were loaded and had exchanged some cigarettes with the eager natives, then said our goodbyes. There was a moment of tense anxiety as the starters whined and the engines just weakly sputtered, but they caught and we circled a bit to warm them and get into position for our downwind takeoff. It was longer than usual, but she never even bounced, and shortly we were winging our way to Mindoro.

"Frisco Gal" insisted on a refueling stop at the tender there, during which time Ensign Roccaforte from the USS Intrepid explained how he was over Clark Field on Oct. 29. "A Jap made a pass at my TBF (torpedo bomber) and happened to hit the oil system. As he sailed past, I cut it hard and squeezed a burst from my wing guns. The Jap trailed flame, but my engine was dying too, and both of us ended up side by side in a rice paddy. I got in OK with a belly landing, but the other plane blew up. The Japs had spotted the plane and were right away after us, so we had to keep our eyes peeled all night." Eventually he stumbled onto some villagers, who in turn took him to a guerrilla colonel. The colonel showed them a short cut, and as they escaped he became separated from his crew. After considerable wandering, he found his way to Nasaza Bay.

Ensign John Doyle, the fellow with the beard and bolo knife, was an SB2C (Helldiver)* pilot from the Ticonderoga. He and his gunner and radioman, William King, went down off Luzon near Santa Cruz. They had been hit twice as they made a run on a heavy cruiser, scoring a hit of their own and disabling it. It later sunk.

"Bill had the raft out in seconds," Doyle began. "I had a small one-man raft in

---

* SB2C Helldiver was a single engine Navy dive bomber with a two man crew, often based on carriers.

my parachute and climbed out on the wing and into the other raft. We spent two days on the water. A pair of Jap seaplanes spotted us and we had to flip the raft and dunk! These rafts are blue on the bottom to blend with the ocean, but they could see us down there anyway. We tried to stay underwater and I don't know if they shot or not, but we didn't have any holes in the rafts."

Once the planes had left, they paddled near the shore of a small island, hoping to find a safe place to sleep. They could see a sloping white image, perhaps a roof of a barracks, in the dim moonlight, so they continued cautiously toward the shore. To their amazement, the white area was not a roof, but a beach, so they quickly made their way up and across it. It suddenly occurred to them, "Could this be an unfinished Jap airstrip?" It was wide enough and firm, and there along the edges were the dark silhouettes of the dozers and equipment they had been using when they knocked off for the day. The two quickly made for the foliage, wanting to put plenty of distance between themselves and the strip.

After a restless night made worse by swarms of mosquitos, they climbed a hill in the morning light and peered back at the same location. They were a bit embarrassed to see it was indeed a beach with some rectangular, squatty boulders here and there around it.

They made their way along the beach and stumbled into an old man who was scavenging around the water's edge. He spoke little English, but led them to a guerrilla leader who did, and they followed him to a small village where the friendly natives supplied them with rice. "At first, we ate it three times a day, but they took such good care of us, soon we were up to six!" Doyle went on. "You develop a taste for the stuff, if you can believe that."

After a week, they were driven out by the enemy and traveled nearly seventy-five miles over difficult terrain. "It got pretty rough and the hunger is always there," King continued. "John told me when we hit San Francisco, we'd both visit the Drake and gorge ourselves and he'd pick up the tab, and if I complained, he'd put me on report. I told him, 'O.K. then, I'll eat you out of a month's flight pay!'"

Eventually, they found their way to a Lt. Colonel Merrill who had escaped during the Bataan Death March and had been holding out in the jungle for nearly three years. The Colonel appeared to be quite a character, living a Robinson Crusoe-type existence deep in the rain forest. One day he took them both to an even more remote location, finally crossing a stream on a water buffalo to what he described as

> "Then today when you flew by and the natives yelled, 'Flyin' boat ... look! Flyin' boat!' I just couldn't believe it, I still can't."

his "office." Here, he had a war room set up, using a bicycle-powered generator peddled by his Filipino sidekick, Marcello, to power a radio and light. He would study the charts and listen to radio broadcasts while poor Marcello peddled faster and faster in the tropical heat. It was Merrill who told them about the others some fourteen miles away at Nasaza Bay.

Ensign Maurice Naylon was also shot down over Clark Field. He spoke glowingly of the wonderful treatment they received from the guerrillas and native Filipinos. "They treated us like gods. Anything you were wearing or had on you was of the utmost value to them, especially shoes. They would look for the man in your group wearing the best shoes and figure he was the boss. At first, we gave away our stuff, survival gear and knives and stuff to pay for these favors, but then we found we didn't have to. They considered it the highest privilege to take care of you. Sometimes they would feed us. One time, a guerrilla colonel showed up with a bottle of prewar gin. When it was gone, he shifted over to the awful tasting native beer that was like 200 proof. I passed out and someone put me to bed."

At this point, Doyle chimed in, "That's another thing, when we were inside we always slept on the floor with mats. I don't think I could sleep on a mattress any more. And they got the biggest kick out of watching us sleep. Several times, we would awaken to find a whole circle of people we had never seen before that had gathered during the night, just watching the American sleep."

"The Japs kept us moving, though," Naylon added. "The natives were gossips, they would want to display you to their friends, and the word would spread. One time, some old gal even sold us out to the Japs and we just made it out of there in time. Then some friendlies told us about this place by Nasaza Bay, and we made our way over there. It was rice three times a day from then on, and that came over the hills by porter. They helped us get through it. We had the mirrors and held 24-hour watch, except when the Japs were in the bay. Two days ago, there were two destroyers anchored there all morning. They hid there until our planes passed from strikes, and then steamed north."

"But what got me," Doyle went on, "is when the planes we signaled would fly over, maybe fifty feet above us, and you felt them saying 'hi, guys,' and then they would fly off to warm food and a clean, dry place to sleep and we would never really get any closer to getting out of there." Naylon patted old "Frisco Gal" and grinned. "Then today when you flew by and the natives yelled, 'Flyin' boat ... look! Flyin' boat!' I just couldn't believe it, I still can't.

We lifted off again for the last 250 miles to Leyte Bay and our tender there. Five tired but happy Americans would be taken aboard, head down to medical for a check up, and then be whisked away to some clean clothes, dry shoes, and a square meal. Rocky brought his coconut shell rice bowl along with him. It would now be full of ice cream.

They spent a week aboard the tender, were clean shaven and posed for countless pictures together with us and with members of her crew. Fairy tales do come true.

But not always. Doyle came down with malaria and joined Schelitsche, who was being treated in sick bay for anemia. The orders for their "survivor's leave" came through, and they were feeling really dispirited when Naylon, King and Roccaforte came in to say goodbye. It seemed to me a shame to break up the five now.

The other three, each holding their priority papers, were ferried in to the airstrip where they climbed aboard the NATS R4D, a big C-47 transport bound for Palau. We assembled at a prime viewing spot high upon the Tangiers and could see the big plane racing down the runway. What we didn't know was that an army lieutenant was taking his new girlfriend for a joyride in a L-4 cub and picked that moment to buzz the runway. It clipped the C-47's tail and they both quickly fell to the ground and exploded. All perished, including the girlfriend, a young nurse from the hospital ship that had just arrived.

Moments like that stay with you for a lifetime. I knew this one surely would for me. Doyle, with his malaria, and Schelitsche turned out to be the lucky ones I guess. I heard they eventually made their way home safely.

Mt. Lopevi-4747' Volcano

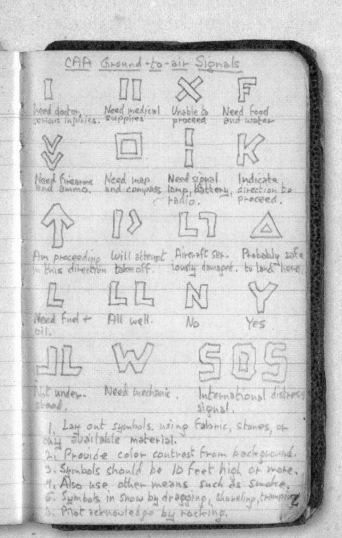

Ground-to-air signals for rescue

Odd juxtaposition of coconuts, enemy artillery shells, and "bones"

5 survivors, three later involved in fatal runway crash

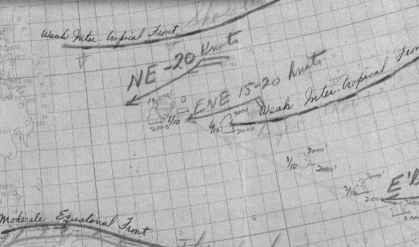

Weather report for South Pacific Islands

Palawan Island survivors with escort

Thirteen and Three?

Time was dragging along. Something was afoot in our area and I felt a gnawing apprehension. We were eight months into our second tour. Indiana seemed like a distant memory, and I wondered, "Is this battle fatigue?" I found I was even envying, a little, my friend Jack, back in the states. When we were in Espiritu, Jack and I were between missions and decided to try our hand at tennis. A tropical storm had passed through, and the full sunshine quickly cleared the court of water, save a few small puddles. We hacked away at each other, laughing as much as playing, when Jack suddenly reversed direction to chase a volley and hit one of those wet spots. He fell hard and while obviously hurt, I didn't realize the extent of his injuries at the time, but he deteriorated rapidly from a combination of the nerve injury suffered in the fall and from the mental strain of his flying duties. He was officially diagnosed with "battle fatigue." The guys and I all dropped in often, sneaking occasional banned refreshments in to him to his great delight, but he was eventually sent stateside and never fought again. He was probably my closest friend.

We were spending much more time in enemy territory now, and I hoped MacArthur would return to Manila soon. The crew and I had just completed a roundtrip from the northwest coast of Siquijor Isle where a P-51 pilot, 2nd Lt. Robert Guttlieb, was wounded in a crash. We had gone out to bring him back. Today a patrol plane searching along the southeastern shore of northern Palawan had been

> Ensign Babb looked for the entire world like a civilian, even a tourist, sitting hatless with a borrowed white island shirt.

in contact with a downed Navy FM-2 pilot and promised to return in a few days. We were sent out to find him and headed west toward Mindoro to pick up our P-38 escort.

"Playmate One, this is Possum White, is that you directly in front of us?"

"Affirmative, Possum White, how many hours fuel do you have in a slow cruise, over?"

Our Wildcats had a good four and a half hours flight time, and we had reasoned that gave us an extra hour to play with, so we continued west and sighted Palawan in only an hour. The Japanese held island of Dumaran was ahead as well, and I wanted to cling to the coast and make for a point of land where we expected to start the serious searching. Almost instantly there was a flashing mirror, a nice surprise that called for a closer look. A winding, muddy river lay ahead, flowing down out of the mountains and into the calmer shoreline waters, creating a large, brownish colored area. My first impulse was to land close to our objective in the smoother seas, but some instinct pressed me to head for the choppier, blue water farther out. Of course, a full stall landing was now required and a much longer taxi toward shore. A strong crosswind was blowing and "Frisco Gal" was shipping quite a bit of water, even with bilges on high. Just ahead, I could see the demarcation line of the muddy river water and continued eyeing this area suspiciously, when suddenly she went aground! We abruptly swung into the wind and applied full power. She scratched her way free. An unlucky landing there might have put us on that delta for the remainder of the war. Circling was just complicating things, the bilges were not keeping up, so there was no alternative but to shut down and restart later. A canoe was already well on its way toward us.

Ensign Babb looked for the entire world like a civilian, even a tourist, sitting hatless with a borrowed white island shirt. Behind him, puffing on a large stogie and wearing an oversized, white Panama hat, was the oddest looking character the Pacific has probably ever produced. Babb told us his sidekick was a beachcomber and that they had nicknamed him "Minnie the Moocher" for his propensity for procuring free meals. Minnie claimed he was a prewar millionaire with a large schooner and several estates here and there around the islands. "He hung on to me like a leech," Babb continued. "Seemed to want to use me to further his own prestige. We'd pass a house and he'd say, 'Let's stop here!' and we'd go in and try for a meal. Then he'd talk your arm off."

At this point, the large swells were threatening the transfer of our passenger and then abruptly, the PBY stopped bobbing. Another sandbar. This made getting him alongside easier, but each successive swell would lift the plane higher onto the sandbar. Eventually, we were going to be sitting high and dry, hoping for a tide.

Consequently, there was little time for rewarding the natives this trip, the crew pitching a few packs down to them and clearing them out for start up. As soon as we were warm, I began working the inboard engine and when a swell would lift us a bit, would give it another burst of power and move a little. In this way, she inched out into the deeper water adjacent to the bar, and we wasted no time getting away from it.

Babb now startled us with information that another pilot who had been trying to make it to a guerrilla radio station was somewhere further down the beach. It would be a long trip, taxiing clear around the point while sweeping with binoculars as some natives and even small villages slid by along the way. It was slow going, and it seemed sensible to get the fighters involved dragging the beach farther up the shoreline. One of them spotted a signal flare in a cove ahead, but we were only creeping now in a heavy thunderstorm. Visibility was nasty. Somehow they saw us first and had already maneuvered a small sloop well out in our direction.

The passenger, Lt. James Fallon, was anything but what we were expecting. He was not the other FM2 pilot, but a PBM (Mariner seaplane) flyer, who had been shot down on the night of Dec. 26 by the same task force that Lt. Ellenberger had strafed in his P47. Furthermore, he said his entire crew of ten was safe and sound. The Navy had been searching in vain for these guys since that night and was gravely concerned. "What about the other FM2 pilot?" I asked.

"Lt. Hobson? He's on his way down from the radio station right now and should be here in no more than forty-five minutes."

A guerrilla officer in the canoe with Fallon was a small shriveled man sporting a Fu Manchu mustache. He was obviously very happy. "All my boys go home now!" he said with a twinkle in his eye. He went on to say he had three Japanese prisoners, all officers, and would greatly appreciate it if we could deliver them to MacArthur for him. His companion in the canoe, another guerrilla fighter, said with a smile that if we would just let him have one of our .30 caliber machine guns, he would get us fifteen more in one hour. I politely thanked him, but sixteen extra passengers would be quite enough. I decided it was time to shut down the engines again. This was going to take a while.

The fighters still lingering overhead were beginning to worry about fuel, so they tried to arrange for some fighter relief to meet us on the way back, but couldn't raise the base on voice. We dismissed them and they darted low, tipping wings and wishing us good luck, and then headed for home.

The canoe continued back and forth, delivering survivors two or three at a time. They were a tired but happy bunch. Now on board, in addition to Babb and Fallon, were Ensign Robert Harper, 1st pilot; Lt. (jg) Erhard Runner, navigator; James Kupper, AMM 1/c; Francis Thierer, ARM1/c; James Walters ARM3/c; Eldred Enloc, AMM 3/c; Raymond Gorea, AOM2/c; Herbert Wells S1/c; Royal Duplontis, S1/c; and Melvin Frank S/1c.

A sloop carrying the Jap prisoners arrived, a sad looking trio all stripped to the waist. They seemed perfectly willing to cooperate and really were no trouble, although it could have been because they were surrounded by carbines and pistols. We sat them side by side on the ammunition container in the blister, and an officer and two of the survivors were detailed to watch them.

The canoe made its way to the sloop for the last of the men, Hobson, and Fallon, who had returned to help with the prisoners. There was a brief delay when the shuttle craft sunk beneath them and needed to be re-inflated, but before long, everyone was on board and the anchor was weighed. The guerrilla officer smiled and saluted as the heavily laden plane pulled away.

The engines had fired nicely and I maneuvered around to gain a better heading with plenty of takeoff room. We were loaded, twenty-five in all, and the passengers all moved aft, with instructions to come quickly forward once she was "on the step." The plane shuddered, edged forward, and slowly staggered into the air as Roger plotted a course for home.

It was late afternoon and light was becoming a problem. It seemed it was always a race with darkness. We decided not to go by way of Mindoro and dispensed with the fighters, preferring to head directly across Panay, trying to stay low enough to avoid being detected by Jap positions along the way. While we weren't exactly out of danger, the scenery seemed particularly stunning in the dwindling light, the leafy deep ridges of the mountains with rivers forming intricate networks and patterns as they emptied into the viridescent shallows of the small bays. A rich wide rainbow showed itself, gracing us with a complete circle instead of the familiar arch that is usually interrupted by land or clouds. Ahead, the big round island of Jintotolo was capped by the picturesque little white lighthouse on the central heights. It overlooked the lush farmlands with their herds of cattle and horses, and signified that we were nearing home. It was a long day, but a good one! First Radioman Lambert sent a message ahead advising them of thirteen survivors and requesting a Marine guard to escort our three Japanese prisoners of war.

He took particular delight in "Rogering" the base when they slowly repeated our message to him, then still sounding puzzled, asked, "Playmate One, I thought you said thirteen pickups and three prisoners, could you confirm that?" But when we landed about fifteen minutes before dark, there was a launch with three armed Marines waiting for us alongside our buoy.

This night required a little medicinal alcohol. It took some doing, though. In Espirito we had managed to stockpile a sizable beverage cache, but now that we were aboard ship, regulations required that our liquor be confiscated and stored in the ship's locker (we wondered if it was actually the 'Captain's locker') until such time as we should have shore leave. In lieu of the "job well done" accolade, I persuaded them to allow a special dispensation, and before long my personal bottle of Scotch appeared and we all happily retired for the evening.

A few hours later, "General Quarters" sounded and an orderly scramble ensued, all of us heading to our battle stations. It was a total blackout, and there were easily a million more stars overhead than usual. The Tangiers guns were all trained skyward as the radar screen rotated wildly on the mast. We whispered among ourselves. Here we were aboard this enormous steel battle machine and we were whispering so the enemy wouldn't hear us. I searched the sky but nothing moved. Apparently, the radar scope was watching what we couldn't see, and with a colossal explosive burst, all hell broke loose! On all sides, a complete 360-degree panorama of fire strikes, it was like a thousand ships had decided to pull the trigger all at once, creating this one singular, thirty-second detonation. It was deafening. If something was up there, any evidence was by now surely obliterated by this array of heavy guns and newly acquired rockets. We had come a long way since Pearl.

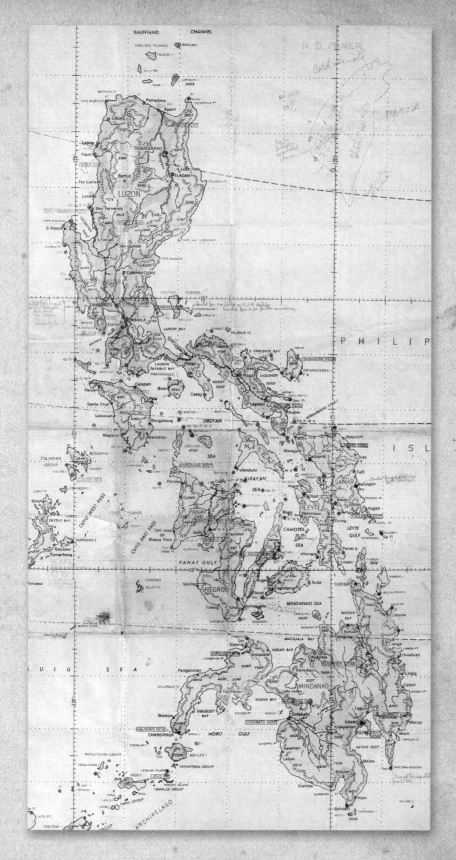

"Original" map with handwritten locations of survivor pickups. In the corner is a hand drawn image of Formosa, detailing concerns about enemy positions and landing challenges.

Towering plume near Subic Bay

Picture recovered from Japanese soldier

Native outrigger approaching blister hatch

Japanese prisoners being escorted across runway

Approach photo for pilots

Mac Attack

VPB-54 was on the move again, at least for a short while. This time it was north to the Lingayen Gulf and a much smaller but familiar tender, the Orca, a converted destroyer escort. Orca had recently had several run-ins with a group of Japanese buccaneers bent on blowing up the ship by planting explosives under the fan-tail. Refusing to surrender, the attempts continued until this bunch was finally dispatched by the ship's .20 mm cannon.

For the next few days, I shuttled between Leyte and our new home near Lingayen. There was less formality here and that agreed with our small band.

A little island was but a stone's throw from our berth, and it was in need of a party, primarily because our access to the necessary provisions had improved. Gewin suggested we visit the galley for some olives, and they scrounged up a gallon jug with about an inch of the things in the bottom. As the volleyball game got under way, we broke out the refreshments, added a fifth of gin and some vermouth to the olive jug and voila — the tyrannosaurus of martinis! It was a near bottomless jug and of course, it was necessary to freshen up the gin until the last of those pesky olives was gone, some time considerably after the game had fizzled out. It was about then that Gewin and I decided to sit down in the surf to recuperate. The cool water was soothing, and we both quickly conked out. Moments before Davy Jones claimed us, Willie happened by and, taking hold of our shirt collars, dragged us up to higher ground. Later on, I awoke with a well-earned headache, lying fitfully in my upper bunk. Del saved the day, arriving a few minutes later with a life saving canteen of ice-cold water.

The next morning, I was assigned to the mail plane. This was an arduous task under the best of circumstances and these were not even close. I was probably in no condition to fly, but this was war! I guessed I had no choice. I gripped the yoke as the teeny waves of the gulf bounced the PBY around like a toy, and then gaining speed, the choppy stuff nearly finished me off just as we finally got airborne. I steeled myself as I reached for what we called "autopilot" — three cone shaped knobs on the instrument panel and a long stick with a rubber cup on the end. I sort of invented the long stick part to eliminate the strain of bending forward and named it the "no strain pilot stick." Within a couple of hours, the device had given me enough relief that I was reasonably recovered. Lesson learned.

Japanese resistance was still strong south of the gulf and throughout much of Luzon. We had Mindoro Island now and continued to pound away at enemy forces in preparation for an invasion of the stronghold in Manila, where some 20,000 Japanese troops were waiting. The Lingayen Gulf was now a critical staging area for supplies and its location on the north end of Luzon gave us positions above and below, effectively straddling Manila. The squadron headed south again to Leyte and the USS Currituck, our tender there.

The tenders typically had an array of buoys to secure our PBYs. Between the rescues and parking arrangements, we were spending much more time in the salt water than our planes were accustomed to, and even with routine washing of our aircraft, there were sometimes problems. On Tacloban airstrip over in Leyte, a PBY came in for a runway landing only to discover one of the landing gear was locked up, causing the plane to dramatically pull to one side. The wing began brushing the parked planes all along the strip, finally hitting one B-24 and ripping the glass bubble housing of its gun turret cleanly off the top of the fuselage and spinning, one at a time, each of the four props. As it continued along, the Cat racked up varying degrees of damage to each plane, depending on their size and specifics. From that time on, when landing on a runway after a sea takeoff it became our habit to bounce once and have the blister guys peer down at the wheels to make sure they were spinning before settling in for the landing.

There was nowhere to go for shore leave during our stay on the ship, but Leyte airstrip with all its military planes was clearly visible and beckoned. I knew my younger brother, Mac, was based somewhere on Leyte in an Army medic outfit, so I requested permission on my scheduled day off to go ashore on the mail launch and try to locate him. Permission was granted.

Once on the island, I started asking around, beginning with some MP's and checking at the motor pools. Bit by bit, I pieced together a direction and thumbed my way along from jeep to armored vehicle and from base to muddy jungle road. Finally, through the trees in the distance was the barely distinguishable big red cross of his M.A.S.H. unit.

At that point it wasn't too tough locating him. And then, there it was. His unmistakable grin lighting up the camp as I appeared unexpectedly across from the mess tent. There was plenty of hearty hand shaking and backslapping, much to the surprise of everyone around, a Navy flier in an Army camp, after all.

Mac showed me around the camp and we talked a while about his life here in the jungle. He worked in the major surgery tent and told me of the struggles of practicing medicine in this primitive place. The weather was a constant challenge, the frequent rain storms kept things muddy, and twenty-four hours later, the mud would all turn to dust. Then another two nights of three inches of rain each would return the camp to a mucky swamp. The wind blew over the surgery tent one night, creating a mess that was days straightening out. The native Filipinos were always eager helpers, especially if they were given food, and they thoroughly hated the Japs. They were always exchanging Japanese souvenirs with the camp population.

As we compared notes, I told him about the marathon trip that landed us in Hawaii last year. It was like I'd let the genie out of the bottle. "At least you got to fly over here," he began. "Here was our average day on one of YOUR Navy transports. You are sleeping on deck because it is too hot below. Beneath you is one army multipurpose poncho and one army blanket that you crawl under if it ever got cold. Under that are solid steel deck plates, a comfortable enough bed, I suppose, until they blow soot out of the stacks and you are dusted black. Just as you get in a good position, the loud speaker blares out, 'Reveille! Reveille! All hands heave out and lash up!' It's black dark, but you get up because people will step on you if you don't, especially since you're now all sooty black. You grab a towel before your eyes are open and get in line to shave in fresh water, which they turn on only once in a while. About this time you remember you forgot your razor, run back into your compartment knocking people down all along the way, climb up to the fifth bunk right smack against the overhead, and spend fifteen minutes looking for the damn thing. About then, a voice bellows down that the water is now cut off.

"You grab your canteen, cup, and fork and spoon and run up the companionway/stairs just as the PA announces, 'All troops in D compartment pipe to breakfast.' You run out to the fantail and go down the chow line hoping to see somebody you know in the line, but no such luck. So you head to the rear of the now 300 yard long line that circles the deck once or twice.

"You eat breakfast, which actually wasn't that bad, I'll give you that, only the mess hall is way too hot to enjoy your food. Back up on the deck you find a swell place in the shade to play cards with three of your buddies, who you couldn't find in the chow line, and as you deal, the ship changes course and now you're in the sun full blast. It can knock you over. Then the PA again, 'Sweepers, start your brooms! Clean sweep down fore and aft. Hose down all weather decks.' So you stand up for another hour while they shoot hoses all around everywhere.

"They order you aft for physical exercise consisting mostly of push-ups on a deck that is so hot you can't touch it. That over, you spread your poncho out again in a decent spot, play some cards again and just about forget about the heat when the PA says, 'Now hear this. All troops, lay below to your compartments immediately and stand by for debarkation drill.' You go below, get into full fatigues instead of the shorts you had on, and put on steel helmet, pistol belt, canteens, trench knife, jungle aid kit, life belt, and even the damn carbine. You stand by your bunk, sweating, and wait to be called. The temperature is, conservative now, 110 degrees.

"Finally you get called to your stations. It's over and you can strip the wet clothes off again and once more try to play cards. Then it is already 11:15, time for chow again. And you thought the mess hall was hot last time. It is a real pleasure enjoying that bowl of hot soup, hot potatoes, and hot tea.

"The afternoon is interrupted by an abandon ship drill and a stimulating bout of target practice by the Navy gunners.

"Come evening, the ship is blacked out and you find a spot on the deck to sleep ... just as it starts to rain. You pull on your poncho, muttering all kinds of words to yourself, and await reveille.

"Yes, I'm quite sure that life aboard a transport is what makes you glad to climb into the landing boats and hit the beach. Part of the strategy that's getting these islands back from the Japs."

His rant completed, I asked if there was any chance he might return with me to our ship. He talked with his base commander and, it not being an every day occurrence to run into one's brother out here, was given not one, but four days leave. Once we were back aboard the Currituck, I realized Mac's enlisted rank would be somewhat of a problem for us, so I promptly promoted him to line officer, giving him one of my tans and some J.G. bars. Now we had run of the ship, took in a movie, and spent considerable time just swapping stories. Tokyo Rose was on the air again, always an interesting listen, proclaiming the extent of our great military defeat in the Philippines. For most of us, it really was having quite the opposite of the intended effect. Mac chimed in, "They sink an average of about one battleship, three cruisers, and eight destroyers every day. At that rate, I guess they'll be invading California before long, since we have no Navy or Air Force left to protect it."

The next morning, we had fresh eggs, courtesy of John (Love). John hailed from Colorado Springs, was a University of Denver grad, and was well on his way to becoming a lawyer when the war interrupted things. He was a very sharp fellow, articulate, handsome, and well liked. He was married on the same day he received his Navy wings and popped a champagne cork back in December when he got news of the birth of his son, Andy. About a week ago, his plane had been forced down and he and his crew lived with some natives for a few days while it was being repaired. They then gave him a fine send off, loading him up before he left with some local eggs. After breakfast, Mac and I sat down to write the folks a "joint" letter.

About an hour later down at operations, we ran into Pete who was just finishing up his turn as duty officer. He looked a little blurry to both of us and proceeded to explain that Art Bonnet was flying a radar mission from Tacloban yesterday in their countermeasure plane. It was equipped with a spool of metallic material that would be released from the rear of the plane like a long coiled hundred-foot tail. When it was extended, it interfered with radar detection and theoretically made the plane hard to see. Bonnie had been taxiing out and a few minutes later came roaring back into the operations office "Shaking like a hula girl," saying one of his engines had conked out on takeoff. Pete told him to cool down. "Let's go have a quick shot, it'll calm your nerves." Twenty minutes later, they were both plastered.

We had a good chuckle and I looked over the mission board to see what was in store for me today. I discovered I was assigned to fly medical supplies into a leper colony on the westernmost island of Culion. The colony had been established to isolate the incurable disease from the Philippines at large and, periodically, planes or boats were dispatched with provisions and sometimes additional "patients." This seemed irresistible enough, so Mac joined the crew. It was a good three hours out and, after landing, a small sailing vessel promptly headed over for the pickup. One of the party graciously invited us to come ashore for lunch, but under the circumstances, we declined. A few moments later, there was a close call as the bobbing boat struck the underside of our engine mount with neither vehicle suffering any damage. It was time to bid our new friends goodbye.

Winging our way home, Mac was really enjoying the aerial view of the Philippines and he even logged a couple of hours as "copilot." We touched down and made fast to our buoy but, oddly enough, the launch to the ship was very slow in coming. Poor brother Mac, his face now a lovely green, had yet to gain his sea legs and made his way very cautiously up the gangway. Otherwise, it had been a refreshing visit!

The news came suddenly. I somehow expected it to feel different, more like a rite of passage or a "graduation" from combat. But this was like becoming a surprise contest winner. We had received new orders. We were going home! The next few days were filled with anticipation. Our remaining shifts seemed uninteresting, presenting needless obstacles to our desire to ready ourselves and do a little proper celebrating. I had one more flight to make, down the line to a remote island called Woendi. The assignment was to swap one of our black amphibious planes for a Catalina seaplane version with heavy sophisticated radar gear. The camp down there included a group of tents in a palm grove. A particularly large tree was leaning rakishly over my quarters and, naturally, during the night we had a violent storm. I was startled awake by the familiar swish of a falling tree and dove for the deck. It was an adjacent tree, and concluding that it was unlikely that two side-by-side trees would fall in the same storm, I managed to sleep through the night.

The new plane was not only a Seacat, but came complete with its own crew of radar specialists. The lieutenant of the group, some kind of electronic wizard, was fond of spouting symbols and model numbers: "Yes we should use the R4-66B, but a 1032 model 6 Mark VIII will do," or something like that. As we began preparing for takeoff, it was plain to see that finding a path through the anchored ships and floating debris was a ticklish prospect. We considered a circular takeoff, but Bob and I agreed on a channel past the bow of a tanker. Glancing back, we saw the six radar men were busy studying their scopes and the Lieutenant circulated and continued spewing statistics.

Our checklist completed, it was time to head out. As we were nearing takeoff speed, the "ship's boat" started moving out from behind the tanker and into our path, its coxswain waving to someone back on board and oblivious to what was unfolding. The plane was now going too fast to abort and was unable to turn left because we had not yet passed the towering prow of the tanker. My copilot caught his first glimpse over our bow gun turret of the launch crossing left to right in front of us and began yelling and gesticulating wildly, at one point nearly seizing the controls. I was frantically yelling back, "I know! I know!" over the blare of the engines behind us, as scores of scenarios flashed through my mind. As the plane cleared the arching bow of the tanker, I pulled as hard as I could, virtually begging us off of the waves and then immediately kicked rudder. Peering over at the wing tip float, I cranked in the left aileron, turning us on edge, just enough to avoid dragging it in the water and prayed the right float would be high enough to miss the boat. By now the coxswain saw us and stood there, frozen, as we thundered over him and into the clear. After we had collected ourselves, Bob and I looked at one another, then began laughing hysterically over what we supposed was now the condition of his jeans. The lieutenant was mysteriously quiet for the balance of the return trip.

A big empty Navy troop ship called the "Wharton" was anchored in the harbor, our transportation home in the morning, and we busied ourselves packing and negotiating with the stay behinds over our liquor library. For some reason, Art's orders were not yet cut and he inherited the lieutenant and his electronic operation. This new officer was a very "gung-ho" character intent on ending the war single handedly. He worked out all sorts of elaborate missions with flight operations including a venture into the China Sea to flirt with the Japanese Navy. Bonnie wasn't willing to risk his crews so recklessly when their orders were perhaps hours away. For the next couple of evenings, as they taxied out into the darkness, he would discover that the "mags" didn't check out properly or something and then ground the aircraft, to the intense frustration of the lieutenant. Thankfully, Art got his orders in a couple of days.

The morning we thought would never come had finally arrived, and excitement was running high as we assembled at the gangway. Slowly each of us filed down into the launch and took a seat for the short run over to the troopship. Behind us were the islands that represented our world for the last two years — the crews that would continue the work, the forests and ships that had served as our encampments, our trusty Catalinas. It would all be a distant memory. Our weary Dumbos remained by the wayside, parked here and there where some were stripped for parts and steel for manufacturing, and others would blend into the jungle and likely never be seen again. Slow but sturdy, they had plodded ahead doing their level best to keep ahead of the smaller, swifter, and more dangerous predators that lurked throughout these islands. Much was asked of them and they bore their wounds without complaint. Our episode was now coming to a conclusion, and the entire parade of fifteen PBYs that carried us from Hawaii in June had miraculously endured, only to suffer the indignity of abandonment as their usefulness in the tropics ended. These noble creatures deserved a better fate.

For twenty-seven days, the ship meandered in a serpentine antisubmarine pattern across the Pacific and past a huge task force assembling at Ulithi Atoll that was preparing for the planned attack of Japan. Of course, it never occurred.

Our route wound eastward, making a brief stop at Pearl Harbor where all this mess began. On deck, our daily ritual was a study in monotony, but who cared? Life was growing sweeter by the mile. Three times a day the canteen opened for business, and most of us went for Cokes and ice cream cups, two of each, and enjoyed them on deck amid the salt spray and the sounds of the ship's band. It represented simple pleasures rediscovered, heralding the return to times that we could understand, family and familiar surroundings. For the second time I looked up from beneath the Golden Gate, this time with tears, and shared the moment with my "two-tour" friends as our time together grew shorter.

We headed straight for the Sir Francis Drake Hotel. Our old buddy, Jack, was waiting for us, eager to rejoin the group and swap sea stories again. It had been some time since his discharge for medical reasons and he was now employed by General Foods in the Frisco area. We booked rooms, gathering in one to get decked out for the evening's adventures and spinning yarns about the events of the Pacific tour. I completed my uniform, and while the others were dragging their collective feet, I was eager to get going. I told them I'd meet them in the Orchid Bar, but by now they were busy taunting Jack about his tendency to pick up much "older" women. What delicious luxury. Quickly locating just the right bar stool, I ordered a

> Tomorrow is the big day! We'll be shedding a few tears perhaps as we sail under the Golden Gate Bridge around 9:00 AM. There's a hundred dollar pool on the exact minute of the hour we pass beneath the bridge. I never win these things but think they're fun

Scotch and soda. As I tipped the glass to my lips, I heard a female voice behind me, "There's one now ..." It seemed odd, and as I tried to make some sense out of the comment, an elderly lady seated herself on a stool beside me. "Please forgive me for intruding," she began, " but you see, my son was a Navy pilot, too. He was killed in action just about a month ago."

"I'm so sorry ..." I whispered back sympathetically.

"It kind of helps to talk to one of you, if you don't mind, of course."

"Not at all," I replied honestly. "Where was he stationed?" We chatted together intently, my hand on her arm. Slowly she gave me more of the details. It could have been my own mom. I couldn't imagine what she must be going through. Glancing up at the smoky glass behind the bar, I could see the image of the near half dozen leering faces — Del, Gewin, Pete, Ray, and Jack — with their eyes all on me.

They closed in, grinning and remarked coyly, "So aren't you going to introduce us to your friend?"

The initial flush of embarrassment quickly left me, and after a moment, I slowly responded, "This is Mrs. Williamson. I think we weren't able to find her son last month, only the plane."

Over the course of the evening, the awkwardness of the moment subsided, and we were soon again entertaining ourselves with stories, drink, and humor. These were, after all, my friends for life.

This time, I flew home to Indianapolis, about a hundred dollar fare for 2,000 miles. It was an old DC-3, a midnight flight that made at least six stops. I drank hot chocolate the entire night. My several weeks of leave were welcome indeed and seeing my folks and friends again — what a feeling. I was relaxed and finally got a car, used because the automakers were still emphasizing weaponry and machines and weren't making anything I wanted. But times were good.

My new orders were for instructor's training back at Pensacola, about a 700 mile drive. I was back in the air again — still in PBYs — and guessed I would never get a crack at one of those hot shot fighters, but that was OK. Flying these big planes through the skies, hobnobbing with clouds, rainbows, gorgeous sunsets, even occasional frightening weather probably brought me as close to God as a person can get. You come to feel at home in the Cats, and I found there was a lot more to learn.

The instructor was an old friend from my first squadron who had been teaching here a year and a half. He had incredible skills and taught me finesse and how to make a Catalina do things they shouldn't be able to do. I learned a "full slip," a maneuver that had us flying over a landing spot on the water at 1,000 feet. As it disappeared under the nose, he cranked the plane up on its side with crossed controls until we were again staring at the target, then suddenly dropped like a rock. At the last minute, he gently rolled out into a nose high full stall landing attitude and set her down right on the mark. Subsequently, I probably demonstrated the same feat a hundred times. Stateside duty was a different animal, indeed, and it was starting to agree with me. And Pensacola was not a seaplane tender! I was a twenty-six year old Navy bachelor in a place swarming with women. By late July, a few of us had set up a bachelor bungalow off base and even started looking for beach front property. The work days were spent enjoying stress-free flying, something for which I had developed affection. Some of our trips would take us to destinations like New York for overnighters, and sometimes those finicky planes would develop a little problem that would keep us up there an extra day.

> The war had taken its toll on him just as surely as if he'd been in combat.

On Aug. 6, there was an explosion unlike anything the world had ever seen. Two days later, it happened again. It was stunning. We weren't yet sure what it would mean. Then suddenly it was V-J Day and everyone poured into downtown Pensacola and danced in the streets, a wild celebration that continued through the night. The war was finally over!

Things changed fast around the base. Many put in for discharges and the daily instruction and workload dwindled. I decided to hang in there a while longer and put in for my discharge, effective for Jan. 29, exactly four years after my induction.

My remaining time turned more administrative and the idiosyncrasies of military regulation and discipline became increasingly more stifling and unnecessary. It was becoming clearer with each passing day that military life, at least for the long haul, was not for me.

I received an emergency call from my high school principal. He was a close friend of my father, who was still a teacher, and the news wasn't good. My dad had passed away. The war had taken its toll on him just as surely as if he'd been in combat. With two sons overseas and so many of his beloved ex-students killed in action, he had suffered from his own form of battle fatigue. I flew home for the funeral.

Four years to the day that I first put on my Navy uniform, I took it off again and dressed in civilian clothes. I arose that memorable morning with my bags already packed and considered the future with a mixture of excitement and trepidation.

What would I do next? Where would I go to work? Who would I marry and would I have kids?

I didn't yet know that I would take a trip to California in a few months, passing through Salt Lake City. There I would have dinner with the parents of one of the rescued fliers who died in that unfortunate accident right on the runway. I would tell them about the last hours I had spent with their precious son, and later we would drive up to a ridge above the city and be witness to a spectacular meteor shower, a fitting tribute to a fine young man who died much too young.

I didn't know that I would finish college and become interested in oceanography, or that I would continue flying for another thirty plus years, some as a small flying school owner and most of them with Eastern Airlines as a pilot.

I would indeed get married and have four wonderful children, and one day I would even fulfill a childhood ambition of "piloting" a train as its engineer.

I was waiting, still lost in my reverie, when the yeoman opened the office. He went right to work processing the discharge papers. It seemed appropriate to experience, one last time, the process — the countless duplicates and filling out of redundant forms, the military way that was now so familiar. When the completed packet in its manila envelope was ready, right on top was a rather artistically impressive document, and I proudly saw the words "Honorable Discharge."

I drove out of Pensacola a free man, thankful for each breath I was taking. I cruised along the high bluffs just on the edge of the city and cast one last look over my shoulder. The waters of Pensacola Bay were lovely, ripples forming tiny whitecaps. "About twelve knots of wind, I should say." And I drove home.

The Seven
Del Fager, Howard Miner, Jack Beuttler, Gewin McCracken,
Ray Peckham, Art Bonnet, Pete Maravich

1965 "Cat" Reunion-Howard, Art, Del, Peck, and Jack

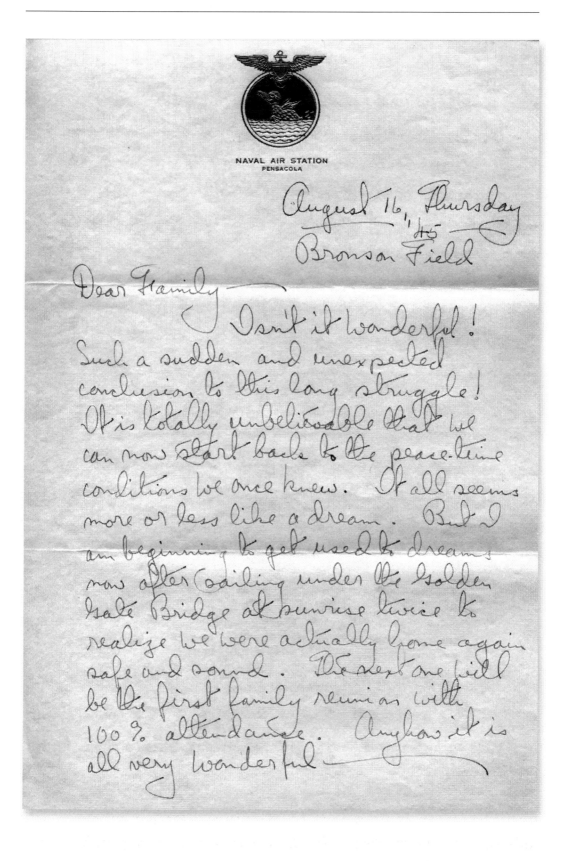

NAVAL AIR STATION
PENSACOLA

August 16, Thursday
45
Bronson Field

Dear Family

Isn't it wonderful! Such a sudden and unexpected conclusion to this long struggle! It is totally unbelievable that we can now start back to the peace-time conditions we once knew. It all seems more or less like a dream. But I am beginning to get used to dreams now after sailing under the Golden Gate Bridge at sunrise twice to realize we were actually home again safe and sound. The next one will be the first family reunion with 100% attendance. Anyhow it is all very wonderful.

Epilogue

"When I had the pleasure of addressing a word to you just before we left the states, I told you that I had not the slightest doubt as to how your men would acquit themselves in battle. How right I was!

"They have met a skilled and battle-wise enemy, and they have beaten him. They have met mud and rain that are beyond my power to describe and they have conquered it. I cannot begin to express my admiration for them. To them, and to you who are giving them strength by your faith, I offer a soldier's salute.

"Inevitably, we have lost some of our comrades. Others have been hurt. To those of you whose men have made the ultimate sacrifice, nothing I can say can make up to you your sad loss. I know they would want you to carry on in the same way they gave their lives - bravely and proudly. I am sure you will.

"Our men - yours and mine - now are seasoned soldiers, poised and confident. Nothing can stop them, for they know they are on the road to Tokyo, and beyond Tokyo, lies home."

J. L. Bradley
Major General, U.S.A.

The above quotation was included in a 1944 letter from my Uncle Mac to my grandfather. He felt it might be included in the local papers in Indianapolis, and whether or not it made it into print then, I thought it should now. The war effort indeed required unimaginable sacrifices on so many levels. We would do well today to remember that. We live in a world where the everyday drone of the current news cycle minimizes the conflicts that our military men and women are involved in through saturation, political spin, statistics, and posturing. Often that misses the realities that members of the armed forces and their families face daily. At home, very little is asked of us in support — no draft or rationing, no war bonds or tax increases, no victory gardens or laws against profiteering, or any of the other characteristics that were part of everyday life during World War II. Times are very different, to be sure, but the toll of a war effort on troops is still very much the same.

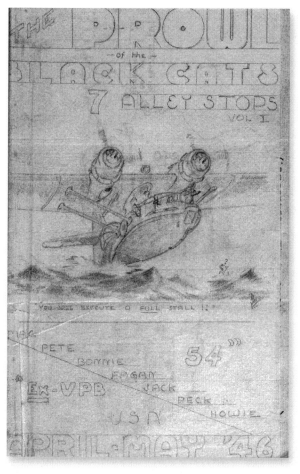

When VPB-54 folded up tents in 1945, the conflict was in its final phase. The Dumbos were tired, full of holes, and generally beaten up, but proud nonetheless. They had operated largely without fanfare, slinking around the seas disrupting supply lines, bringing home survivors, and aiding other air force efforts. VPB-54 rescued 225 men and assisted on thirteen more during their second tour alone. This was accomplished without the loss of a single plane. Sadly, by war's end most were so worn down they were simply left by the wayside because they were no longer flyable.

Dad celebrated with the squadron at reunions until at least the year 2000 and other members continued the traditional until 2006. When he passed away in September 2015 at 96, Del Fager became the last surviving member of "the Seven" to do so.

Since the publication of the first book, I have had the pleasure of sitting down and talking with quite a number of Dad's Squadron mates. Their contributions have helped fill many voids and further immersed me into the story. They have allowed us to save their interviews on camera and all have become good friends. We are well on our way to compiling what promises to be a new short documentary film about the Black Cats of the South Pacific, perhaps the first since the old Navy black-and-white newsreel film made back in the forties. The completed project will be available to the public and have a place in the Library of Congress archives.

I've also spent some time reading a number of issues of the "Black Cat Prowl," a hand drawn newsletter Dad developed in hopes of beginning a conversation in 1946 about staging a reunion of the Seven and any other squadron members who wanted to join them. Four issues (at least) were produced over six years or so with a different PBY cartoon on the cover of each. Dad would get it started in his finest "pilot-speak" and then mail it on to the next of the Seven buddies. Each would add their thoughts, family news, humor, and try to develop it a bit further.

Eventually, over several months, it would travel around the country and return to Dad with a sample of writing from each of them. It was, in effect, a journal of the changes in their lives over those years. This gave me a synopsis of things as they were up until the early 50's.

By 1947, Dad was the only unmarried member of the group. The rest were already well on their way to starting families. Del and Shirley Fager lived in the Orinda area of California and had two children. Initially, he worked as wholesaler of fruit and produce. He later remarried and moved to San Francisco with his new wife, Bebe, and enjoyed a career marketing and selling fitness equipment and saunas. He wouldn't fly again after the war. While visiting with Del and Bebe in 2014, he told me a dramatic tale of a time, aboard one of the tenders in Leyte Gulf, when he watched as a row of allied ships stretching out on both sides of him were pounding away during the assault of the island. Kamikaze fighters suddenly appeared and began their diving runs at the ships as they fired back wildly. An Australian cruiser alongside the tender was miraculously able to shoot down nearly all of these planes before they struck anything on either ship, and when the smoke cleared, there were four large holes in the cruiser but the tender was intact. "We were sitting there, almost helpless and nothing but gas! If anything had hit our ship it was over. I've never been so scared."

And from *The Prowl*: *"Howie, are you still in as good a shape as you used to pretend to be? Chasing those crates of oranges around has left me in pretty good condition. You'll have to watch that waistline since you're pushing a pencil instead of a yoke!"*

While Gewin McCracken wasn't thrilled with his government job, after he and Francis were married they entered a government sponsored lottery that awarded eighty-six homesteads in Oregon and Northern California to lucky WWII veterans. Gewin's was the second name selected. They packed up their truck like a prairie schooner and with their new son, headed west to Tule Lake, Calif., amazing the rest of group by trying to make a living off the land. They planted nearly eighty acres of barley and potatoes, and he proudly raised his family on the farm, thrilled with this change in lifestyle. Tragically, he was killed in his car at a traffic light when it was struck by another vehicle.

"Pete, I could bust your punkin head for not looking us up when you were in Washington playing ball. Marguerite found us. You should have been able to!"

Art Bonnet and his wife Ginny had two girls and lived in Glenview, Illinois. He and Dad flew a PBY-5A onto Lake Michigan together in 1947. He spent much of his working life as a sales manager in real estate. The guys continued to remind him of his receding hairline, which was in full retreat by the first reunion. Alex Catlow, his copilot, had a close relationship with Bonnie, and spent many hours telling me about his mischievous ways during the second tour. Art had beautiful handwriting.

"If any of you fellows stop through Chicago, we'll have a room for you — that is if you promise to give Susie her bottle and change her when she needs it. You're right, Peck, she already has more hair than I have."

Ray Peckham lived in Arcadia California before enlisting and was always a musician at heart. He helped organize a twenty-two piece band that played at clubs and various locations where people enjoyed dancing. Ray was a kind and thoughtful man. After completing his Navy service, he had attended an Army-Navy event and entered a drawing, winning a new car. He promptly gave it to his mother.

When Ray met Virginia in a music shop, she was already a war widow. Her husband completed his flight training and had just entered the conflict when his plane struck a mountain, killing him and his entire crew. She was still deeply in love with him as she and her young son, Tim, struggled to make it on their own.

For Ray, it was love at first sight, and he finally persuaded her to go out with him. Unfortunately, he had to borrow a car…from his mother.

Virginia wanted to have a man in Tim's life and was honest with Ray about her feelings. Soon they were married and had a second son, Jerry. Ray worked in the lumber business in Arcadia for years and proved to be a wonderful father and talented artist in wood and stone. Virginia played saxophone and sometimes joined Ray in the band. Tim went on to become a State Senator in California. I briefly spoke with Virginia in May 2015. She and Ray had been married sixty years when he died in 2008.

"Glad to hear Press is doing so well in basketball. You must have improved since you left the Canal, Pete, or else you had tougher competition then. Hi fella ..."

Jack Beuttler also continued to live in the Bay area with his wife, Sybil, and they had two boys, John and Doug. Although he had learned to fly before the war began, his days in the cockpit were behind him. Or so the family thought. It turned out Jack learned to fly a glider, a hobby that was as secret as it was silent.

For a while after the war, he sold a variety of products and lotions to an assortment of resorts in California. Later, he began a long career with General Mills and, after the boys were grown and away at school, he and Sybil sold the house and moved to a condominium in Saratoga, near San Jose. Jack was a regular at reunions. He and Dad remained close friends and stayed in contact for many years until his unexpected death at the age of 60.

"Beuttler Tower reporting to all Black Cats. It is sure good to hear from you guys again ... I'm now selling for General Mills, so don't forget to eat your Wheaties!"

Pete (Petar) Maravich remained a basketball bachelor for a few years after the war. He played professionally with several clubs, notably Youngstown and Pittsburg, before beginning his college coaching career. He finally found the right girl, Helen, a war widow herself with a young son, Ronnie. Pete surprised the group with both the announcement of his marriage to her, and soon after, the birth of their first child together, Pete. During the war years, the Seven knew their buddy as "Pete," although Maravich was christened at an early age with the more familiar "Press," a name he inherited not because he or his teams played great defense, but due to his characteristic banter. Depending on the story's version, he probably gained the nickname as a child who had more to say than the *Pittsburg Press* or from simply peddling the papers and yelling his employer's name at the top of his lungs.

When I was twelve or thirteen, I remember Dad joining me on the driveway while I was shooting baskets. He had invited an old friend of his to our house for dinner in a few weeks, someone who had a son around my age who was a pretty fair player. This throw down was a huge motivator, and I intently went to work sharpening my skills. Turns out the dinner date was cancelled and it took several more years before I realized how lucky I was.

Of course, Pete Jr. grew up to eclipse his father's career as a player, becoming an NBA All Star and Hall of Fame member. The two of them would struggle unsuccessfully to find a cure for the older Maravich's prostate cancer and he passed away in 1988.

"As you know, I saw Bonnie quite a few times this past season. Lo and behold, guess what he did. He bought a house for 11 g's, and I don't mean gravity either. Heard via the grapevine that the location of the house is atop quicksand, so if you pay Bonnie a visit and see a chimney sticking out a little, you'll know you've found the place."

John "Dugie" Doyle sported a "fine Abraham Lincoln beard" when Dad first laid eyes on him in Nasaza Bay. He was one of the two surviving airmen afflicted with malaria and avoided the fateful flight that killed three of his fellow fliers. He went on to graduate from the University of Nebraska and was awarded the Navy Cross at a "Navy Day" ceremony at the university in 1945. He also competed for the Cornhusker football team, and after completing law school, became a successful attorney in his father's law firm. He and his wife, Barbara, settled in the Lincoln area and had two children, Timothy and Louis. His brother, David Doyle, was a familiar face in television and movies throughout the 70s and 80s. Dugie was active in many local, state, and national organizations, including the National Council on Alcoholism, and stayed in touch with his squadron mates for the remainder of his life. He died in 2013.

Mac (Macarten Miner, Dad's brother) joined the Army and a hospital unit after just a single semester of college, served three years, and returned to DePauw University where he graduated in 1949. He went on to med school at Northwestern, where he met and married his wife, Carolyn. They lived in the Chicago area. He completed his studies and, for a time, went to work as a prison doctor. He did his residency at Charity Hospital in New Orleans and later worked in a clinic in Lynch, Ky., treating coal miners. These early influences likely inspired his deep-seated, compassionate approach to medicine.

The two of them moved to Carlsbad, N.M., and he set up a practice in 1954. They raised three children — Alan, Shelli, and Laura — and he continued to serve his community as a family doctor, making house calls as routinely in the 1990s as he did in the 1950s. To Mac, medicine was never a business, but rather a way to care for people in need. Even a cancer diagnosis and chemotherapy didn't deter him from continuing to see patients with a smile, finally succumbing in 1997 at age 73. From a letter sent to the *authentic* John Caldow, Jan. 27, 1945:

"I believe it rained more in the month of November than it does in a year back home. When we reached our final position where we knew we would stay for some time, we dug a well for our water supply, and most of the time, the water level was only four feet below the surface."

I attended a service for Del Fager in San Francisco in October 2015. He was 96. His ashes were scattered over the bay from a seaplane.

My father's artwork and photos have graced the walls of university art galleries, finally finding their way into the Evergreen Aviation and Space Museum in Oregon and the National Museum of the Pacific War in Fredericksburg, Texas, for three months in 2014. I look forward to continuing that journey with other national museums around the country. Who would have ever thought?

Dad went on to start a small flying school, marry Mom and raise a family. He hired on with Eastern Airlines, but for a time he hesitated to fly, suffering from a self described "burn out," and it cost him valuable seniority that hounded him through much of his early career before becoming captain. He never touched another coconut. And his retirement in 1979, after thirty years, came disappointingly soon. He felt he was at the top of his game when the FAA told him he was "too old" at 60.

Too old? Dad continued skiing until nearly 90, made a couple of trips from Florida to Massachusetts each year while actively landscaping his properties in both states, and he was thrilled to be a part-time railroad engineer for most of that span.

The Black Cats are fading now, but they and all the World War II veterans deserve our respect and attention. As for Dad, I'll be forever grateful for his sketches, his words, and for giving me these insights into his past. It is a lesson for all of us in leaving a legacy of family history to those who will survive us.

Dad would want to be sure I acknowledged, again, the fine crew of the "Frisco Gal." He was very proud of them:

Ens. Robert White - copilot
Ens. Roger George - Navigator
ARM3/c Robert Synan - 2nd Radioman
AOM3/c Roswell Combs - 1st Gunner and Bombardier
AMM2/c Billy Keene - 2nd Mechanic
ARM1/c Duane Lambert - 1st Radioman
AMM1/c Norris Townsley - Plane captain and 1st mechanic
AOM3/c Harry Richardson - Gunner
ACMM(AA), (CA) Roy Doull
AOM3/c Robert Knecht - Gunner

Crewmembers Doull and Knecht were not listed on the official roster but are mentioned in Dad's own crew lists. My conversation with Bob Knecht confirmed this. He remembers the "Frisco Gal," but flew with four crews during the two tours.

Crew 1943 — John Erhard, Howard Miner, Mel Goers, Frank Shackelford, Wendall Brock, Charles Hammett, Welham Garber, Don Elliot, James Cloud, George Keen, Glen Lindgren, and John Kiner

Crew members were often moved between planes in the first tour. By August 1943, the roster in Lt. Cmdr. Schoenweiss' Report lists: Lt. Erhard, Lt. Hyland, Ensign Miner, Garber, Jackson, Keen, Hammett, Williams, and Lynch. Mel Goers now flew with Lt. Apgar's crew.

Glossary

NAS — Naval air station

starboard — right side facing bow or front **port** — left side facing the bow (front) **fore** at the front or bow

aft — at the rear or stern

CB's seabees — construction battalion

banka — canoe

Tender — vessel that services seaplanes

Wasp — USS Wasp, carrier

the hack — place of confinement for punishment

amidship — middle (of the ship)

slipstream — "wake" of turbulence behind a moving plane

abeam — at right angles to the plane, across the middle waist

waist — narrowing of the plane's fuselage

yoke — the control or "steering wheel" of an aircraft that adjusts the attitude of the plane, side to side (roll) or up and down (pitch).

Acknowledgements and Notes

What a fascinating journey this has been and I still don't know where it is leading. I am grateful to so many who have helped encourage and guide me along the way. David Sanford has been and continues to be an unselfish mentor. My brother, Mike, has helped me with both elbow grease and enthusiasm for the project, and we confer and travel to interviews and venues often. Military author Don Keith has patiently provided advice and a willing ear.

My appreciation, also, to J. A. Prusick for helping provide additional details about one of the rescue episodes and to my proofreaders, Lloyd, Ginger, John, and Win who were willing to donate their time not fully realizing what they were getting into.

To my Aunt Marian, my wife Heidi, and all the members of the family who have been so supportive and helpful in more ways than I can count, you have my sincere thanks, as does Anneli Anderson, who again helped get me through the painstaking process of turning all this material into a book…and once again found the right amount of "sparkle."

(Win Stites, above left, VP-91, VP2-1, flight engineer who served in both the Atlantic and Pacific regions. He is the author of **Cat Tales**, a humorous collection of WWII crew experiences aboard a PBY, and **Gigi**, a coloring book for children and adults alike).

The opportunity to meet squadron members and their families has been invaluable: Alex Catlow, Del Fager, Bob Pinckney, Harold Koenig, Win Stites, Elliot Schreider, Virginia Peckham, Paula and members of the Sneed family, Becky and Andy Love, Gary Goers, and John Beuttler.

This book is built primarily around my father's words and writings and gleaned from his extensive collection of documents, news clippings, war records, and keepsakes. My aim has always been to remain true to his voice, so familiar to me over the years in stories and conversations that it seemed to become a part of my own. I felt the *first-person*, narrative style of the original book did the best job of telling the story and related it in a more reader-friendly way. It was important to me to share the Black Cats' legacy with as many readers as possible, and especially with younger readers and those who may not ordinarily find conventional nonfiction accounts their cup of tea.

In some instances, I believed a particular reference or anecdote might benefit from additional clarification, expanding, or the simple weaving in of a little history for context. Where this required research, I have tried to include and give credit to those sources. As I became acquainted with many of his friends, I found the interviews often included some of the same shared experiences and locations and whether at Black Cat Base or at a reunion, story swapping was a favorite pastime. Dad was no doubt very familiar with the exploits of his buddies, and the continuity of the book relies on relating these parts of the squadron's history in a way that made it part of the action of the story. I am, again, especially grateful to the VP-54 and VPB-54 members who contributed wonderful new storytelling and corroborated old: Alex, Del, Bob, Elliot, and Harold.

Footnotes and Credits:

Many resources were helpful for general information and history about the Black Cats including:

Official US Navy War Diary

Reunion version of diary (Willie Sneed)

Black Cat Raiders by Richard Knott

The Retired Officer, July 1986 article by Michael Martin:
   The Black Cats~Unlikely Heroes of the Pacific by Michael Martin.

Wings of Gold feature by Ens. John Leads 2010:
   A perspective on MPRF and the Black Cats

PBY: The Catalina Flying Boat by Roscoe Creed

Details about various aircraft were found on the navalaviation.org website, acepilots.com website, and Wikipedia

Dave's Warbirds - daveswarbirds.com

pg. 13 An illuminating article by Carl Zebrowski called *"Your Number's Up!"* in the Dec. 2007 issue of *WW II Magazine* discusses the draft in much more detail.

pg. 15 Details of the "Macon" courtesy of a 1942 letter home.

pg. 33 Footnote R4D from interview with Stewart Bailey, *Evergreen Aviation Museum* and Wikipedia.

pg. 41 Queen Mary and Elizabeth - According to the QM (now a floating hotel) website (queenmary.com/history/) a record for troops transported aboard ship was set on a voyage from NY to Great Britain when 16,085 were aboard the QM. At that point she was stripped of her luxurious amenities and outfitted for wartime. A more complete WWII history is detailed there.

pg. 43 An interview with Black Cat Lt. Cmdr J.O. Cobb, USN from April 26, 1943 is available in the Bureau of Aeronautics archives. His fascinating insights about the Black Cats include a discussion of red goggles and red light. In addition to my father's descriptions, a host of PBY details are available in Jim Busha's article about flying the Slattery PBY in the May 2014 issue of *Sport Aviation* and another in *AOPA PBY-5a Catalina: Stand Up and Salute* by Barry Schiff (aopa.org/News)

pg. 50 Photo courtesy of John Bickford found at *"Dave's Warbirds"* (daveswarbirds.com/) and is attributed to Marine Colonel W. C. Lemley.

pg. 51 Major Roosevelt account is from one of Dad's letters home. More about his war record is available at valor.militarytimes.com and James Roosevelt, Wikipedia

pg. 53 Poem from *"We've Got a Fighter Up Tonight."* A hand typed version was in Dad's scrapbook. Full version is available from the American Folklife Center, Library of Congress, #AFS 8763 B1. There is no mention of an author.

pg. 54 Additional descriptions about PBYs can be found in a variety of locations. *Black Cat Raiders* by Richard Knott is the "go-to" resource for PBY information and the article in *Sport Aviation* magazine (May 2014) written by Jim Busha elaborates on many of my father's details provided in his notes.

pg. 55 My photo taken inside PBY at the *Evergreen Aviation and Space Museum*

pg. 57 Dad mentioned this in his writing and additional information can be found on the Library of Australia website.

pg. 59 SNV Valiant trainer by Vultee . Information is available at navalaviationmuseum.org

pg. 69 From *Black Cat Raiders*: Pg 115 discusses Lt. Erhard's crew and using the countermeasure equipment.

pg. 83 From the Cobb interview, additional details on glide bombing and the "low altitude Cat."

pg. 84 The entire story of Lt. Anderson's crew came from numerous sources including Elliot Schreider, *Black Cat Raiders*, Willie Sneed's writing, the War Diary, and my father's notes.

pg. 85 R4D - from interview with Stewart Bailey, *Evergreen Aviation Museum* and Wikipedia explanation

pg. 91 Photo Noumea from Schreider collection

pg. 95 This compelling account was from the Elliot Schreider interview and Dad's notes. Photo from Elliot Schreider collection.

pg. 98 Many good websites on rationing including amesihistory.org . My Aunt Marian provided some personal details.

pg. 107 GO-9 transmitter was part of discussions with Alex Catlow, Bob Pinckney, and Win Stites.

pg. 112 Lt Cobb's interview covered the reconstruction of the PBYs and the level of security the patrols in the Solomons were providing.
Discussion of this carrier duty is mentioned in the VP/VPB-54 War Diary.

pg. 113 Specifics about the Battle of Midway from Elliot Schreider, history.com/battle-of- midway and navy.com/battle-of-midway

pg. 114 Swan account of Nell 96 from the *Catalina Chronicles* newsletter, Vol II, Feb. 24, 1995 PBY Catalina Foundation.

pg. 117 This account differs from the contemporary account and Lt. Gordon's own retelling of the story of the rescues. It was reported in an interview with Gordon by Charles Rawlins in the *Saturday Evening Post* in Dec of 1944 and corroborated in article by Don Wharton, Look Magazine, (Feb 1945). These articles were part of my father's scrapbook and Library.

pg. 118 Gibson Girl hand cranked transmitters involved an H2 generator, a metal cylinder containing granular material that when mixed with sea water would produce hydrogen gas. It was part of a kit that included a box kite, the hydrogen generator, and even a small light that was strapped to either the kite or balloon. The gas was used to pressurize the balloon if there wasn't enough wind to fly the box kite. Courtesy Henry Rogers, historian - **WHRM**

pg. 122 Photo from Del Fager collection

pg. 145 Photo Del Fager collection

pg. 156 F4U Corsair see acepilots.com
Photo courtesy Harold Koenig

pg. 159 Photo courtesy Paula Sneed

Pg. 160 Largely taken from a letter by Willie Sneed provided by Andy Love

pg. 163 Photo from Schreider collection

pg. 167 Leaflet from Fager collection

pg. 173 P-38 - see acepilots.com

pg. 179 Photo from Alex Catlow collection

pg. 188 SB2C - see acepilots.com
A letter written by Doyle to the King family was printed in the *Historic Huntsville Quarterly* 1992 and supplements my father's account. This was provided to me by J. A. Prusick. Adam also provided a copy of *Nebraska History Magazine*, Vol. 95/4/Winter containing an interview with Doyle by Samuel Van Pelt. I was pleased to discuss the article with Judge Van Pelt by phone in May 2016.

pg. 201 and 204 Photos of Japanese Del Fager collection

pg. 205 Attempts to bomb the Orca are addressed in the VPB-54 War Diary.

Epilogue: The explanation of the name "Press" is slightly different in the two books I've looked at on the subject, so I've included both. *Pistol: the Life of Pete Maravich* by Mark Kriegel and *Pete Maravich: the Authorized Biography of Pistol Pete* by Wayne Federman and Marshall Terrill.

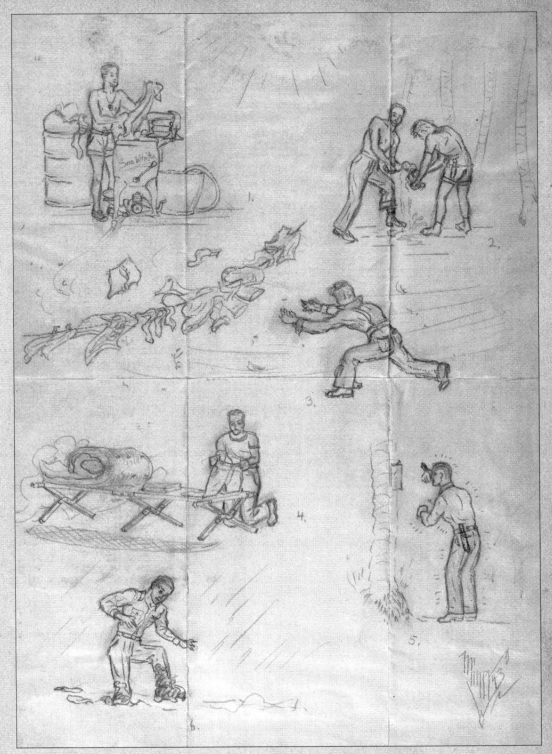

Wash day at Guadalcanal

Thanks for reading *Sketches of a Black Cat*.
Please consider leaving a review on Amazon. This is extremely helpful for authors and titles that might otherwise be skipped over without them.

Made in the USA
Columbia, SC
22 February 2021